The Great Big Prayer Book For Schools

2000 Prayers

Compiled by Alison Evans

Illustrations by Melody-Anne Lee

kevin mayhew

kevin
mayhew

First published in Great Britain in 2010 by Kevin Mayhew Ltd
Buxhall, Stowmarket, Suffolk IP14 3BW
Tel: +44 (0) 1449 737978 Fax: +44 (0) 1449 737834
E-mail: info@kevinmayhewltd.com

www.kevinmayhew.com

The publishers wish to thank all those who have given their permission to reproduce copyright material in this production.

The material in this book has been published previously.

ISBN 978 1 84867 239 0
Catalogue No. 1501217

Compiled and edited by Alison Evans
Illustrations and cover by Melody-Anne Lee

Printed and bound in Great Britain

Contents

School life

Our school

1 Father God,
thank you
for our time at school,
for our teachers
for our dinnerladies
for our cleaners
for our school secretaries
for our caretakers
for our friends
who all make us
happy and glad
that we can all come back
tomorrow.

Tony Bower

2 We pray for those we see and talk to
every day or every week;
for those we often argue with
or misunderstand;
for those who brighten our lives
and make us smile;
for a greater thankfulness and appreciation
of those we usually take for granted.

Susan Sayers

3 Lord, come into the daily relationships
we so easily take for granted,
and enable us to value one another,
delighting in one another's richness,
and responding to one another's needs with love.

Susan Sayers

4 Almighty God,
may our school be welcoming.
May our school be encouraging.
Let friendship flourish here.
Let learning fill our day.
Give us the strength to do our best.
Give us the hope to carry on.
Be our guide in all we do.
Lord, make this school your home too.
We ask this through Jesus Christ, our Lord.
Amen.

Rupert Bristow

5 Almighty God,
we give thanks for our school.
For us it is a special place.
Make it special for you, Lord, and bring your peace, love and friendship to everything we do here.
As we learn and as we play, may we always be in your safe keeping.
We ask this through Jesus Christ, our Lord.
Amen.

Rupert Bristow

6 Heavenly Father,
be with us in our learning.
Be with us in our playing.
Be with us in our laughter.
Be with us in our tears.
Be with us when we get things right and when we get things wrong.
Be with us as we come to school and when we travel home.
We know that you will always be here for us, Lord, at . . . . . . school.
We ask this in Jesus' name.
Amen.

Rupert Bristow

7 Heavenly Father,
help our learning and our knowing and bring us friendship and fellowship.
Take us to new places, Lord, as our teachers show us the wonders of your creation.
May we help each other at . . . . . . school so that we can learn from everyone around us.
We pray also for our families and our homes; keep them safe while we are safe at school.
We ask this in Jesus' name.
Amen.

Rupert Bristow

8 Thank you, God,
for this school.
Thank you for
the pupils and staff.
Thank you for
the helpers and friends.
Thank you, God,
for this school.

Nick Harding

9 Father God, help us here.
Help us to work hard and enjoy learning.
Help us to play and enjoy having fun.
Help us to respect each other and enjoy friendships.
Help us all to make this school even better.

Nick Harding

10 This school is great, and that's how we want it to stay.
This school is great, and we make it better every day.
This school is great, and we want to learn God's way.
This school is great – be with our work and play.

Nick Harding

11 May the peace of the Father fall on this school.
May the love of Jesus fill this school.
May the Spirit of God give energy to this school.

Nick Harding

12 God who cares, we ask you to care for this school.
We ask you to care for all of us.
We ask you to care for all visitors and friends.
We ask you to care for our families.
God who cares, we ask you to care for this school.

Nick Harding

13 Thank you, Jesus, for all of us here.
Thank you that we can learn and enjoy ourselves together.
Thank you for all the groups and clubs we belong to.
Thank you that you want us to be together.
Amen.

Nick Harding

14 Thank you, God,
for our
school,
teachers,
families,
homes,
food,
clothes
and our lives.
Amen.

Ashley Guest

15 Generous God, you have been good to us.
You have given us a good school.
You have given us great students.
You have given us a clear vision.
Generous God, you have been good to us.

Nick Harding

16 God, we are a busy school.
We have work to do, and new skills to practise.
We have friends to help, and games to play.
We have sadness to remember,
And achievements to celebrate.
God, we are a busy school.

Nick Harding

17 Make us your school, God of everything.
Make us your students, God of everything.
Make us your staff, God of everything.
Make us all your servants, God of everything.
Make us your school, God of everything.

Nick Harding

18 Lord, in our school there is so much to do,
and so little time.
Lord, in our school there is so much work going on,
and so little time.
Lord, in our school there are so many tired children,
and so little energy.
Help us, Lord, in our school, there is so much need
and so much trust in you.

Nick Harding

19 Lord,
I'm watching,
observing,
looking at all these people
who don't seem to have very much in common.
But I'm still watching,
observing,
looking at such a variety of life passing by.
There are all sorts
of people
with their peculiar ways,
their idiosyncrasies,
their own way of doing things.
I really can't imagine
what you see in all of us.
We're such a ragbag of emotions,
of tastes, of styles.
(Not that many people have a sense of style!)
We're all so opinionated,
so devious,
so human.
But you love us just the way we are
and that knocks all my preconceived ideas about love
straight out of the window.
I don't know how you do it.
I think I know why you do it.
And I'm really glad you do
love me and him, and her and every single
twisted, hassled, frightened,
lonely, drained, wrecked, soiled, bedraggled, cracked,
phased, emotionally bankrupt
one of us.
I'm glad your heart is big enough
and your arms wide enough
to love and hold on to each one of us.
Thanks. Amen.

Pete Townsend

20 Father God, thank you for this school.
Thank you for all the
teachers,
cleaners,
and other helpers
who work here.
Thank you
for all the children
who learn here.
Help us all to think more,
listen more,
and learn more this year.
Amen.

Nick Harding

Starting a new school

21 Dear God,
you know that I'm going to a new school.
You what it's like to be
unknown, nervous and worried.
You know that I've got to settle
in a new place.
But I know that you are with me.
I know that you'll help me
whatever may happen, good and bad,
and I'm pleased you're there.
Amen.

Nick Harding

22 Change is hard.
God was with you in the past
and he will be with you in the future
– put your hope in him!
Amen.

Nick Harding

23 I'm starting a new school, God.
I'm a bit nervous about it,
but I'm excited too.
It'll be good making new friends.
And I know that you'll be there for me,
wherever I am.
Amen.

Anon

24 Thank you, God,
for new friends

and for the love and fun
I will share with them every day
in my new school.
Amen.

25 Dear Lord,
starting a new school
can be very
difficult. Please
help us to know
that you are
always with us
and will help us.
Amen.

Denis O'Gorman

26 Jesus,
it's not easy
moving to a new place,
a new school
or church
or home.
Lots of new faces.
Lots of strange places.
You have to meet
new people
and often leave behind
those people
who are your friends.
I pray, Jesus,
for all those people who are moving
to a new place.
Help them to feel at home, Jesus,
and be happy
where they are.
Amen.

David Gatward

27 Jesus,
making friends
can be difficult.
You have to do so much.
You have to listen to them
and get to know them
and learn about them.
And you have to help them
get to know who you are, too.
But new friends are great!

David Gatward

28 Jesus,
it's not nice being lost.
You feel alone
and helpless.
You don't know what to do
or where to go.
I've felt like that before, Jesus.
Most people do.
But, when we do feel lost,
you're still there, aren't you, Jesus?
Thank you!
Amen.

David Gatward

29 Dear Lord,
sometimes new
pupils come to
our school. Please
help us to make
them welcome
with words of
friendship.
Amen.

Denis O'Gorman

30 Lord,
help us as we move
to different classes or schools
to be careful to take
the important things with us.
Help us, Lord, never to forget
that you promised to go with us
wherever we go, should we ask you.

Ashley Guest

Leaving school

31 Almighty God,
we ask for your blessing on all who are moving on to their next school.
We give thanks for what they have contributed to this school, what they have learnt and what they have left behind them.
May they be a credit to our school in all that they achieve in their future lives and may they remain grateful for what this school has given them.
We ask this through Jesus Christ, our Lord.
Amen.

Rupert Bristow

32 Almighty God,
we thank you for the achievements and hard work of all those who are leaving this term; for the friendships they have made; for the service they have given.
We ask, Lord, for your protection and inspiration as they move on to the next step in their education, the next development of your purpose for them.
May they remember the Christian values they have learnt in this school and may they always follow your ways.
We ask this through Jesus Christ, our Lord.
Amen.

Rupert Bristow

33 Changes are coming,
and we often fear change.
Challenges are coming,
and we often fear challenge.
Doubts are coming,
and we often fear doubts.
God is here with us,
and we have nothing to fear.

Nick Harding

34 It is time to move on.
Time to move on to
a new school.
Time to move on to
new teachers.
Time to move on to
new learning.
It is time to move on.

Nick Harding

35 Looking back
we remember good times.
Looking forward
we hope for good times.
Looking back
we remember challenges.
Looking forward
we hope for challenges.
Looking back
we remember security.
Looking forward
we hope for security.
Looking back
we remember.
Looking forward
we hope.

Nick Harding

36 As the clouds float through the sky and move on,
so we move on to new things.
As the seasons change and new growth comes,
so we change and grow.
As the stream becomes a river, and the river becomes the sea,
so we go forward to bigger things.

Nick Harding

37 As we leave we give thanks
for all we have enjoyed here.
We give thanks for the jokes
and the laughter that has made us smile.
We give thanks for the success
and the sense of achievement we have known.
As we leave we give thanks.

Nick Harding

38 Lord, we pray for you to
walk with us all,
but particularly with those
who are moving on to a new school.

Ashley Guest

39 Jesus, when you said goodbye to the disciples
you promised to be with them always,
to the end of the age.
This has been true for us too,
when we acknowledge you,
you will never leave us.
Bless us all,
especially those of us moving to a new school.
Amen.

Ashley Guest

40 We thank you for our time here.
We thank you for the years
when we have been safe and secure.
We pray for our futures,
we pray that you would keep us safe and secure.
We thank you for our time here.

Nick Harding

41 Lord, God of the past,
thank you for it.
Lord, God with us now,
help us today.
Lord, God of the future,
walk with us into the unknown.

Nick Harding

42 The time has come to step forward,
to step forward into the unknown.
To step forward into new experiences.
The time has come to step forward,
to step forward to new friendships,
to step forward to new learning.
The time has come to step forward.

Nick Harding

43 Father God,
you take us from the old to the new.
You take us from the past to the future.
You take us from the memories to the challenges.
Take us to our next school, we pray.

Nick Harding

44 We are ready, Lord, to move on.
To remember the fun and the games,
to remember the teachers and the friends.
We are ready, Lord, to move on.
Move on to more laughter,
Move on to new teachers and friends.
We are ready, Lord, to move on.

Nick Harding

45 Opportunities are spread before us
like paths across the fields.
Opportunities are so many
like pebbles on the beach.
Opportunities are challenging
like climbing up a hill.
Opportunities are waiting –
help us make them real.

Nick Harding

46 May the Father who made
us watch over us,
the Son who died for us
be alongside us,
and the Spirit which fills
us give us life.
Today as we leave,
and every day.

Nick Harding

47 Father God,
be with us all as we move on.
Help us to look back and remember
the good times we have had.
Help us to look forward to
the good times we will have.
Help us not to fear what is ahead,
or yearn for what has gone.
Amen.

Nick Harding

School year begins

48 Almighty God,
as we begin this new school year, we ask for your blessing on all who study and work here. May those who are new be helped by those who are returning.
May we accept new challenges with eagerness, new risks with courage, and new insights with openness.
Above all, Lord, assist us, in all our learning,
to do our best
and to grow in understanding of your world.
We ask this through Jesus Christ, our Lord.
Amen.

Rupert Bristow

49 Almighty God,
at the start of another year we come together to commit ourselves to our school community; to our learning and playing; and to each other.
Help us to bring forward all we have learnt last year
to make the most of our time in this year's class.
Give us the strength and purpose, Lord, to be a good neighbour and a good Samaritan when others around us need our help.
We ask this through Jesus Christ, our Lord.
Amen.

Rupert Bristow

50 Father God,
thank you
for this brand-new school year.
We pray
that we will make the most of it,
do our best,
try our hardest,
listen well,
do what we are told
and always remember to say
'please' and 'thank you'.
We pray
that you will bless our teachers.
Give them wisdom,
grant them patience,
give them strength,
grant them grace.
Thank you
for them,

Continued overleaf

for the wonderful work they do,
for the special things
they teach us,
the special people that they are.
Please help all of us
to make you
the centre of our community
and listen to you,
the greatest teacher
of them all.

Tony Bower

51 Father God,
you have chosen this time for a new beginning.
This new beginning can help us
to begin afresh and try harder.
This new beginning can help us
to do new things and try out new skills.
This new beginning can help us
work together for the good of everyone.
Help us all make the best of this new beginning.

Nick Harding

52 We are grateful, Lord,
for all the good things we did last year.
We are sorry for the times when we have done wrong.
We ask for strength to pull our socks up;
to make a new start; to begin again.

Nick Harding

School year ends

53 Almighty God,
we give thanks for all that has been achieved
in our school this year.
We remember our successes in competitions, as members of teams and as individuals. We recall the special occasions during the year when we went on visits, took part in a school production, involved visitors and contributed to a fun project.
Let us not forget the new things we have learnt
during the year and the friendships we have made.
Prepare us, Lord, for all that the next school year will bring by granting us and our teachers and everyone in our school a great holiday.
We ask this through Jesus Christ, our Lord.
Amen.

Rupert Bristow

54 Almighty God,
may we look back on the year with pride at the things achieved, awareness of where we have gone wrong, and thanks for all that our teachers and parents have done for us.
We look forward to the holidays, remembering the friends we have made and all the new things we have learnt and experienced.
Bring us back refreshed and ready for all the next year will offer.
We ask this through Jesus Christ, our Lord.
Amen.

Rupert Bristow

55 Thank you, Father God,
for this school year,
for all we've learned,
for all we've done,
for all the fun,
for all the smiles
from all of our friends.
Thank you
for this our school,
for all who've worked
so hard this year.
We pray you will bless them
and help them to rest and be
refreshed.

Tony Bower

School term begins

56 Heavenly Father,
as a new term begins, we promise, with your help,
to bring new energy to our work at this school.
May we always be aware of the needs of others in school and in the local community, including our church.
Help us to listen and learn in our classes; do our very best in our homework; and play our full part in school and class sports.
We ask this in Jesus' name.
Amen.

Rupert Bristow

57 Heavenly Father,
thank you for the refreshment that the holidays have brought, for the people we have met and the places we have been.
As we gather again at the start of a new term, give us the energy to do our best, the desire to aim high and the ability to learn from our mistakes.
We pray for our teachers and our parents and ask that you care for them as they care for us.
We ask this in Jesus' name.
Amen.

Rupert Bristow

58 God above,
thank you for our school.
Thank you for our friends
and thank you for our adults.
Thank you for our fun
and thank you for our learning.
Help us this term
to do more, learn more, and enjoy more.

Nick Harding

59 We are gathered here
to begin again together.
We come here
to learn more together.
We are united
to go forward together.

Nick Harding

60 Time passes, the time has come
to rest and to learn,
to think and to have fun,
to grow and to move on.
Time passes, and our time has come.

Nick Harding

61 God, you gave us a rest,
now is the time to be lively.
God, you gave us a break,
now is the time to think.
God, you gave us others,
now is the time to be friends.
God, you give us now –
help us to make the most of it.

Nick Harding

62 New things can be a challenge,
new friends can be a pain,
new terms can be quite scary,
help us through this term again!

Nick Harding

63 Creator God, you gave us minds
to help us understand and know.
Creator God, you give us time
to do our best and learn to grow.

Nick Harding

64 Father God,
in this new term we ask your help
to keep us safe, to keep us strong,
to help us become more
the people you want us to be.

Nick Harding

65 We thank you for our school, Lord.
We thank you that we are back together.
We thank you for our school, Lord.
We thank you for everyone here.
We thank you for this new start, Lord.
We thank you for our future.

Nick Harding

School term ends

66 Heavenly Father,
we are ready for the holidays. You know, Lord, that we have done our best and learnt a lot. Thank you for the fun we have had and the hard work we have put into this term.
Help us to carry on learning after this short break.
We ask this in Jesus' name.
Amen.

Rupert Bristow

67 Heavenly Father,
as we complete another term, we give thanks for this school community, our class, our friends, our teachers, our teaching assistants, our parents and all who support the school.
Bring us back safely next term.
Just as we look forward to the holidays, so may we look forward to returning here to . . . . . . *(school)*.
We ask this in Jesus' name.
Amen.

Rupert Bristow

68 Father,
keep these children safe
this school holiday
and help them with
the choices they make.

Ashley Guest

School day begins

69 Thank you, God,
for this fresh new
day to live in!

Susan Sayers

70 Dear God, I want to live
this day in the very best,
most excellent way.

Susan Sayers

71 Here I am, Lord God, your friend,
happy to work with you today,
and looking forward to
what we'll do.
The Lord is my shepherd.
There is nothing more I need.

Susan Sayers

72 Almighty God,
as our school day begins, we meet to dedicate ourselves
to you.
May our hopes for today reflect your hopes for us.
Help us to face the challenges and take the opportunities
that this day brings.
And in a moment of silence let us prepare ourselves
for the tasks ahead . . . .
Be with us, Lord, in all that we do and say, and give us
the time for reflection on our learning.
We ask this through Jesus Christ, our Lord.
Amen.

Rupert Bristow

73 Almighty God,
may this new day bring light as well as heat; help to overcome the hurdles; fun alongside the struggles.
Help us to put things in perspective, not to rush to judgement, and to listen hard to what others are saying.
May this school be a real learning community today.
We ask this through Jesus Christ, our Lord.
Amen.

Rupert Bristow

74 Here we are at the start again,
gathered as a school again.
Be with us today, God, we pray,
help us do our best again.

Nick Harding

75 Gracious God,
a new day is beginning:
new opportunities are coming,
new ideas are growing.
May we make the best of all things new.

Nick Harding

76 There are only a few hours before home-time,
only a few hours to learn.
Only a few hours for friendship,
only a few hours to think.
Help us make the most of each minute.
There are only a few hours to home-time.

Nick Harding

77 Thank you that we are here,
thank you that my friends are here.
Thank you that you are here.
Be with us all today.

Nick Harding

78 There are things we must do,
and things we should do.
There are things we want to do,
and things we need to do.
There are things we have to do,
and things we choose to do.
In all these things be with us.

Nick Harding

79 God of all, Father,
Son and Spirit,
be with your
people today.

Nick Harding

80 Helpful God, help us today.
Help us in all we do.
Help us in all we say.
Help us in all we learn.
Help us in all we play.
Helpful God, help us today.

Nick Harding

81 Loving God, we pray
that your love would help today.
Loving God, we need
your help to write and read.
Loving God, we seek
your help in all we speak.
Loving God, we pray
that your love would be here today.

Nick Harding

82 The day is just beginning,
be with us we pray.
There is work to be done,
be with us we pray.
There are challenges to face,
be with us we pray.

Nick Harding

83 We offer thanks for this new day.
We offer thanks for those walking with us.
We offer thanks for those working with us.
We offer thanks for those waiting for us.
We offer thanks for this new day.

Nick Harding

84 We've arrived, we are ready,
we are happy, we are strong.
We are learners, we are teachers,
help us all to get along!

Nick Harding

85 As the light replaces darkness,
bring light to our learning.
As spice adds flavour,
bring spice to our thoughts.
As life replaces death,
bring life to our working.

Nick Harding

86 Lifegiver, give us life.
Give life to new ideas.
Give life to our teaching and learning.
Give life to our friendships.
Give life to our day.
Lifegiver, give us life.

Nick Harding

87 God of time, help us to use our time well.
Help us to use each moment wisely.
Help us to use each minute with purpose.
Help us to use these hours effectively.

Nick Harding

88 We offer thanks for food and drink.
We offer thanks for time to eat.
We offer thanks for all your gifts.
We offer thanks.

Nick Harding

School day ends

89 Heavenly Father,
we offer you our day's work.
As we prepare to go home, help us to reflect on what we have learnt, what we have seen, what we have said, what we have struggled with, and what we have enjoyed.
We are sorry for any angry words or unjust actions.
We thank you, Lord, for the whole day and look forward to what tomorrow will bring.
We ask this in Jesus' name.
Amen.

Rupert Bristow

90 Heavenly Father,
thank you for our school day.
Thank you for revealing more of your world to us.
Thank you for all the experiences this day has brought.
May our school always be a learning community with you as its focus, Lord.
Give us rest tonight so that we can return refreshed and ready to resume our studies.
We ask this in Jesus' name.
Amen.

Rupert Bristow

91 Here we are at the end again,
ready to go to our homes again.
Be with us this night, God, we pray,
help us rest in peace again.

Nick Harding

92 Thank you that we have been here,
thank you that our friends have been here.
Thank you that you have been here.
Be with us all at home this night.

Nick Harding

93 May the God of the clouds and sky,
the God of the leaf and petal,
the God of life and love
be with us this night as we leave.

Nick Harding

94 We have had a time to rest,
and now we are full of energy.
We have had a time to think,
and now we are full of ideas.
We have had a time to stop,
and now it is time to get going.
Be with us, God, we pray.

Nick Harding

95 As the day moves
closer to darkness,
thank you for the light
in our learning.
Help us to think more,
remember more,
and move forward
more after today.

Nick Harding

96 May God go with us into the community,
may God go with us into our homes,
may God go with us into our sleep,
may God come with us here tomorrow.

Nick Harding

97 Thank you, God,
for a great day,
thank you, God,
that in every way
you made today better,
thank you!

Nick Harding

98 We are grateful for the day you gave,
we are grateful for the people we've shared it with.
We are grateful that you kept us safe.
Father God, we are grateful.

Nick Harding

99 The end of a good day,
we all say 'Thank you'.
The end of a tiring day,
we all say 'Thank you'.
The end of another day,
we all say 'Thank you'.

Nick Harding

100 We give thanks for all we have discovered today.
Help us to become more aware of the
miracles around us.
May we grow in awe and wonder and treat
creation with love and respect.
Amen.

Jill Fuller

School trips

101 Lord,
thank you
for school trips,
educational visits,
to libraries and museums,
entertaining visits
to the theatre and cinema,
exciting visits
to the countryside and seaside;
for all the places
that we go.
Please keep us safe
and help us to learn
as well as enjoy
school.

Tony Bower

Our teachers

102 Forgive us, Jesus,
when we only see the rules and not the love behind them.
Help us to remember that they're made for people
– and it's the people that matter!

Michael Forster

103 May all our teachers
be directed, inspired and upheld
by the living Spirit of God,
and may there be a deepening
of love and commitment
in all Christians the world over.

Susan Sayers

104 Heavenly Father,
we thank you for all those who remind us
to be kind and loving by their words and example.
We pray that as a school
we may get ready to welcome you
and put right whatever blocks us from your love.

Susan Sayers

New head teacher

105 Almighty God,
we ask your blessing on our new head teacher . . . . . .
Give them wisdom and strength in the leadership
they exercise.
May the school, the church and the wider community
assist them in this role through personal, practical and
prayer support.
And may their vision be your vision, Lord, as the school
begins a new chapter in its history.
We ask this through Jesus Christ, our Lord.
Amen.

Rupert Bristow

106 Almighty God,
we give thanks for the arrival of our new head teacher . . . .
May they feel welcome and at home here at . . . . . school.
Help them to meet your high expectations, Lord, and help
us to show confidence in their leadership, renewing our
commitment to the school's mission, and encouraging
them through our support and prayer.
We ask this through Jesus Christ, our Lord.
Amen.

Rupert Bristow

Retiring teacher/ head teacher

107 Heavenly Father,
as we say goodbye to . . . . . . we thank you for their tireless work for this school.
We remember the special ways in which they have made their mark on our school and our community – and how they have been special to each one of us.
Only you, Lord, know how hard they have worked on our behalf.
Bring them a long, happy and fulfilling retirement in the knowledge that they have carried out your purpose here.
We ask this in Jesus' name.
Amen.

Rupert Bristow

108 Heavenly Father,
we celebrate all that . . . . . . has meant to us here at . . . . *(school)*: in the classroom, in the hall, in their office, on the playing field, and also in the community.
Thank you, Lord, for the special gifts they have shared with pupils and staff over . . . . . . years at this school.
Bring them happiness and good health in retirement, fond memories of this place and a sure knowledge of firm friendships made and a job well done.
We ask this in Jesus' name.
Amen.

Rupert Bristow

109 Loving God,
you have created people to care for others.
You have given them love and concern in their hearts.
Today we thank you for . . . .
We thank you that you sent them to us
and we ask that . . . . will find rest
as they move on to do new things.
In your name we pray.

Nick Harding

110 God, there are many people in this world
and some are special people.
There are many people in this community
and some are special people.
There are many people in this school
and some are special people.
Thank you for one special person, ...

Nick Harding

111 May the God of peace walk with you
in the valley of peace.
May the God of love rest with you
in the field of rest.
May the God of hope stand with you
on the mountain of hope.

Nick Harding

112 God, you made us all as a family.
You made this school to be a family.
Help us to remember . . . .
and always know that they were part of this family.

Nick Harding

113 Loving God,
you know our needs.
You offer us rest in green fields,
next to quiet, still waters.
Give us rest now we pray.

Nick Harding

114 Jesus, you called yourself a servant.
Jesus, you called us to be servants.
Jesus, we thank you for your servant . . . .
We thank you that this servant
cared for us and many others.
Jesus, we pray for this servant,
that they may rest in you.

Nick Harding

115 We give thanks for . . . .
We give thanks for patience,
we give thanks for love,
we give thanks for humour,
We give thanks for hard work.
we give thanks for . . . .

Nick Harding

116 As the single leaf falls from the tree,
and slowly floats to the ground,
so you gently move us on, O Lord.
As the leaf finds rest
on the soft grass below,
so you give us rest, O Lord.

Nick Harding

117 Father God,
in all of our lives the time comes to change.
We pray for . . . . and the change they face.
We pray that the change would be a good one.
We pray that the change would be a calm one.
We pray for . . . . and the change they face.

Nick Harding

118 Lord of all we do and say.
Please be with . . . . today,
and be there in *his/her* heart we pray.

Nick Harding

You made us all, and you give us talents.
119 We thank you for . . . ., and all those talents.
We thank you that we have received
from those God-given talents.
You made us all, and you give us talents.

Nick Harding

New birth

120 Heavenly Father,
as we welcome back our *(head)* teacher we celebrate the arrival of their child. We thank you for the gift of a new life and ask that the family of this school be an extension of their own.
Bring happiness and a bright future to . . . . . .
We ask this in Jesus' name.
Amen.

Rupert Bristow

Getting married

121 Teacher, we have heard it said
your wedding will be soon.
And then you'll get a fortnight off
to spend on honeymoon.
We'd like to come along with you
and stay at your hotel.
But if we can't, we'll wait for you.
Till then, we wish you well.
Teacher, we all wish you luck,
so have a happy day.
And all of us will think of you
and some of us will pray
that you will have a lovely time,
with blessings from above.
May God, with joy, watch over you
and fill you both with love.

Teacher, may we thank you now.
these flowers *(presents if for groom)* are for you.
Each child has brought a special gift,
so here's another too.
So may God bless you with his love
and make you both as one.
And may your days you share from now
be filled with joy and fun.

Denis O'Gorman

Death of a teacher/ head teacher

122 Almighty God,
you know that it will be difficult for us at . . . . . . school without . . . . . .
Bring us the strength and the hope to carry on, as they would have wished.
We thank you, Lord, for the special gifts they brought
to this school and shared with us.
May the church and the wider community give thanks
for their contribution to the life of . . . . . . *(village /town)*
and may we redouble our own efforts to serve each other,
in honour of their memory.
We ask this through Jesus Christ, our Lord.
Amen.

Rupert Bristow

123 Almighty God,
as we remember all that . . . . . . has meant to us at . . . . . . school, we pray that they are now at peace with you in your eternal kingdom.
Only you know why they have been taken from us at this time,
but we give thanks for their special place in our hearts at our school.
We pray for their family and friends at this difficult time.
Show your love for them and for us as we struggle to cope with the loss.
May your church be a comfort and a strength to us all.
We ask this through Jesus Christ, our Lord.
Amen.

Rupert Bristow

New priest

124 Heavenly Father,
as our new priest starts their ministry in this school and this community, we thank you for the gifts and experience they bring.
We look forward to their presence among us.
Help us to be responsive to their efforts to bring us closer to you and to your Church, O God.
May they feel welcome and at home in our school and may our church be a place of worship, exploration and celebration for pupils, parents, staff and governors.
We ask this in Jesus' name.
Amen.

Rupert Bristow

125 Heavenly Father,
we celebrate the arrival of . . . . . . in our school community and in our church.
Give them energy, insight and patience in their ministry.
May our school play a full part in the church's life and worship and may our new priest always find a warm welcome in the school.
Through their words and work help us to know you better, to worship you joyfully and to give thanks for the love you have shown through your Son, Jesus Christ.
We ask this in Jesus' name.
Amen.

Rupert Bristow

Retiring/leaving priest

126 Almighty God,
we thank you for the ministry of . . . . . . in our school.
As we say farewell to them we remember the many ways in which they have supported the school, leading worship at our assemblies, making us feel at home in the church, and being available in good times and difficult times.
May . . . . . . continue to serve you, Lord, in your Church, knowing that they leave us firmer in our faith and with a closer relationship with you.
We ask this through Jesus Christ, our Lord.
Amen.

Rupert Bristow

127 Almighty God,
we are grateful that you sent . . . . . . to this school
and this community to be our pastor and our friend.
We celebrate their ministry amongst us as we say farewell
to them *(and their family)*.
Through them we got to know you better, Lord.
May the link between the school and the church continue
to flourish, building on the firm foundations which you
have laid here through the ministry of . . . . . .
Bestow your blessings on them in the next stage of
their work in your service.
We ask this through Jesus Christ, our Lord.
Amen.

Rupert Bristow

New board of education

128 Almighty God,
as our new Board gathers we ask for your strength and
purpose to be clearly apparent in our deliberations.
Help each one of us to seek your will as we give direction
to our work and the tasks ahead.
Keep us focused and alert; keep us open to the Holy Spirit.
Create in us a willingness to learn from each other, that we
may grow your kingdom through our awareness of the
needs of the children and families in our diocese, our
educational communities, and our world.
We ask this through Jesus Christ, our Lord.
Amen.

Rupert Bristow

129 Almighty God,
we know that every child matters in your sight.
Help us as a new Board to see where we can bring the light
of your love to shine on children, families and the work of
education in our diocese.
Direct our thoughts, open our minds and empower us to
take risks for your sake.
We ask this through Jesus Christ, our Lord.
Amen.

Rupert Bristow

Staff

New

130 Heavenly Father,
we celebrate the arrival of our new staff member(s) . . . . . .
and ask your blessing on their contribution to our school.
May they bring new insights and gifts to our school life
and may we welcome and support them in this new step
in their career.
We ask this in Jesus' name.
Amen.

Rupert Bristow

131 Heavenly Father,
we ask for your guiding hand to be extended to our new
staff member(s) . . . . . .
Let them flourish here as they become part of our team.
Give them firmness of purpose, generosity of spirit and
willingness to listen. Give us the commitment to show
hospitality, provide support and offer a Christian welcome.
We ask this in Jesus' name.
Amen.

Rupert Bristow

Leaving

132 Heavenly Father,
we give thanks for the contribution that . . . . . . has made
to the life of this school.
As we say farewell, we remember all that they have meant
to us previously, all that they have done for the school as a
whole, and their contribution to the wider community.
As they move on from this school, Lord,
may they be aware of your love in all their future endeavours.
We ask this in Jesus' name.
Amen.

Rupert Bristow

133 Heavenly Father,
we will miss . . . . . . in our school.
We will miss all the things that make them special:
their sense of humour,
their . . . .
We will laugh when we remember . . . . . .
Please, Lord, look after them when they leave,
and may they have many good memories of us too.
We ask this in Jesus' name.
Amen.

Rupert Bristow

Governor leaving

134 Almighty God,
as . . . . . . steps down from being a governor here, we celebrate their commitment to this school during the past . . . . years.
You know, Lord, the late hours and many days they put in and you know the difference they have made.
In asking for your blessing on them we also ask for your continued inspiration in the work of governors in the years to come.
We ask this through Jesus Christ, our Lord.
Amen.

Rupert Bristow

135 Almighty God,
we will miss the contribution . . . . . . has made to our deliberations, our decisions and our debates.
We ask, Lord, that you will continue to use their ministry in other ways to extend your kingdom.
We thank you for their lasting legacy to our school and our community.
May their contribution be an indication of our desire to serve you always.
We ask this through Jesus Christ, our Lord.
Amen.

Rupert Bristow

New school building

136 Almighty God,
we give thanks for our new school; for all those who planned, designed and built it; and for the vision that sustained the project.
May the learning and the teaching within these walls reflect that vision and your glory. And let us not take for granted our new surroundings, but appreciate them and allow them to enrich this learning community.
Wow . . .
We ask this through Jesus Christ, our Lord.
Amen.

Rupert Bristow

137 Almighty God,
bring to these new buildings a sense of your presence.
Bring to our hearts a new purpose.
Bring to our learning and teaching a renewed commitment.
We give thanks for the dedication and expertise of all those who have contributed to this project and we ask for your blessing on those who will benefit from this school, now and in the years to come.
We ask this through Jesus Christ, our Lord.
Amen.

Rupert Bristow

138 Heavenly Father,
may this new building be an extension of your kingdom, a passport to new learning opportunities and a focus for excellence.
Help us to integrate what it can offer into the fabric of the school.
Inspire all those who use it with your purpose for them.
In sharing these facilities may the school and the community grow ever closer.
We ask this in Jesus' name.
Amen.

Rupert Bristow

139 Heavenly Father,
with this new building to inspire us, set our sights high.
With you as our guide, help us to enrich the education that goes on in this place.
May many people benefit from the new facilities and may skills learnt here reflect the skills which went into the building's design and construction.
We ask this in Jesus' name.
Amen.

Rupert Bristow

School amalgamation

140 Heavenly Father,
as our two schools come together, please bless our new creation.
May we become stronger as we grow larger.
May we care for each other and share what both our schools have.
Above all, Lord, may we know you better through our worship together.
We ask this in Jesus' name.
Amen.

Rupert Bristow

141 Heavenly Father,
as we now become . . . . . . *(school)*, help us to respect our different origins.
May we learn to think of ourselves as one community; our teachers, teaching assistants and support team as one staff; and our school aims as one shared vision.
Bring unity and purpose to our work and learning.
We ask this in Jesus' name.
Amen.

Rupert Bristow

School closure

142 Almighty God,
we give thanks for . . . . . . *(school)*:
for the vision of those who founded it;
for the head teachers and governors who have had charge of it;
for the Church which has supported it;
and for all the children who have been educated here.
We ask that all those who have learned and taught and administered in our school, and the parents who entrusted their children to the school's care, will know your lasting love through their time here and will always have . . . . . . *(school)* in their hearts and minds.
We ask this through Jesus Christ, our Lord.
Amen.

Rupert Bristow

143 Almighty God,
in the ending of this chapter in our community's history,
we give thanks for the education . . . . . . *(school)* has provided for the pupils here.
May all who have learned, taught and worked here be proud of those gifts they have shared and received.
Wherever people move on to, let a little part of . . . . . . *(school)* be carried with them to help them on their way.
We ask this through Jesus Christ, our Lord.
Amen.

Rupert Bristow

Federation of schools

144 Almighty God,
create in us the will to work together and give us the means to collaborate effectively; enable the gifts of both our schools to flourish in our wider school community.
May your name be honoured and your Son's example followed in all that we do individually and together.
We ask this through Jesus Christ, our Lord.
Amen.

Rupert Bristow

145 Almighty God,
bring to us new insights and new ways of working together.
May our schools bring to each other new opportunities for learning and growing forward together.
We ask that the collaboration we seek provides the challenge and change you ask of us all, through your transforming love.
We ask this through Jesus Christ, our Lord.
Amen.

Rupert Bristow

Inspection reports

146 Almighty God,
as we receive and celebrate our school's inspection report(s),
we acknowledge and give thanks for all the hard work represented and recognised in the report(s).
You know, Lord, the strengths of this school community.
You know our weaknesses too.
May we grow forward together in confidence and in faith
so that we can continue to be worthy of your purpose.
We ask this through Jesus Christ, our Lord.
Amen.
Rupert Bristow

147 Almighty God,
great news!
We pray that these reports are read and valued by staff, governors, parents and pupils and recognised as part of your 'good news' too, Lord.
Help all those in our community to see our school as we really are and to support us in all our activities.
May we continue to grow as a learning community.
And may your Church be at the heart of our school life.
We ask this through Jesus Christ, our Lord.
Amen.
Rupert Bristow

Significant anniversaries

148 Heavenly Father,
as we celebrate the school's . . . . . . years of service to our community,
we give thanks for those who have learned about you here;
those who have grown in faith here and those
who have made . . . . . . a special place.
May the staff and governors, parents and pupils always value their time and each other's efforts at this school.
May they look back in appreciation and forward in hope.
Give to this learning community the confidence to make a difference, to challenge what is wrong and champion what is right, and to grow daily in our love for you.
We ask this in Jesus' name.
Amen.
Rupert Bristow

149 Heavenly Father,
on this special day for the school we give thanks for all those who have contributed to the life of this place.
Thank you for the commitment of the people who founded the school and for all the teaching and learning that has taken place here.
We ask that your Church continues to provide us with support and prayer, inspiration and love.
We ask this in Jesus' name.
Amen.

Rupert Bristow

150 Almighty God,
it's a great day.
Please be with us as we celebrate and have fun.
Help us to value what we have and not worry about what we don't have.
Thank you for all those who have built up our school and the community around us, and we ask you to bless everyone in our school today.
We ask this through Jesus Christ, our Lord.
Amen.

Rupert Bristow

151 Almighty God,
it is only . . . . . . years since we became . . . . . . *(school)*.
We have enjoyed the journey so far and we look ahead with confidence and expectation.
Be with us on our journey, in our church, in our community, in our school and in our hearts.
We ask this through Jesus Christ, our Lord.
Amen.

Rupert Bristow

At a governors' meeting

152 Almighty God,
may we bring reflection and wisdom to our meeting.
Use our expertise and our judgement, Lord, in directing our contributions.
Let us be listeners more than speakers.
And may we always have in mind your will for the well-being and the future of the school.
We ask this through Jesus Christ, our Lord.
Amen.

Rupert Bristow

153 Almighty God,
we pray for our school and our meeting: grant us the wit and the wisdom to conduct our business in a good spirit, open to the views of others but firm in the purpose of our endeavour, and guided by your will.
May our decisions always support the mission of this school and your Church.
We ask this through Jesus Christ, our Lord.
Amen.

Rupert Bristow

At a staff meeting

154 Heavenly Father,
be with us as we meet.
Guide us as we talk.
Stay with us as we plan.
Open our ears as we listen.
Open our eyes to your vision.
We ask this in Jesus' name.
Amen.

Rupert Bristow

155 Heavenly Father,
in our meeting, help us to focus on what is important rather than just what is urgent.
May everything we discuss have a bearing on the children in our charge.
Let us never forget that it is both a privilege and a responsibility to play a part in the education of the young.
Grant that we always support each other in that process.
We ask this in Jesus' name.
Amen.

Rupert Bristow

At an annual/occasional meeting with parents

156 Almighty God,
as we mark another year of effort and achievement at our school, we gather to hear the report of the governors and questions of parents.
We pray that in our report and in our questions we can reflect the mission of our school and your purpose for us.
Guide all those involved in the school in the paths of righteousness and the search for truth.
We ask this through Jesus Christ, our Lord.
Amen.

Rupert Bristow

157 Almighty God,
we pray for this school.
We give thanks for the staff and pupils.
We ask for your encouragement to governors and parents.
Help us to take stock of the past year, to acknowledge achievements and to be clear-sighted about improvements under way.
Bring insight to our meeting and understanding to our hearts.
We ask this through Jesus Christ, our Lord.
Amen.

Rupert Bristow

Death of a pupil

158 Heavenly Father,
we give thanks for the life of . . . . . . ; for the smiles, the fun and the friendships she brought to our lives.
Through our tears we ask, Lord, that as she is welcomed into your loving arms she also stays in our hearts.
She will always be special to . . . . . . school and to . . . . . . church.
Help us all, family, friends and community, to say farewell to . . . . . . but never to forget her.
We ask this in Jesus' name.
Amen.

Rupert Bristow

159 Heavenly Father,
at present we can only feel the loss of . . . . . .
We want to be strong and we want to understand why
he is no longer here with us.
We pray that . . . . . . is safe in your arms, in your heavenly kingdom.
Help us to remember what he meant to us and what
he left behind – the laugh, the smile, the favourite
comment, the things he struggled with.
Bring us happy memories in the tears.
Bring him the peace only you can give, Lord of love
and mercy.
We ask this in Jesus' name.
Amen.

Rupert Bristow

160 We have lost someone special,
someone who was part of us,
someone who was here with us,
someone who was one of us.
We have lost someone special,
someone who made us complete,
someone who added so much.
We have lost someone special.

Nick Harding

161 There is a time to be sad,
that's the way you made it, God.
There is a time to remember,
that's the way you made it, God.
There is a time to look back,
that's the way you made it, God.
There is a time to feel sorrow,
that's the way you made it, God.

Nick Harding

162 In our tears may we find relief,
in our heavy hearts may we find hope,
in our memories may we find truth,
and in our prayers may we find God.

Nick Harding

163 For all the things we can't understand,
we trust you, Loving God.
For all the people left sad and lonely,
we trust you, Loving God.
For all those in pain and injury,
we trust you, Loving God.
For all those who can only see darkness,
we trust you, Loving God.

Nick Harding

164 We pray for those who have left us,
and for those left behind.
We pray for peace in their hearts,
and understanding over time.
We pray for those who have left us,
and for those left behind.

Nick Harding

165 God in your plan,
there is a time to be born, and a time to live.
A time to fight, and a time to be peaceful.
A time to love, and a time to die.
God, in your plan
there is a time for everything.

Nick Harding

166 Bring healing where there is pain,
bring memories where there is emptiness.
Bring hope where there is despair,
and bring love where there is hurt.

Nick Harding

Success

167 God, we know that we were all made by you,
and we are all special.
God, we know that sometimes we do well,
and we are all special.
God, we know that sometimes we do badly,
but still we are all special.
God, we know that success or failure
doesn't change how you see us:
still we are all special.

Nick Harding

168 Every one of us has gifts and abilities
given to us by God.
Every one of us has talents and skills
given to us by God.
Today we celebrate with those
who have fully used their gifts
given to them by God.

Nick Harding

169 God in heaven,
we thank you for the good things we celebrate.
We thank you for the success we have known.
We thank you for the joy this has given.
We thank you for this blessing.

Nick Harding

170 Father God,
you teach us to run the race of life and to do our best.
You teach us to run the race of life and try our hardest.
You teach us to run the race of life and keep on keeping on.
Father God, thank you for all that you teach us.

Nick Harding

171 David was good at playing his harp,
Gideon was good at fighting a battle.
Noah was good at building a ship,
Mary was good at hearing God speak.
We are all good at something,
thank you for our gifts.

Nick Harding

172 We celebrate our success today.
We celebrate our skills and talents today.
We celebrate our abilities today,
and we celebrate your love for us today.

Nick Harding

173 God who made us,
who gave us music to enjoy,
skills to develop,
matches to play
and success in many things,
give us both the joy of winning,
and the pride in trying.

Nick Harding

174 For all our gifts and talents,
we thank you, God.
For all the times we try hard,
we thank you, God.
For lifting us after failure,
we thank you, God.
For celebrating our success,
we thank you, God.

Nick Harding

175 We are your seed in the ground,
O God our maker.
We are a small shoot of growth,
O God our helper.
We are a bright, strong plant,
O God our sustainer.
We are nothing without you,
O God our friend.

Nick Harding

Setbacks

176 Heavenly Father,
we pray for our school community at this difficult time.
Help us to recover and rebuild our confidence.
Give strength to our teachers and governors
as they meet the challenges ahead.
May pupils and parents join them
in preparing for a better future.
Make us proud in our school and in all the people who contribute to our learning community.
We ask this in Jesus' name.
Amen.

Rupert Bristow

177 Heavenly Father,
help us to come to terms with . . . . . .
that has hit our school so hard.
Give us the help and the hope
from all around to put us back on our feet.
We put our trust in you, Lord,
to bring out the best in us at this time.
May our neighbours in this community act as good neighbours and may we repay them by redoubling our efforts in all that we do.
We ask this in Jesus' name.
Amen.

Rupert Bristow

178 Lord,
thank you
for all the people
who visit our school,
ministers,
nurses,
police,
guest speakers,
parents
and all kinds of helpers
who care about us
and come to teach us
so many different things;
please help us
to show respect
to those who so generously
give their time
to help us.

Tony Bower

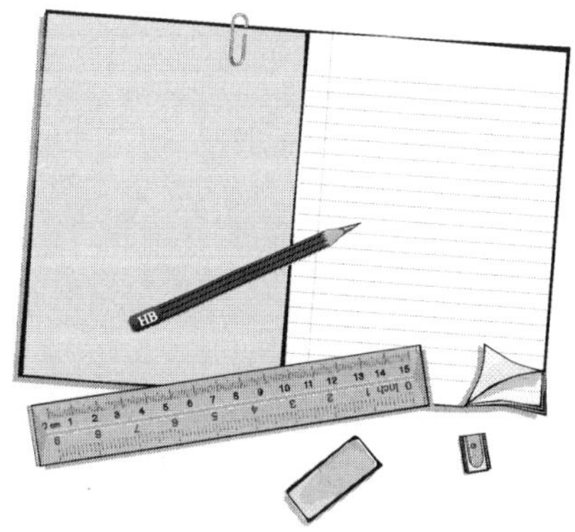

Exam time

179 I know this exam's important, God,
and I'd like to do well.
Please help me
to remember what I've been taught,
and not to be nervous.
And thank you for loving me just as much,
whether I do well or not.
Amen.

Anon

180 Help me, Lord,
to be able to pass the test,
to run life's race and never give up.
To do my best – for you.
When I'm confused by all those books and questions,
then help me to pause and to give thanks
that in all the stress, the work and the pain,
I have at least the chance to try to do well.
Thank you, Lord.
Amen.

David Gatward

181 Heavenly Father,
we pray for all those taking exams today/this week.
You know their capability, Lord.
Help them to do themselves justice as they are put
to the test.

Continued overleaf

Give them the confidence and strength to show what they have learnt, to demonstrate their ability to analyse, and to prove that they can express themselves.
Banish any nerves and give them the peace to show themselves as they really are.
We ask this in Jesus' name.
Amen.

Rupert Bristow

182 Heavenly Father,
help and guide us as we sit our exams.
May we recall what we have learnt.
Keep our minds focused as we analyse and solve problems, let our imagination soar as we express ourselves, but help us to remember to do the simple things well.
May Jesus be our example and inspiration as we are put to the test.
We ask this in Jesus' name.
Amen.

Rupert Bristow

183 Lord Jesus, you faced the crowd,
always calling out your name.
Jesus, you faced temptation,
but you chose the better way.
Jesus, you faced insults,
but stayed calm and determined.
Jesus, you faced it all –
help us to face it too.

Nick Harding

184 I am scared, God of hope.
I am scared of not succeeding.
I am scared of failing myself.
I am scared of letting others down.
I am scared of not remembering,
I am scared of wasting time.
Give me hope, God of hope.

Nick Harding

185 God who made us, you know us.
You know we want to do our best,
you know we want to succeed.
God who made us, you know us.
Help us to do all we can,
help us to cope with the result.

Nick Harding

186 We have so much to think of,
we have so much to do.
Loving God, give us strength,
and help us through.
Show us what is important,
help with every task.
We have so much to do –
help us through, we ask.

Nick Harding

Times of pressure

187 Jesus our friend,
you know what it is like to feel tired.
Jesus our leader,
you know what it is like to feel rushed.
Jesus our hope,
you know what it is like to feel despair.
Jesus, our Saviour,
be with us now, we pray.

Nick Harding

188 God, you made us and you know us.
You know when we are really down
and it all seems to be too much.
You know when we go wrong
and we feel we'll never get it right.
You know when we don't trust you
to help us out of trouble.
God, you made us and you help us.

Nick Harding

189 God, you know we can only do our best.
God, you know we can only give our all.
God, you know how hard we are working.
God, we know that you will help us.

Nick Harding

190 May the God of the quiet and stillness
fill our hearts with calm.
May the God of life and activity
give us energy to serve.
May the God of vision and confidence
give us hope for the future.

Nick Harding

191 There is so much to do
and so little time.
There is so much to say
but not enough words.
There is so much to write
but not enough space.
There is too much, but you are great.
Make all we do as great as you are.

Nick Harding

Playtime and lunchtime

192 Lord,
in our playground
there is lots of noise
from all the boys
and all the girls.
There are shouts and screams,
groans and moans,
cries and sighs,
laughter and fun.
We thank you for
our times of play
and pray
that we will be safe today,
happy in our play.
Amen.

Tony Bower

193 Lord,
thank you for
our break times
and lunch times,
and for all the times
that we can go out and play.
Thank you for
the games that we can play,

and the fun we can have
with our friends.
Please help us
to not just think about
what we want to play
but about what others
want to do today.
Please help us
not to exclude,
but to include,
people,
so that not just some,
but everyone,
can have fun.
Amen.

Tony Bower

194 Lord,
on a day
when the clouds
are grey and gloomy
and the rain is pouring
like a non-stop leaking tap
and we can't play outside,
please help us to make the most
of our nice warm school,
to enjoy playing indoor games,
reading books,
swapping stories and jokes
with our friends.
Please help us
to make the most
of our wet day plays
we pray.
Amen.

Tony Bower

195 Jesus –
thank you for
– grass
– skipping
and running about.
Thank you for
fun and laughter.

Susan Hardwick

196 When I go out to play,
thank you that
it is so much fun.
You are always nearby,
watching over me
and keeping me safe.

George and Angie Allen

197 I got stuck up a tree today.
I called for help.
Thank you, God, that you found a way to sort things out.
Amen.

Heather Ellis

198 Father God,
you give us love and happiness.
Help us to be careful that our games and fun do not hurt others.
Amen.

Denis O'Gorman

199 Father God,
you love us and we are all your children.
Help us to be honest and fair
with everyone we meet
and to be glad to share our fun, play
and happiness with others.
Amen.

Denis O'Gorman

200 Thank you, God, for all good things.
Thank you, God, for all good food.
Thank you, God, for this!

Nick Harding

201 Bless us as we drink and feed,
please help those who are in need.

Nick Harding

202 We've got lots, we are hungry.
We'll enjoy, we are happy.
We remember, we are grateful.

Nick Harding

203 For drinks and sarnies, chips and peas,
for grapes and apples, ham and cheese,
for all this food upon this plate,
thank you God, it's really great!

Nick Harding

204 There's red food and green food,
yellow food and white.
There are sandwiches and platefuls
everywhere in sight.
There's great food and dull food,
tasty food and plain.
All this food reminds us
to say 'Thank you' again.

Nick Harding

205 Make this food special, Lord we pray
so we can enjoy the rest of the day.

Nick Harding

206 You made the food, you made the drink
so as we eat help us to think
of those who nearly starve for real
and those who do not have a meal.

Nick Harding

207 We are grateful for this lunch,
Lord, we give thanks.
We are grateful for all your gifts,
Lord, we give thanks.

Nick Harding

208 Bless this food
as it keeps us going,
may our brainpower
keep on flowing!

Nick Harding

Sports day

209 Almighty God,
you have given us strength and judgement as well as knowledge.
Be with us today as we use your gifts in our races and jumps and games.
Help us to use our individual skills and our teamwork to the maximum.
Above all, Lord, let us have fun on our sports day.
We ask this through Jesus Christ, our Lord.
Amen.

Rupert Bristow

210 Almighty God,
we ask for your blessing on our sports day.
We pray that in all our races, jumps and throws we try to exceed our personal best. Where we are part of a team, in relays and games, may we do our best to support others to succeed in the interests of the team.
And may we compete fairly, perform safely and not laugh too much when our parents take part.
We ask this through Jesus Christ, our Lord.
Amen.

Rupert Bristow

Subjects

Learning

211 You are gentle and kind.
You show your wonderful love to all.
I want to be like you.
God, I am glad I can learn from you
every day.
Amen.

Heather Ellis

212 If I have plenty,
help me to give to those
without.
If I am strong,
help me to help those who are
weak.
If I am good at maths,
help me to be a friend people
can count on.
If I am good at English,
help me to be a friend people
can talk to.
If I have gifts and talents,
help me to use them and bless
others.
If I have a heart,
please help me to care.

Tony Bower

213 You know, God,
it must be really hard for people
who are afraid to ask;
who want to question things
but have been told they shouldn't!
Please help us all to be more curious!

Michael Forster

214 Sometimes, God, we shy away
from the difficult questions.
Probably, we're afraid of where the answers may lead us.
Help us to trust you, even when the answers seem hard.

Michael Forster

215 Teach us, dear God,
to know you better,
explore your world,
learn from mistakes,
understand others,
use our talents,
remember important things,
grow like Jesus.

Ray Simpson

216 Lord,
thank you
for all the times
when people have been patient
with me.
Thank you
for the times
when people have waited
and not rushed away.
Thank you
for the times
when my teachers
have explained things to me
again and again
and have patiently
waited
for me to understand.
Thank you
for your patience
with me
time and time again.
Please help me
to show patience
and be patient
with others.

Tony Bower

217 Jesus,
there is so much
to see and do
in this world,
that I often find
things I want to investigate,
find out about
and discover.
Sometimes though,
this can be dangerous
or a bit silly,

as wanting to discover
can become
being nosy.
I know I won't go looking
down a manhole
or anything daft like that.
But, if there is something
that I want to investigate
that might get me into trouble,
help me to realise this,
and turn away.
Thanks, Jesus.
Amen.

David Gatward

218 Thank you for
school,
and learning,
and brains
to do it with.

Susan Hardwick

219 Dear God,
please help us to be
the sort of people who
find out the full facts about something
and then make the right decisions.
Amen.

Caroline Vallance

220 Dear God,
help us to find out the full facts
about something before
we make a decision about it.
Amen.

Caroline Vallance

221 Father God,
we thank you that all are invited to learn.
Be with us all
as we discover more about your world,
more about ourselves
and more about each other.

Nick Harding

Art

222 Father God,
thank you
for Art,
for the opportunity
of creating,
of making,
of decorating,
of designing,
of painting,
of drawing,
of colouring,
all kinds of shapes,
all sorts of patterns,
all types of pictures;
thank you
for giving us
the abilities
for artistic creativities.

Tony Bower

223 Thank you, God,
for giving us the chance
to be creative with you.
Thank you for making us all so differently,
so that each one of us is special
and of infinite value.

Michael Forster

224 Loving God,
please bless all people who feel left out of things.
Help them to find a sense of value,
and feel that they are important
to your creative work.

Michael Forster

225 Thank you God for thinking of so many
colours for the rainbow.
I love using them in my paintings.
Thank you for colour.
Amen.

Heather Ellis

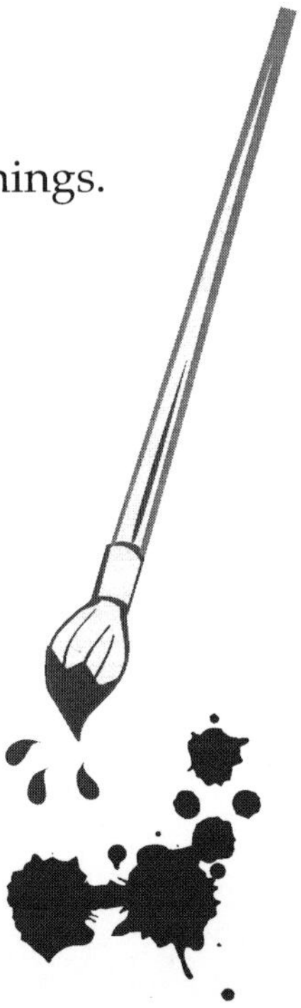

226 I love flowers.
They are so beautiful.
I love their wonderful perfume
and their colours.
Thank you God for making flowers.
Thank you God for colour.
Amen.

Heather Ellis

Design and technology

227 God,
you like making things,
so when I like making things,
I'm being like you.

Susan Sayers

228 Lord,
you love mending things,
so when I enjoy mending things,
I'm being like you.
Amen.

Susan Sayers

229 Father God,
thank you
for food,
for pizzas
and all the different toppings,
for all the food we buy
when we go shopping.
For burgers,
for fish,
for lots of tasty things
we can have in our dish.
For 'cracking cheese'
that would please
Wallace and Gromit.
We thank you
for all the wonderful food
that we can eat
and pray
that we will share
the plenty we have
with those
who have so little.

Tony Bower

230 Loving God,
thank you
for ice creams
on a hot sunny day,
delicious flavours like
chocolate,
raspberry,
cherry,
vanilla,
mint,
strawberry,
chocolate chip.
So many wonderful flavours
that we can savour
and taste
on a summer holiday
lounging on a beach.

Tony Bower

231 Jesus, you helped your dad in a
woodwork shop.
You made nice things out of wood.
I am like wood in your hands.
Sometimes I am hard.
Please make me into a nice person.

Ray Simpson

English

232 Father God,
thank you for English,
for the wonder of words
and the power of words,
please help us to use our speech
wisely and carefully
so our words
bless and not curse.
Please help us
to comprehend
how much you love us
and to read your story
and hear what you
have to say to us.
Amen.

Tony Bower

233 Loving Heavenly Father,
thank you
for words.
With words we can talk
and say what we think,
what we feel,
what we like,
what we don't like.
We can share our secrets
with our friends,
we can share our dreams
and our hopes.
We can share our thoughts,
tell our jokes,
we can say all kinds of things.
Please help us
to be kind
in what we say.
Please help us
to think
about what we are saying
and how others may be
feeling.
Please help us
to help others
with our words
today.

Tony Bower

234 Jesus,
you're an amazing storyteller.
I wish I could tell stories
like you did.
They were amazing.
I love the stories you told,
where crowds of people
listened to you
as you told them
what life was about,
what love meant.
And about heaven, too.
Stories are great, Jesus.
I wonder if I have any stories
that I could tell people
which would be about you?
I hope so.
Help me to tell them, Jesus.
Amen.

David Gatward

235 Thank you, loving God,
for helping us to understand one another,
even though at times we seem to speak
entirely different languages!
Thank you, too, for the wonder of words,
and the way they can help us express your glory.

Michael Forster

236 Sometimes we use all the wrong words,
or just too many of the right ones!
Please, God, send your Holy Spirit
to help us communicate more clearly.

Michael Forster

Geography

237 Father God,
thank you for geography,
where we can learn about distant lands,
hot places with scorching sands,
countries which are mountainous,
and nations that are flat.
Thank you that we can see
the wonder and the beauty
of so many brilliant,
colourfully different places
in this big amazing world
that you have made.
Amen.

Tony Bower

238 For the world you have made,
thank you, God.
For the sky, the earth and the sea,
thank you, God.
For fish and birds and animals,
thank you, God.
For people in every land,
thank you, God.
Amen.

David Adam

239 Father God,
thank you for the lovely world,
which you made.
Help me to know you made everything
out of your love.
Amen.

David Adam

240 Father God,
thank you for the
green,
green,
green
countryside.
It would be no good
for playing hide and seek
because there's so much of it,
and it's everywhere, if we look.
Lots of countryside
in shades of
green,
green,
green,
all there to be seen.
Amen.

Tony Bower

241 Jesus,
I love this world!
I think it's fab!
There is so much to see
and so much to do.
Will I have time?
I hope so.
There are so many animals
and plants.
And then there's the mountains
and rivers
and the sea.
And there's the weather too!
I love it when it's sunny.
Even thunderstorms can be exciting!
(As long as I'm hiding under my duvet!)
This world is a great place, Jesus.
I'm glad I live here.
Help me to look after it.
Amen.

David Gatward

242 God,
thank you for the colours of the rainbow,
and for showing your love to the world
in the sun and the rain.
Amen.

David Adam

243 God,
for a rainbow you both need sun and rain.
You never tell lies so we can trust in you.
Amen.

Susan Sayers

244 Creator God,
thank you
for the rainbow,
that it reminds us
that you always,
always, always, always,
keep your promises.
Please help us
to keep our promises
too.

Tony Bower

245 God, thank you for the colours of the rainbow
and for showing your love for the world
in the sun and the rain.
Amen.

David Adam

246 For a rainbow you need
both sun and rain.

Susan Sayers

247 Dear God,
thank you God for different kinds of weather, we know we need both sun and rain. Thank you for the world that you have created, and thank you for caring for us. Help us when we get frightened, and please help all those in dangerous situations.
Amen.

Gill Thorniley

248 Thank you, God,
for water,
for rivers and streams,
for tap water and well water.
Thank you for giving us water
and for giving us life.
Amen.

David Adam

249 Lord,
giver of life and love,
thank you for the water
that refreshes and revives us.
Thank you for Jesus,
the Water of Life,
who gives us life eternal.
Amen.

David Adam

250 Thank you for
– water
to drink
and to splash in.

Susan Hardwick

251 My lovely God,
thank you for supplying all our needs,
like a fresh, clear spring of water
which never runs dry.
Amen.

Susan Sayers

252 Flow in me, living water of God,
and satisfy my needs.
Flow through me, living water of God,
to bring life and hope to the world.

Susan Sayers

253 Lord, giver of life and love,
thank you for the water that refreshes
and revives us.
Thank you for Jesus, the Water of Life,
who gives us life eternal.
Amen.

David Adam

254 Dear Jesus,
you are the living water
that fills us with life.
May we come to you for this water
and so live for ever with you
in happiness and joy for ever.
Amen.

Denis O'Gorman

255 Almighty God,
thank you for water.
It sounds strange to say, 'thank you' for water,
because it's always there; we never even think about it.
But without water we would die;
just like air,
we need it all day, every day.
Please help us to appreciate water,
and be always grateful for it.
May all those people in the world
who do not have a safe, clean supply of water,
get one soon.
Amen.
Tony Castle

256 We give thanks for the wonder of water:
for cooling drinks on a hot day;
for hot baths on a winter's night;
for the fun of swimming and sailing;
for all the creatures which live in water;
for the miracle of living water.
Amen.
Jill Fuller

257 Father God,
water is great
when we're thirsty, we're hot, we're dirty,
and when we're showing you
that we don't want to hang on to anything
which keeps us away from you.
Not our actions or our inactivity
nor by giving in to thoughts that suggest
we look away from you and your love for us.
We wash our hands
as a symbol of our decision to follow you;
as a symbol of love for your ways;
as a symbol of thanks for your Son.
Amen.
Pete Townsend

258 Father God,
thank you for the sea,
it's a lot, lot bigger than me.
It's deep and it's wide,
deeper than a hole in the ground,
wider than a house
and a building
and a plane

and a field
and a lake.
It's amazing to see
how huge,
how vast
the ocean is
compared to me.
Amen.

Tony Bower

259 Father God,
thank you for the sea,
sparkling bright blue,
under a hot summer's sun.
Thank you for the sound
of the surf as it rolls
onto the shore,
a sound as old as time,
the steady rhythm of creation.
Thank you for life
under the sea
that lives and swims
deep down in the ocean's depths,
brilliant creatures
with fascinating features,
a rainbow of colours,
a rich mixture of textures,
all giving glory
to the artist of the ocean,
the creator of the sea
and all that we can see.
Amen.

Tony Bower

260 Heavenly Father,
thank you for the waves
that lap the sandy shore.
Thank you that the waves
never get tired
or find it a bore,
but keep on rolling in
and in
and in.
Day in,
day out,
day in,
day out,
year in,

Continued overleaf

year out,
year in,
year out,
the waves
keep waving,
keep coming,
keep going,
and I love it!
Amen.

Tony Bower

261 Life-giving God,
thank you
for waterfalls
that splash
and crash
onto rocks
and stones,
that splash
and bash
over pebbles
and twigs,
that dash
and rush
over mountains
and hills.

Tony Bower

262 River, wash over me,
cleanse me and make me new.
Bathe me, refresh me and fill me anew.
River, wash over me.
Amen.

Susan Sayers

263 Creator God,
thank you
for rivers
that sparkle and shine
in the bright, summer sun.
Thank you
for rivers
that burble and murmur
and sing their own song.
Thank you
for rivers
that run on
and on and on.

Tony Bower

264 Dear Creator God,
thank you
for the rain
that makes the flowers grow,
that helps the rivers flow,
that helps the harvest grow,
that helps the world we know
to flow with LIFE!
Tony Bower

265 Thank you God for making rain.
Thank you for the puddles.
I love jumping in them!
Amen.
Heather Ellis

266 Father God,
thank you
for your love,
your faithful love.
As reliable as sunrise,
as dependable as sunset,
deeper than the oceans,
higher than the mountains,
bigger than the universe,
gentler than a summer breeze,
warmer than the sun and
brighter than the moon.
Tony Bower

267 We give thanks for the mystery of the wind;
for the movement of the clouds in the skies;
for the refreshment of gentle breezes on
hot sunny days;
for the power and strength of the wind.
Help us to be more aware of things which
we cannot see but which change our lives.
Amen.
Jill Fuller

History

268 Father God,
thank you for history,
where we can learn about our ancestors,
wars, famines and earthquakes
and all kinds of disasters
from far-away countries, foreign cultures,
kings and queens from the past,
Ancient Rome and Egypt,
civilisations that didn't last.
Thank you that there are so many lessons
we can learn from history.
Please help us
not to repeat the mistakes of yesterday
but build a better future
and a bright tomorrow
by the way we live today.
Amen.

Tony Bower

269 Loving God,
in our learning about events of the past,
help us to hold on to what we believe,
exploring and celebrating what is new
alongside what the works of our ancestors teaches us.
May we always respect those who have worked hard
to make our world a better place today.
It is an honour to read about them.
Someday, people may be reading about us.
What will we do to make them proud?
Amen.

270 Loving God,
bring to us an understanding of different cultures and events through time.
Help us to recognise what binds us together as human beings, what divides us through background and history, and what we can do to understand each other better.
May we push back the limits of our learning, knowing that there are no boundaries in your creation.
Amen.

Rupert Bristow

271 Thank you, God,
that we can know about
how people like us lived in the past.
Our learning from them helps us
be who we are today.
Help us all to fight bad things
by trusting you, and doing good.
Amen.

Nick Harding

IT

272 Father God,
thank you
for IT
and for computers,
it's great to learn
how to use them
and see how clever they are,
and all the amazing things
that we can do on them.
Thank you
that each one of our minds
is more complex
and far cleverer
than the smartest computer.

Tony Bower

273 Loving God,
thank you for the gift of technology,
all the games we can play
and the way we can find out anything
or talk to people all over the world
at the touch of a button.
Help us to be careful
and use this wonderful gift
wisely and safely so that
we will not be hurt but will learn and grow.
Amen.

Maths

274 Father God,
thank you for maths,
please help us to have
a positive attitude to learning,
and not to be negative in our studying.
Thank you that you want to add
good things to our lives
and take away
all that is negative and bad.
Thank you that we can
always count on you
to help us.
Amen.

Tony Bower

275 Creator God,
thank you
for sums,
a multitude
of many numbers,
a way to busy ourselves
on a rainy day and
add up our blessings
every single day.

Tony Bower

276 God, thank you for numbers.
I am grateful that I can see,
I can read,
I can enjoy adding and subtracting.
This gift will help me to work out
that I can count on you always to help me.
Amen.

David Adam

Music

277 God, thank you for ears to hear
and a mouth to speak and sing.
May I listen carefully to what I am told
and enjoy singing songs for you.
Amen.

David Adam

278 We give thanks for the praise we can offer
through our bodies,
through dance,
through movement,
through gesture and mime.
May all our being praise our God.
Amen.

Jill Fuller

279 God, thank you that you have given me hands.
I clap my hands to thank you:
CLAP, CLAP, CLAP, CLAP.
I clap my hands because I love you:
CLAP, CLAP, CLAP, CLAP.
God, I clap my hands because you are here:
CLAP, CLAP, CLAP, CLAP.

David Adam

280 God, thank you for ears to hear
and a mouth to speak.
May I listen carefully to what I am told
and enjoy singing songs about you.
Amen.

David Adam

Physical education

281 Father God,
thank you for physical education,
learning how to play all kinds of games
like football, netball,
hockey and cricket,
how to bowl a ball
and try to take a wicket,
how to kick a ball
and try to score a goal,
how to catch a ball
and not let it fall,

Continued overleaf

how to keep our bodies nice and fit
with so many exercises
that we can jump to it!
Amen.

Tony Bower

282 God never thinks children are
too young to be on his team.

Susan Sayers

283 As you grow stronger
and can do more
things, thank God for
making it possible.

Susan Sayers

Religious education

284 Father God,
thank you for RE,
for learning about faith,
stories that are thousands of years old
and yet as up to date as our daily papers.
Thank you for the lessons of life
that we can learn from these timeless tales
which teach us how to treat one another
and respect each other
and help each other;
thank you for faith.
Amen.

Tony Bower

285 Thank you, God,
for people who show real faith,
and who use that faith
to change the world around them.

Michael Forster

286 Some people are afraid to turn back to you, God.
They're afraid they'll be punished
– often because of what your 'friends' have told them!
Please give us all a better vision of your love,
and help everyone to feel they can turn to you.

Michael Forster

287 We all do it, sometimes, God:
get so hung up on doing the religious stuff
that we forget just to listen to you.
Help us to take time
to hear what you're trying to say to us.

Michael Forster

288 Thank you, God, for those special moments
when you really cut through all the nonsense
and help us to see things differently.
Would that happen more often, perhaps,
if we cut the cackle and gave you a bit of space?

Michael Forster

289 It's sad, Lord.
Some people spend all their time
trying to please you by doing religious things,
when what you most want us to do
is be good to ourselves and each other.
Please help us all to know you better.

Michael Forster

290 How is it, God,
that some people have the idea
that religion's all about not enjoying life?
Who's given them that kind of idea, we wonder?
Please forgive us if we've ever forgotten
that life is your gift, to be celebrated.

Michael Forster

291 I lift up my eyes to the hills:
but where shall I find help?
My help comes from the Lord:
who has made heaven and earth.
He will not let your foot stumble:
and he who watches over you will not sleep.

From Psalm 121

292 We pray for a fresh outpouring of the Holy Spirit
on the people of God
all over the world,
and in all worship traditions.
For a readiness to be changed and made new;
for a softening of the ground of our hearts
to receive without fear.

Susan Sayers

293 Almighty God,
as we gather as people of faith, we thank you for
the different paths we have been given to follow;
the different ways in which we can worship you;
the different ways we have experienced your love.
In our lives and in our minds, may we remain true to you
and respectful of each other's different contributions;
may we always be aware of, and celebrate,
the rich diversity of your world.
Amen.

Rupert Bristow

294 Lord God,
in our learning about different religions,
help us to hold on to what we believe
and reach out to explore and celebrate what is new.
May we respect the views and beliefs of others.
Create in us, Lord, the capacity to understand and reflect.
Help us to learn fresh ways of being still and knowing that
you are God.
Amen.

Rupert Bristow

295 Lord God,
on this day when the festival of . . . . . . is celebrated, we
thank you for the richness of cultures and religions in your
world.
We pray especially for all those in our community and all
those worldwide for whom this is a special day.
You gave us all the gift of hospitality. Let us offer and
receive that gift as we celebrate and give thanks.
Amen.

Rupert Bristow

296 Jesus,
it's not easy being a Christian.
There is so much to think about.
So much to do.
You have to be nice to people,
even when you don't really like them.
That really isn't easy, Jesus.
Especially when someone's annoying you.
But there's more to it
than that.
You have to help each other
and love each other.
Help me to do that.
Amen.

David Gatward

297 Lord, we pray that all
who open their hearts and minds to your Word
may allow you to lead them towards deeper faith,
greater hope and more generous love.

Katie Thompson

298 Dear God,
help us to take time
to discover for ourselves
whether you are real or not.
Amen.

Caroline Vallance

299 Dear God,
help us make a church without walls:
help us to pray all over the place.
Help us to have parties all over the place.
Help us to play.
Help us to visit and tell stories.
Dear God, who is with us all,
put your love in our hearts
and draw others to you.

Ray Simpson

300 Please forgive us, God,
when we act as though we (and often only we)
know all about you.
Help us to be more humble
and to wonder at your greatness.

Michael Forster

301 Lord God, bless all who truly seek to know you,
and help all people to realise
how little we can ever really understand you.

Michael Forster

302 Thank you, God,
for people who trust you
and challenge us to see the new things
that you are doing among us.

Michael Forster

303 We pray for religious leaders,
for parents and teachers,
for all whom you use to expand our minds.
Give them the courage to stand up for what they believe,
and open our hearts and minds to their challenge.

Michael Forster

304 Sometimes, God, we try to box you in
and make you predictable.
Sometimes we act or speak
as if you could only work in our ways.
We're sorry for doing that:
help us to remember how great you are.

Michael Forster

305 Loving God,
we pray for people who are surprised
when you include them in your work.
Give them the grace they need
to fulfil your purpose.

Michael Forster

306 Dear God,
help us to treat places of worship with respect.
We pray that you will bless all those who work in
churches, mosques, synagogues, temples
and other places of worship.
Help them keep them clean and beautiful.
May all places of worship
be places of peace and prayer.
Amen.

Gill Thorniley

307 Almighty Father,
you are the God who loves and created all people,
whatever their religion;
you are not just the God of Christian people.
You know all, you love all,
and receive praise and prayer from everyone
who sincerely seeks and turns to you.
May we always respect people
who have a different religion from us.
May we respect their culture and their ways,
and be ready to learn new and good things from them.
Amen.

Tony Castle

308 Lord, be fair –
it isn't easy you know,
and it's really difficult
with a hot sausage roll in your mouth!
I can't help it,
it's just . . . well, you know,
not easy.
It's not that I don't care
or that I can't be bothered;
that's just not true,
even though it may seem like it.
I want to chat about you
and what you mean to me,
but it's just not very easy.
And it's really difficult
when the jokes get out of hand;
and it's really difficult
when I can't take my eyes
off the spot on her chin.
But I'm not giving up,
I'll give it a go.
But promise me one thing –
you'll back up everything I say!
Amen.

Pete Townsend

309 God,
a lot of the time,
I just can't get a handle on you.
I can't find answers to the questions
that rumble around my head

Continued overleaf

making everything appear unclear,
difficult to see, hard to understand.
If only I could speak to you
face to face;
ask some of those questions
that are burning my tongue;
see what it is you want me to see;
put things into perspective
so that my image of you
isn't quite so distorted.
I don't want to feel afraid
that my honesty
causes you, and other people,
a problem.
I think that
if my questions cause them a problem,
that's not my problem but theirs.
I'm waiting, listening.
Please tell me what you think
and that way
at least we're talking
which, if what I hear is right,
is what you wanted
in the first place!
Amen.

Pete Townsend

310 Lord, it feels, at times,
that I'm walking through treacle.
Each step takes so much effort,
and I know that the next time I put my foot down
it's going to be messy . . . again.
I want to follow you,
but when the going gets tough
my feet get stuck.
It wouldn't be so much of a problem
if everything was OK here, right now.
But, well, it's sort of sticky, you know how it is.
What with this and that, that and this,
and plenty of bother.
I think I need you, Lord,
to help me out.
Providing you've got
a bucket of hot soapy water,
scrubbing brush and a towel.
Amen.

Pete Townsend

311 Dear God,
who made us all and loves us all,
teach us not to hate those of a different nation, colour,
or religion, but to see them as being like us,
your children, and as brother and sister
whom we should love and help if we can.
Amen.

John Wright

Science

312 Father God,
thank you for science,
learning to understand some of
the wonders of the world around us,
doing experiments,
watching and seeing
how things work
and why things work.
Thank you that you
had the ability to create
and to make our world
and everything in it,
including us.
Amen.

Tony Bower

313 Thank you, God,
for a wonderful world,
for all the animals, birds and fish.
Thank you for mothers and fathers
and thank you for making me.
Amen.

David Adam

314 God,
thank you that I can grow and change.
You have given me a strong body
and you make me new.
I love you because you give me life.
Amen.

David Adam

315 Life-giving God,
thank you for the air we breathe.
We cannot see it
but we know
we cannot live without it.
Thank you that we have been given
the breath of life through you.
And although we cannot see you,
we cannot live without you.
Amen.

Tony Bower

316 Father God,
thank you for the sand
that gets between my toes,
that goes up my nose,
sticks on my face,
and gets all over the place.
Thank you that sand
is good fun to play with,
make sandcastles with
and all kinds of creative creations.
Thank you for every grain
which isn't the same
but wonderfully unique
and beautifully made.
Thank you for creating the sand
that gets stuck between my toes.
Amen.

Tony Bower

317 Father God,
thank you for sand,
soft and running through our hand,
thick and squidgy,
when it's wet and squishy;
sand that we can transform
into a castle
surrounded by a moat
or a car or a boat,
sand that's sometimes
as hot as burning coals,
and sometimes

as cold as ice,
sand that says to the sea
'stop'
and sand that says to me
'come'
and have some fun.
Amen.

Tony Bower

318 Heavenly Father,
thank you for pebbles,
so smooth and so round,
stones that are found
on the sand,
that we can hold
in our hand
and throw into the sea,
skim across the water
and watch them bounce,
see the ripples they make
as we drop them
and watch them
fall into the deep blue sea.
Amen.

Tony Bower

319 Creator God,
thank you that you
are bigger than me,
bigger than all I can see,
bigger than the universe,
bigger than the galaxies,
bigger and bigger
than anything
because you
created everything.
Amen.

Tony Bower

320 Our world
is BIG
and round,
so the scientists
have found.
It's filled with
land, sea and air,
all kinds of animals
who share
our planet,
our earth,
our world,
with us.
The great BIG
family of God's creativity.

Tony Bower

321 Thank you, God, for an ordered world.
Thank you for 'scientific laws' – like gravity
that stops us floating off into space!
Thank you for everything that helps us to be safe
and truly to live.

Michael Forster

322 Creator God,
Thank you for all the animals
that live in our world.
Thank you for the lions and
their super claws.
Thank you for the pandas
and their big, black eyes.
Thank you for the polar bears
and their furry, white coats.
Thank you for the seals
and their slippery skin.
Thank you for the penguins
and their waddling walk.
Thank you for the crocodiles
and their snapping jaws.
Thank you for the orangutans
and their swinging arms.
Thank you for all the animals
that live in our world.

Tony Bower

323 Creator God,
thank you
for daffodils,
tulips,
roses,
carnations
and all colourful
flowery creations
that smell so well
and look so swell.

Tony Bower

324 Father God,
thank you
for the sun
that feels warm on our face,
and shines brightly
from far-away space.
Thank you
that it's parked
in just the right place
to give us light
and help us see
that everything was created
the way it should be.

Tony Bower

325 Loving God,
thank you
for light,
whether it's brilliant and bright
or murky and grey,
it's always with us,
every single day,
and means that we can see
this wonderful world
that you created.

Tony Bower

326 Father God,
thank you
for the stars
at night
that shine
so bright,
glow with
brilliant light,
a wonderful
glorious sight,
shining from a
great height,
shining millions
of light-years away
TONIGHT.

Tony Bower

327 Creator God,
thank you
for our bodies.
Thank you for
long legs,
short arms,
red hair,
brown eyes,
big ears,
little noses,
white teeth,
freckled faces,
blue eyes,
blond hair,
short legs,
long arms,
small ears,
rosy cheeks,
pale skin,
brown skin,
red skin,
yellow skin,
black skin,
skinny legs,
scabby knees
from climbing trees!
We all have different bodies,
and no body
is the same . . .
. . . thanks to you!

Tony Bower

328 Father God,
thank you
for our hands.
With our hands
we can make things,
write stories,
throw a ball,
catch,
shake hands,
stroke a dog,
paint a picture,
eat an apple,
make a snowman,
cook food in a pan,
decorate a Christmas tree,
hang up a stocking,
open presents,
play with our toys,
press the keys on our computer,
feel the coolness of a sparkling river,
touch the furry caterpillar,
put them together
and say a prayer.

Tony Bower

329 Father God,
thank you
for our feet.
With our feet
we can kick a ball,
run on the grass,
stand up,
walk up
a mountain,
cross the road,
go and see our friends
who live on a different street,
dance to the rhythm and beat
of a song,
feel the sand between our toes,
splash in the sea,
run wild and free
on our two wonderful
feet.

Tony Bower

330 Father God,
thank you
for our eyes.
With our eyes
we can see the clear blue sky,
the vast ocean,
the smallest flea,
a bird in a tree,
a buzzing bee,
blades of grass blowing in the breeze,
the colours of the rainbow,
a crimson sunset,
the winter frost on the icy ground,
the rain running down the window pane.
With our eyes
we can see
our family
and friends,
people who love us
and care for us.
We thank you
for our eyes
which help us to see
this wonderful world around us.

Tony Bower

331 Father God,
thank you
for our ears.
With our ears
we can hear the birds singing,
the cat meowing,
dogs barking,
the hamster's wheel running,
rivers gurgling,
waves surfing,
aeroplanes flying,
cars revving,
children playing,
teachers teaching,
phones ringing,
and if we listen very, very

quietly
maybe
the sound of the earth
rotating.

Tony Bower

332 Life-giving God,
thank you
that you made me
the way I am.
The colour of my eyes,
the shape of my face,
the length of my legs,
the colour of my skin,
every single thing
about me
is all down to you
thinking of me,
even before
I was born.
Father God,
that thought
AMAZES me!
And all I want to say
is a great, big
THANK YOU!

Tony Bower

333 Life-giving God,
thank you
for the birds of the air
that can fly anywhere
and seem to have nothing
to worry
or care about,
not when you
feed them
and give them
enough to eat.
They don't have to go out to
work
or buy meals from the shops
or put bread in their baskets
at the supermarkets.
Thank you
that you have provided food
for the animal world.
Please help us

Continued overleaf

to make sure
that we don't take away
the food
that they need
because of our greed;
please help us
to think about
the animals
that you have created
and the ways in which
you have made the world
their meal table.

Tony Bower

334 Jesus,
what type of roots
do I need to grow?
I need food
and water
because they help me to grow.
I need family
and friends
because they love me
and care for me.
I need school
and church
because that helps me
to learn about
so many things.
But I need other things.
I need to talk to you,
and read about you,
and learn about you.
These are my roots, Jesus.
Help me to grow.
Amen.

David Gatward

335 Thank you for
– my warm, woolly
winter coat.
Your grateful
Lamb.

Susan Hardwick

336 Thank you for
sky and sun.

Susan Hardwick

337 Thank you for
birds and animals
Thank you for
flowers,
and telinths
with their
sparkly,
shining leaves.

Susan Hardwick

338 For the world you have made
thank you, God.
For the sky, the earth and the sea
thank you, God.
For fish and birds and animals
thank you, God.
For people in every land
thank you, God.
Amen.

David Adam

339 God, thank you for good seeds,
for the seeds of flowers, fruit and vegetables.
Thank you for seeds from which trees grow
and seed from which bread is made.
May I grow to love you and to do good
and be part of your kingdom.
Amen.

David Adam

340 Father God,
thank you for making me strong and healthy.
Keep me safe from all illness
and protect me from evil.
Amen.

David Adam

341 God, thank you that I can grow and change.
You have given me a strong body
and you make me new.
I love you because you give me life.
Amen.

David Adam

342 Thank you, God,
for making me
and loving me.
Help me to love you always.
Amen.

David Adam

343 Jesus,
bless my eyes – so I notice others.
Bless my heart – so I love others.
Bless my hands – so I help others.

Ray Simpson

344 As you learn more about the
universe, thank God for it all.

Susan Sayers

345 Thank you, Creator God,
for giving us eyes to see with,
and for giving us minds to interpret what we see.
Please help us to use them both
to your glory.

Michael Forster

346 Dear God,
You made the
stars to shine
when the sun
goes down.
Please help us,
now and then, to
stand aside and
let others shine.
Amen.

Denis O'Gorman

347 We give thanks for all the gifts we enjoy:
gifts of sight and seeing;
gifts of ears and hearing;
gifts of speech and communication;
gifts of a healthy body
to enjoy movement and sport;
gifts of a mind to imagine, invent and think.
In a moment of quiet we particularly give thanks for a gift which is most special to us.
Amen.

Jill Fuller

348 We give thanks for growth and new life;
for the miracle of life contained within each tiny seed;
for the wonder of seeds
reaching towards the light;
for the mystery of waiting
in the darkness for life to begin;
for the pattern of seeds in fruit and flowers.
Amen.

Jill Fuller

349 As we look at our hands . . .
may we remember all those we have prayed for.
May we trust them to God's loving care.
May we commit our hands, our hearts and our lives to serving those in need.
Amen.

Jill Fuller

350 We thank God for the lights which surround our lives:
for the blazing sun, the shimmer of moonlight, the sparkling of the stars;
for the lights which comfort us when we are sad;
for lights which lead us safely when the days are dark;
for celebratory lights which help us to be joyful.
Amen.

Jill Fuller

Personal, social and health education

Aspirations

351 Lord God,
on the way of goodness,
when I fall,
forgive me and lift me up.
Help me to do your will
and to seek to bring in your kingdom.
Give me the strength to resist temptation
and to do what is right and good.
Amen.

David Adam

352 God, thank you for your love.
When I am down you lift me up,
when I stray you seek to bring me back,
when I fail you forgive me.
Lord, help me to lead a useful life
and to serve you faithfully.
Amen.

David Adam

353 God, you have made me for a good purpose
and to be useful to you and to others.
When I fail to do what you want
forgive me and help me to start again.
Amen.

David Adam

354 Lord Jesus,
as the fishermen listened to you
and obeyed you,
help me to be ready to do
what you want me to do.
Amen.

David Adam

355 Lord God,
you are always more ready to hear
than I am to pray.
Forgive me when I have been deaf to your call
and when I have failed to proclaim you to others.
Open my ears to hear your word to me
and my lips to sing your praises.
Amen.

David Adam

356 Lord Jesus,
guide me into the way of peace.
I give my hands to work for you.
Let my feet always be on your path.
Let me speak your praises
and do your will
this day and for ever.
Amen.

David Adam

357 Lord Jesus,
let your peace fill my heart,
my actions and my days.
Let your peace
be known in my life
and in everything I do.
Help me to be an instrument
of your peace and
to share your peace with others.
Amen.

David Adam

358 Creator God,
thank you for the gift of life
and for the wonders and mystery
of your world.
Help me to use what you have given me
to your glory and the benefit of all.
I ask this through your Son,
Jesus Christ, my Saviour.
Amen.

David Adam

359 God, thank you for giving us life
and making each one of us special.
May I use the talents you have given me
to your glory and to the benefit of others.
Amen.

David Adam

360 God, you have given me many good things;
my life is rich because of you.
Help me to be generous with what I have
and to be willing to give to others.
Amen.

David Adam

361 Jesus,
thank you for the gifts
you have given me.
Sometimes
I don't think I have any,
that I'm not very special.
But, Jesus,
everyone is special to you,
aren't they?
That's why
you made us all
so different.
We all have different gifts,
from playing music
to listening to people.
Please, Jesus,
help everyone
to use their gifts
in the right way.
Amen.

David Gatward

362 Creator God,
thank you
for the talents
that you have given us,
for the abilities
that we have.
Please help us
to use them
and develop them
as we should.

Tony Bower

363 Please forgive us, Lord,
for stopping looking when we think we've seen.
Help us to look more deeply at life.
Help us to see your greater value and purpose
behind the 'ordinary' things.

Michael Forster

364 We all want to do well in life.
There's nothing wrong with that, is there, God?
Sometimes, though, that's just not enough
and we start wanting to control others
for our own benefit.
Please forgive us.

Michael Forster

365 Sometimes when you call us
we say, 'No!'
We know we ought to do something
to help someone else,
but we make excuses.
Please forgive us.

Michael Forster

366 Loving God,
please forgive us when we lose sight
of what really matters.
We're sorry for the way we sometimes go
chasing after things that aren't worth it
when we could put all that energy
into our friendships.

Michael Forster

367 We've done it again, God!
It's so easy, isn't it?
We get hung up on things
and forget that it's people that matter.
Please help us to keep our values straight.

Michael Forster

368 It's the sheer kindness that gets to us, God!
Some people just seem so content with so little
and have so much to give to others.
And they seem so happy about it!
Thank you, God, for people like that.

Michael Forster

369 We pray for people whose vision is limited,
who are so blinded by wealth and things
that they've lost sight of what really matters.
Please God, help all of us
– because we all do that sometimes –
to keep our values focused.

Michael Forster

370 We pray for people who are powerful,
and for those who are famous,
especially those who are finding
it's not all the way they expected.
Please help people under pressure
to remember the ones who love them
and the things that really matter.

Michael Forster

371 We're good at daydreaming,
and getting big ideas.
Then we end up by not valuing the little things.
Please forgive us, God, for getting things out of proportion,
and teach us to value the ordinary stuff.

Michael Forster

372 You know, Lord, it would be a terrible world
if it weren't for 'ordinary' people,
doing 'ordinary' things!
Thank you for people who are happy to do them!

Michael Forster

373 Some people are so unhappy, Lord,
because they want to be 'great' or 'famous'.
Some of them get their wish,
and sometimes they seem even unhappier!
We pray for all people who are unhappy
with who they are, or what they do.
Please help us all to value each other
and ourselves, too!

Michael Forster

374 Wanting to avoid trouble of any kind is natural,
isn't it, God?
And sometimes we try to avoid trouble
by not facing up to things.
Please forgive us, and help us to have real faith.

Michael Forster

375 We've all done it, Jesus:
wanted to be the 'top dog',
maybe even been secretly a little pleased
about someone else's failure.
We're not proud of it.
Not proud of it at all.
Please help us to do it less.

Michael Forster

376 Even when we get it wrong, though,
you love us
just as you loved those disciples!
Thank you, Jesus!

Michael Forster

377 We pray for people
who think coming second is failure.
We also pray for those of us
who can never even get anywhere near second!
Please help us all to find our true greatness
in caring for one another.

Michael Forster

378 Please forgive us, God,
for getting such big ideas that we neglect
the important things.
Help us to remember the value
of simple kindness.

Michael Forster

379 Dear God,
thank you for the gifts and abilities
you have given us.
Help us to use them
to the best of our ability.
Amen.

Caroline Vallance

380 Thank you, loving God,
for all the opportunities you give us.
Help us to use them to make the best
not only of our own lives
but of your whole creation.

Michael Forster

381 It's easy to get carried away
by what we want to achieve,
and forget the needs of others
as well as their hopes and dreams.
Please, Lord, help us to share.

Michael Forster

382 Thank you, God, for challenging us,
for enabling us to do more
than we thought we could.
Thank you for helping us
to help one another.

Michael Forster

383 Sometimes we want power too.
It's just too tempting, Lord,
when we get the chance to be powerful
at someone else's expense.
Please, God, forgive us,
and help us make better choices.
Michael Forster

384 Loving God,
help each and every person you have created
to live as fully as possible
the special life you have given them.
Michael Forster

385 Thank you, Lord God,
for giving us talents
and helping us to achieve things.
Help us always to use your gifts well,
and always to thank you for them.
Michael Forster

386 Please forgive us, Lord God,
when we get so full of our own importance
that we forget to say, 'Thank you' to you.
Help us to remember that
however well we may have used them,
all the skills we have come from you.
Michael Forster

387 We thank you, God, for clever people:
people who invent things
or find cures for illnesses,
people who create great works of art,
all who use the skills you have given them
to make the world even better.
Please continue to bless them
and help them to be not just great
but human too!
Michael Forster

388 Lord God, here is my life!
Lead me your way
and I will follow you
wherever and however you want.
Amen.
Susan Sayers

389 Living God, our life is in your hands,
and we offer you all that we are,
all that our past has made us,
and all that we may become.
Build us up by the power of your Spirit
into a spiritual temple
where you are glorified day after day,
in all our praise and worship,
and in our love for one another.
Susan Sayers

390 Follow Jesus, follow Jesus
walk his way, walk his way,
loving one another, loving one another
every day, every day.
Susan Sayers

391 Lead on, Jesus, I will follow!
I want to live your way,
loving you and loving other people.
Amen.
Susan Sayers

392 Lord,
thank you for the
gifts you give to
each of us, please
help us to use
our talents well.
Amen.
Denis O'Gorman

393 Dear God,
you have given
every one of us a
special gift which
is deep inside us.
Please help us to
see the good in
others and be
happy with what
you have given us.
Amen.
Denis O'Gorman

394 Dear God,
sometimes we
want to become
famous. Please
help us to be the
kind of people
you want us to
be and do the
things you want
us to do.
Amen.

Denis O'Gorman

395 Dear Lord,
you give us all
good gifts. Help
us to use them
wisely and be kind
to everybody.
Amen.

Denis O'Gorman

396 Lord,
thank you for all
the gifts you have
given to me.
Please help me to
keep doing my
best and not to
give up when
things get difficult
or when I am
disappointed.
Amen.

Denis O'Gorman

397 Dear Lord,
we know that we
can't do
everything but
thank you for the
things we can do
well.
Amen.

Denis O'Gorman

398 Dear Lord,
let us see and be
happy for the
talents you have
given to our
friends.
Amen.

Denis O'Gorman

399 Heavenly Father,
thank you for everything
that you give us.
Please help us
to use our gifts
to help other people
to be happy.
Amen.

Denis O'Gorman

400 Lord,
help us to grow up and find out
the things you want us to do.
Help us to find the things
that we are strong at
and the ways we can help
those around us.

Ashley Guest

401 Dear Lord,
thank you for the people you have made us,
with our different abilities and skills.
Help us to appreciate ourselves
and use our talents well and to work
well and be friends with those around us.

Ashley Guest

402 Lord,
thank you for each one here,
their uniqueness, their talents, their struggles,
their value to you.
Help us to realise both that we are special
and that we have so much potential.
Amen.

Ashley Guest

403 Holy Spirit,
we ask that you would bring
your inspiration and help to us.

Ashley Guest

404 Lord,
help us to live life well
and to follow the good ways
that you have set out for us.
Amen.

Ashley Guest

405 God in heaven, some people are chosen by you.
We thank you for St David, and all people
who do hard things because you call them.
May we learn from all who do your work,
and may we be like them.

Nick Harding

406 God in heaven, some people are brave.
We thank you for St George, and all people
who do extra things to help others.
May we learn from all who do more.

Nick Harding

407 Dear God,
we are all good
at something.
Please help us to
see that we can
all be good at
caring for one
another.
Amen.

Denis O'Gorman

408 Dear Lord,
please help us to
be happy to be
the people you
have created us
to be and not to
want to be
something
different.
Amen.

Denis O'Gorman

409 Thank you, God, for the things that we can do,
help us to make wise choices and good decisions.
We ask for your help in situations
we can do absolutely nothing about.
Amen.

Ashley Guest

410 We are lights for you, our God.
Lights in this place, lights in our homes.
Lights on the streets, lights in the shops.
We are lights for you, our God.

Nick Harding

411 Moses became aware of the presence of God
on an ordinary day, doing his everyday work.
Open our eyes to recognise God in the
world around us.
Help us to use our talents and gifts to enable
us to draw nearer to God's presence.
Amen.

Jill Fuller

412 We give thanks for our gifts.
We give thanks for the opportunities we
have to develop and use our gifts.
Help us to be patient when we feel
discouraged,
humble enough to ask for help and advice,
courageous when we need to persevere.
Amen.

Jill Fuller

413 We give thanks for the wide variety
of our gifts.
Help us to recognise our own gifts
and to use them in the service of
others.
Help us to appreciate the gifts of
others and be generous in our
praise and encouragement.
Amen.

Jill Fuller

414 God, it's not easy.
There seem to be so many things that get in the way.
It's difficult to understand,
why you want to work with me.
I can't imagine what you have in mind
when you say, 'Come with me'.
But you know me better than anyone,
although there are some things I would rather
you didn't know!
Even knowing all my doubts and fears,
you still look my way.
I place all my obstacles and difficulties before you.
Deal with them.
Though they appear huge to me,
together we can work through them.
Thank you for trusting me.
Help me to trust you.
Amen.
Pete Townsend

415 Father God,
help us to follow Jesus at all times, hearing what he says,
and doing what he tells us, so that our lives
and those of the people we live with will be happier.
Amen.
John Wright

416 Lord God,
who made us all and loves us all,
help us to share our gifts with people who have almost
nothing,
so no one shall be without food, or drink, or medicine.
For Jesus' sake.
Amen.
John Wright

417 Dear God, thank you for people
and the things that can help us
on our journey through life.
Amen.
Nick Harding

418 Thank you, God, for giving me life.
Thank you for the things I
can do, hear and see.
Help me to treat life properly,
and help me to live it well.
Amen.
Nick Harding

419 Thank you, God,
for all you do for us.
Help us not to get so busy
that we forget you.
Help us to live simple lives.
Amen.

Nick Harding

420 Thank you, Father God,
that you love all of us just as we are.
Help us to make the most of the life you give us,
and help us to
be really happy with ourselves.
Amen.

Nick Harding

421 Thank you, God, for everything that makes me, me.
Help me to use it properly to be the person I can be,
with your help.
Amen.

John Wright

422 Lord God, help me to believe,
and then to live out my belief, so
that others may know my faith from what I do.

John Wright

423 Jesus, be the light we follow, and help us to show your light to others.

John Wright

424 Father God,
everything we have is given by you.
Take back our lives
as an offering to you.
Amen.

Denis O'Gorman

425 Father God,
thank you for all the gifts
you have given to us.
Help us to use them to
help to make people happy.
Amen.

Denis O'Gorman

426 Father God,
being rich and famous doesn't matter.
Help us just to love
and help each other.
Amen.

Denis O'Gorman

427 Father God,
thank you for all the gifts you give us,
and help us to value them and
share generously with others.
Amen.

Denis O'Gorman

428 Father God,
thank you for all the gifts you give us.
Help us to use them to praise you.
Amen.

Denis O'Gorman

429 Father God,
Jesus has shown us the right way to live our lives.
Help us to follow you always.
Amen.

Denis O'Gorman

430 Father God,
you are wonderful.
May all we do bring us closer to you
and make other people happy.
Amen.

Denis O'Gorman

Right and wrong

431 Dear God,
thank you that you are here to help me
put right the wrong things that I do.
Amen.

Heather Ellis

432 Dear God,
sometimes we do and say wrong things. We hurt you and we hurt those around us. We are sorry for all the times we have got things wrong. Please forgive us and help us to get things right.
Amen.

Gill Thorniley

433 Dear God,
sometimes it's hard when our friends do something wrong and want us to join them.
Please help us to make right choices.
Amen.

Gill Thorniley

434 Dear Lord,
please help us to stay away from doing things that we know are wrong.
Amen.

Denis O'Gorman

435 Dear God,
you love us when things go right and when they go wrong. Thank you for your love and for always helping us when things go wrong.
Amen.

Denis O'Gorman

436 Father God,
you know us and you know that we all make mistakes. Please help us to know that you are always with us – especially when things do go wrong.
Amen.

Denis O'Gorman

437 Dear Lord,
we want to do
what is right, but
sometimes others
want us to do
things that we
know are wrong.
Please give us the
courage to say no
to them.
Amen.

Denis O'Gorman

438 Lord,
it is sometimes
hard to be good.
Please help us to
say, 'No' when we
are tempted to
do wrong.
Amen.

Denis O'Gorman

439 Dear God,
we know that
everything you
tell us to do is
meant to make us
happy; but
sometimes we do
wrong things.
Please forgive us
and keep us safe
in your love.
Amen.

Denis O'Gorman

440 Dear Lord,
sometimes we do
wrong but please,
Lord, mend the
wrongs that we do.
Amen.

Denis O'Gorman

441 Dear Lord,
if I want to steal
something
belonging to
someone else,
help me to be
strong and say,
'No'.
Amen.

Denis O'Gorman

442 Dear God,
help us to be
good, caring, honest and kind
to everyone we meet.
Help us to be brave
when we are tempted
to do things that
we know are wrong.
Amen.

Denis O'Gorman

443 Heavenly Father,
give us courage
not to be ashamed
to do what we know is right,
for we know you love us
and teach us what is true.
Amen.

Denis O'Gorman

444 Dear Jesus,
there is a good voice
and a bad voice inside me.
Help me to listen to the good voice
and say 'no' to the bad voice.

Ray Simpson

445 We're sorry, God,
if sometimes we are so obsessed
with rules and regulations
that we lose sight of people's needs.

Michael Forster

446 It's so easy, God,
to become so obsessed with our own goodness
that we end up being terribly good
but not at all nice!
Help us to trust your love
enough to take our minds off ourselves
and think of others.

Michael Forster

447 We pray for people who are frightened to admit
that someone else may be right.
Please, God, help them to feel safe
knowing that right or wrong,
you still love them.

Michael Forster

448 Sometimes we can be really 'blind'!
We can see that someone else is right,
but we don't want to admit it,
so we pretend not to see the truth.
Please forgive us, God,
and help us to be more honest.

Michael Forster

449 God, help me to do what is good
and to walk in the right ways.
When I do wrong
may I turn again to what you want me to do.
Guide me by your presence
and protect me with your love,
that I may walk in the way that leads me to you.
Amen.

David Adam

450 Lord, help me to love you
with all my heart, mind and soul.
Forgive me when I am led astray
and deliver me from evil.
Amen.

David Adam

451 God, thank you that you always love me.
When I do wrong you do not like what I do
but you still love me.
Help me to say sorry when I do wrong
and to give my love to you.
Amen.

David Adam

452 Holy and ever-loving God,
thank you for the forgiveness of sins
and the opportunity to start anew.
I pray that you will fill my heart
with your goodness
and my mind with your love.
Amen.

David Adam

453 Jesus,
being wrong isn't nice,
especially if you thought
you were right,
only to find out
you were wrong.
You have to own up,
say sorry,
and hope for forgiveness.
But when you do,
you can be friends again.
Help me to be like this
more and more.
Amen.

David Gatward

454 Jesus,
I don't mean to be naughty
or mischievous,
but sometimes
I can't help it!
I know that I get into trouble,
and that I shouldn't have done it
in the first place,
but I still do it.
I do learn though, Jesus.
Sometimes I get told off
and that's not nice.
Or I upset people
and that's not nice, either.

Jesus,
help me to do
what I know is right,
and not break the rules
just because I want to.
Amen.

David Gatward

455 Jesus,
what is stealing?
You see, sometimes
if there's some nice food
in the kitchen,
and I know that I'll eat it later anyway,
I want to just have a nibble,
take a little cake,
or stick my finger in the icing.
You see,
I know it's naughty,
but is it stealing?
I guess it is in some ways,
because it's not for me to take,
but for someone else
to give.
Help me, Jesus,
when this kind of thing happens,
because I know it is wrong
to take.
Give me patience, Jesus.
Amen.

David Gatward

456 Jesus,
there are some things
I like doing
that I know I'm not allowed to.
Like jumping on my bed!
That's great fun!
But I know
I shouldn't really do it.
It upsets people,
and I don't mean to.
I just want to have some fun.
But there is a difference
between having fun
and being naughty.
Help me know it, Jesus.
Amen.

David Gatward

457 Dear God,
help us to have the courage
to stand up for what we know is right,
even when the going gets tough.
Amen.

Caroline Vallance

458 Jesus,
saying sorry
isn't always easy.
Sometimes
I don't want to.
I'd rather run away
and hope that what I'd done
would not be noticed,
or perhaps blamed
on someone else.
It's because I'm scared
and because I don't like to see
people upset,
especially if it's my fault.
But saying sorry
is often the only right way out.
Admitting I'm wrong
makes me feel better
and shows that I'm honest.
Help me to be more honest, Jesus,
and to say sorry.
Amen.

David Gatward

459 Jesus,
there are times
when I've made a mistake
that I try to cover up
what I've done.
Sometimes,
when I've done something
I didn't mean to do,
I hide the evidence
to see if I can get away
with what I've done
without being found out
or told off.
That's not nice, really,
is it?

I know I should own up,
and I do,
but I still think, 'What if . . .'
Help me
to own up
and not to run away
from what I've done.
Amen.

David Gatward

460 Jesus,
sometimes
I want to do things
that I know I shouldn't.
It's usually
only small things,
like taking a biscuit
from the kitchen
or watching something on TV
that I know
I shouldn't.
Why
do I feel like this?
Does it mean
I'm really bad?
I don't mean to,
which is why I'm telling you now.
That's good,
isn't it?
Help me, Jesus,
not to give in,
even though I know
how delicious
those biscuits
can be!
Amen.

David Gatward

461 God, I know that you love me.
I am sorry when I do wrong.
I ask you to forgive me
and keep me in your love.
Amen.

David Adam

462 God, thank you
for your love and care.
When I do wrong
you are always ready to give me
another chance
to turn and give my love to you.
Amen.

David Adam

463 Dear God,
please help us to make the right choices today
and not just copy what everyone else does.
Amen.

Caroline Vallance

464 If you are sorry about
something, tell God.
God will forgive you and
help you put things right.

Susan Sayers

465 Be honest and tell the truth.
If you're scared to tell the
truth, ask God to give you
courage and you will grow
strong in God's strength.

Susan Sayers

466 Lord, on the way of goodness,
if I stumble, help me and bring me back.
Give me the courage to stand against evil
and to seek what is good.
May I seek your will
and work for the coming of your kingdom.
Amen.

David Adam

467 Lord God,
help me not to be overcome with evil
but to overcome evil with good.
May I be known as a loving
and forgiving person,
someone with a kind heart
and a generous spirit.
Amen.

David Adam

468 Lord,
now, I'm really lost here,
I've no idea which way to go,
what to do
or whether to do anything at all.
If I turn left
I'll upset those on the right,
and if I turn right
I'll upset those on the left.
If I move forward
people will think
I'm trying to leave them behind
and if I move back
people will think
I'm being evasive.
I try to do the right thing, honest,
but trying to please
so many people
with so many points of view,
opinions,
ideas
(and the occasional plague of stubborn behaviour),
I'll end up doing the wrong thing
at the wrong time
for the wrong people.
I think it's about time
to get a bit of advice.
The confusion is killing me
(or I'll be killing someone if this goes on much longer).
So, as the Creator and all that,
I reckon you might have a few good ideas.
Do you mind sharing some?
Amen.

Pete Townsend

469 Lord,
when I'm honest –
all right, I know that's not all of the time –
but when I'm really honest,
why do I feel that I'm always the loser
when everyone else seems to benefit from the occasional
'I'll borrow this for now and put it back sometime never!'
I'm losing out, aren't I?
You know . . .
from all of those little perks that make life
sort of, well, worth the odd session of honesty?

Continued overleaf

Who is going to know if I'm being honest anyway?
I'm hardly likely to announce the fact that I was thinking,
only thinking you understand,
about helping myself to that box of chocolates;
but I didn't.
If I told everyone, then they'd think I wasn't to be trusted.
Much easier to take the box and keep quiet,
except for the internal combustion noises
that a stomach on chocolate overload makes.
You'd be the only person that knew
and I could chat with you about it
after the chocolate indulgence.
But that's missing the point I suppose.
Much better
to have a chat with you
before my stomach objects to my dishonest behaviour.
Amen.

Pete Townsend

470 Lord,
it's often difficult
to know who's right and who's wrong.
Just as it takes two to argue,
it takes two to agree
to build the bridge
which will join two islands
that have been separated
by an ocean of misunderstanding.
Please help us to learn
how to build bridges,
no matter how far
or how wide
the gap.
Help us to be willing
to realise the loneliness
of anger, of hurt and of damaged pride,
so that we can be a continent of hope
and not a cluster of islands in a raging sea.
Amen.

Pete Townsend

471 God,
help us never to cause pain and hurt.
Help us always to do good.
Amen.

Nick Harding

472 Lord Jesus, when I go wrong, help me to turn to God. Lord God, when I come back forgive me and give me a fresh start. Spirit of God, teach me to do more right things and fewer wrong ones.
Amen.

John Wright

Responsibility

473 Dear God,
when I don't do the jobs that my mum
and dad ask me to do, I'm sorry.
Help me to carry out the jobs given to me.
Amen.

Heather Ellis

474 Dear God,
it is easy to do
the things we
enjoy. Please help
us to be cheerful
when we have to
do things we
don't like doing.
Amen.

Denis O'Gorman

475 Dear God,
you did not give us hands to hang idly by our sides.
You did not give us hands just to take from others.
You gave us hands to work.
You gave us hands to help other people.
You gave us hands to develop our skills and talents.
You gave us hands to give you praise and glory.
May we always be generous in offering to lend a hand.
Amen.

Tony Castle

476 We're sorry, Jesus,
for the times we put off difficult conversations;
the times we've just let bad feelings fester,
because we haven't the courage to deal with them.
Please help us to be the kind of friends to others
that you are to us.

Michael Forster

477 It's not always nice, is it, God,
when people make us face up to things.
True friends sometimes do that, though,
and it feels better afterwards.
Thank you, God, for real friends.

Michael Forster

478 Dear Father God,
please help us
to live our lives
not thinking about
how much we can gain
but how much we can give,
not thinking about how much
we have
but how much we love,
not how much we think
we are the best,
but how we can do
our best for others,
not how much we can
serve ourselves
but how much we can
serve others,
please help us
to be like Jesus.

Tony Bower

479 Dear God,
help us to realise
that our actions and words have consequences
and to think before we speak or act.
Amen.

Caroline Vallance

480 Thank you, God, for loving us so much,
even when we do the most dreadful things.
Thank you for giving us the freedom
to make our own decisions,
so that the things we do really count.

Michael Forster

481 How often we do what we call 'little things'
that turn out to have big consequences!
Please forgive us, Lord,
and help us to learn from our mistakes.

Michael Forster

482 Dear God,
please help us to think before we speak today
and help us to find kind and encouraging things to say.
Amen.

Caroline Vallance

483 Dear God,
thank you that our names
make us the people that we are.
Help us today to think before we speak.
Amen.

Caroline Vallance

Bullying

484 We're sorry, God,
for the way we sometimes make life difficult
for ourselves as well as for others.
Please help all your people to share our space
so that we can have peace in our world.

Michael Forster

485 Please, God, bless all people
who stand up for others who can't.
Give them courage and faith
to keep on trying,
and help us to pay attention.

Michael Forster

486 Dear Jesus,
some people don't notice when I'm feeling sad
and left out.
You were not like that –
you put yourself in other people's shoes.
Help me to put myself in other people's shoes –
to feel what they feel,
to be a friend.

Ray Simpson

487 We're sorry, God, for the times we ill-treat others
because of our own fears.
Help us to get rid of our enemies
by turning them into friends!

Michael Forster

488 Lord Jesus, please bless all people
who suffer unfairly because they're different.
Help them to know that they belong in your world
and help us to show that, in the way we treat them.

Michael Forster

489 If we're honest, God,
we can all be nasty at times.
Some of us actually do it rather well!
Please help us to be kinder.

Michael Forster

490 We pray for people who suffer from unfairness.
Please, God, use us and other people
to show your love.
So that people can believe in your kindness
as well as in their own worth.

Michael Forster

491 Please forgive us, God,
for letting our anger and our prejudice
get the better of us.
Help us to want only good for other people.

Michael Forster

492 There are some people who never seem to hold a grudge,
and who only want what's best for others
– even for 'bad' others!
They really get to us, Lord –
that kind of goodness can be seriously irritating.
But thank you for them, anyway!

Michael Forster

493 We pray for people who feel spiteful,
and make themselves unhappy.
Please help them find happiness
in being more generous of spirit.
Oh, and by the way, God:
can you include us, too,
when we feel that way?

Michael Forster

494 We pray for all people
who think they aren't important,
and that others don't respect them enough.
Please give them confidence in their own value,
and help them find that in valuing others.

Michael Forster

495 There have been times, Jesus,
when people have needed us
and we've left them to cope.
Perhaps we were afraid,
or we just couldn't watch.
Maybe we preferred to pretend
that it wasn't happening.
Please forgive us.

Michael Forster

496 Loving Heavenly Father,
Sometimes
when I pick something up at
home
Mum shouts out:
'BE CAREFUL, THAT'S
REALLY FRAGILE. DON'T
BREAK IT!'
Some things do break easily,
especially if you drop them.
People are fragile too.
If we say horrid things,
it hurts their feelings.
If we hit them,
it bruises their skin.
Please help us today
to be gentle
with one another
in all that we do
and say.

Tony Bower

497 Jesus,
I like it when people
are kind to me.
When they help me
or give me something
or encourage me.
It makes me feel
that they care.
And
I like being kind
to others, too.
Not so that it makes me
feel good,
but because I know
how it feels
when someone
is kind to you.

David Gatward

498 Jesus,
help us to be kind
to one another.
Maybe then
we will be
a little bit more
like you.
Amen.

David Gatward

499 Jesus,
sometimes it is easier
to do what everyone else
is doing.
Like at school
if people are making fun of someone,
it can be easier to join in
rather than help
the other person.
Sometimes
it only takes one person
to persuade you
to do what they're doing
even though
you don't want to.

I need to think
for myself more,
and not be easily led.
Help me do that, Jesus.
Amen.

David Gatward

500 Jesus –
sometimes
I'm not as nice
and kind
as I should be.
Help me
to be more caring
and loving.

Susan Hardwick

501 Jesus –
I was not nice
to my friend
And now I'm feeling
ever so sad.
I've told them
I'm sorry,
and they said it's OK.
But I still feel bad.
So,
now I'm saying sorry
to you.
If I know you
have forgiven me
as well,
I shall feel better.

Susan Hardwick

502 I am so afraid.
I dread going into
school because
of some other
children. I know
you understand.
Please bless
those children.

George and Angie Allen

503 Dear God,
Please help us to stand up for what is right,
even when we find it really hard.
Amen.

Caroline Vallance

504 It's easy to treat well the
people you like. The big
challenge is to treat everyone
well, even those you don't
much like.

Susan Sayers

505 God hates to see any of his
children being badly treated.
It is NEVER God's idea for
you to be hurt.

Susan Sayers

506 Even though other
people may let you down,
God will never let you down.

Susan Sayers

507 God respects you,
so it's good for you
to respect yourself as well.

Susan Sayers

508 When you have suffered yourself
you are more able to reach out
to others in their suffering.

Susan Sayers

509 We're sorry, God,
if ever we've taken advantage of others
so that they've felt hurt.
Please help us to be less like Goliath,
and less like David, for that matter,
and more like you!

Michael Forster

510 Please God, bless all bullies,
and help them to learn to care.
Whether their power is in their strength,
or in their mind or their money,
help them to learn the joy
of using it to care for others.

Michael Forster

511 Loving God,
we pray for people who suffer
because of other people's wrongdoing,
that they may always know that you care
about the injustice.

Michael Forster

512 Please forgive us, Lord God,
when we treat people like toys.
Help us to have Solomon's wisdom
and to know what true love really is.

Michael Forster

513 Please, God, help the people
who know so much pain
that they feel like giving up.
Help them to find hope in you.

Michael Forster

514 Please forgive us, God,
if we've ever made anybody feel
that they don't belong.
Help us to treat everybody
the way we'd like them to treat us.

Michael Forster

515 Loving God, we're so glad
that you are the King of love,
and not just a powerful bully!
Thank you for being King
of all our hearts.

Michael Forster

516 Please forgive us, Lord Jesus,
for sometimes wanting to get our own way
by forcing our ideas on others,
or by misusing our own strength.
Since you are the King of love,
help us to learn your ways.

Michael Forster

517 Some people always seem to get pushed around,
because others always have more power.
Please, Lord Jesus,
help us to find good ways
of showing the power of love to them.

Michael Forster

518 Sometimes, other people find life really bad,
and we're not always as understanding as we might be.
Please forgive us when that happens,
and help us to be more like Jesus.

Michael Forster

519 Lord,
when we see
someone doing
something wrong
to others, please
give us the courage
to tell someone who
can help to stop it.
Amen.

Denis O'Gorman

520 Dear God,
it is terrible to be picked on and bullied.
Your Son, Jesus, was picked on,
tortured and killed;
so you, loving God,
know all about your people
who are picked on;
and those who are bullied.
Every year hundreds of people
die for being Christians.
Every year hundreds of people
are tortured and held in prison,
because of their beliefs.
We pray for anyone, and everyone,
who at this moment,
as we pray now to you,
is being picked on,
hurt and bullied.
Amen.

Tony Castle

521 Father God,
it is so difficult to be brave
when others laugh at us.
Please help us to be strong.
Amen.

Denis O'Gorman

Judging others

522 Loving God, we're sorry
that we aren't always loving, like you.
However hard we try not to,
we do sometimes judge others unkindly
without really knowing them.
Please help us to be more open-minded.

Michael Forster

523 Sorry, God – we've been and done it again!
We see people, and we judge them –
it happens far too often.
Forgive us for being too quick
to jump to conclusions about people.

Michael Forster

524 Please, God,
bless all people who get shoved aside,
because of other people's prejudices.
Teach us all to be more open to others,
and help us to be a sign of your love
to all who are treated like dirt.

Michael Forster

525 We all do it, God,
at least occasionally.
We see someone dressed a certain way,
or living in a certain area,
and we just assume they're bad – or snobbish.
Please forgive us for being prejudiced.

Michael Forster

526 Some people never get the chances they should have
because other people are prejudiced.
Please, God, help us to show your love
to the 'neighbours' whom others don't recognise.

Michael Forster

527 We're sorry, God,
for making snap judgements about people
because of their age, or their colour,
their gender or the way they're dressed.
Help us to be open-minded,
and give you a chance to work through them.

Michael Forster

528 We're sorry that sometimes we're unfair:
sometimes we judge people too quickly;
sometimes we just 'follow the crowd'.
Please help us to be fair to people,
and to make up our own minds.

Michael Forster

529 We're really pleased, God,
that you can make us better than we seem.
Please help us to look deeper
than just the outward appearance,
and see people as you see them.

Michael Forster

530 We're sorry for judging people,
and sometimes for writing them off
just because they don't look or talk
the way we expect.
Please help us to be kinder,
and more like you.

Michael Forster

531 Please, Lord, bless all people
who are badly treated
because of their appearance.
Help them to know that you love them
and can do great things through them.

Michael Forster

532 Please forgive, us, Lord God,
when we think we know people completely,
and we label them as this or that
and don't give them the chance
to surprise us.

Michael Forster

533 Lord God, please forgive us
when we get too concerned with our 'image'
and forget about you.
Help us to project your image
by the way we love one another.

Michael Forster

534 Please, God, help all people
who worry about their 'image',
especially those who feel left out
because they're not 'cool'.
Let them know that it is your love within them
that makes them important.

Michael Forster

535 We're sorry that sometimes we judge people
a little too harshly.
Jesus brought out the good even in Zacchaeus!
Help us to be the kind of people
who bring out the good in others.

Michael Forster

536 It's not always easy
to relate to people we don't understand.
Please help us not to confuse 'different' with 'bad',
and help us to welcome and value
people whose ways are unfamiliar.

Michael Forster

We're all equal

537 Dear God,
thank you for making us different.
Help us to love one another.
Amen.

Heather Ellis

538 Heavenly Father,
help us to
respect and help
everyone we
meet, because we
are all your
special children.
Amen.

Denis O'Gorman

539 Dear God,
please help us to
be friends with
everyone, no
matter who they
are, because you
love all of us the
same.
Amen.

Denis O'Gorman

540 Dear Lord,
thank you for
loving us and
showing us that
we are all valuable
in your eyes.
Amen.

Denis O'Gorman

541 Father Creator,
I want to say thank you for my hands.
They are very special to me;
they are different from my friend's hands
and the hands of everyone here.
The whole of me is specially made by you, dear God.
I think it is wonderful that I am special and unique.
Every boy and girl, every grown-up living in the poor
countries is also special and unique, and dear to you.
Every person should be treated fairly,
should live in peace and be treated equally and fairly.
May all the people around the world who work and suffer
so that the poor may be loved and respected,
be blessed, made strong and kept safe.
Amen.

Tony Castle

542 Lord,
we thank you that you know
and value every one of us here.
Amen.

Ashley Guest

543 We all look and sound different,
but you love us all.
We speak different languages,
but you understand us God.
Thank you God for loving each one of us.
Amen.

Heather Ellis

544 Dear Lord,
thank you for all
your gifts. Please
help us to see the
gifts that others
have and not to
make fun of
people who are
different.
Amen.

Denis O'Gorman

545 Thank you, God, for difference!
Thank you that we aren't all the same!
Thank you for blue eyes, and brown eyes,
for dark skin and fair skin.
Thank you for a wonderful, varied creation!

Michael Forster

546 Jesus and
God –
how ever so clever
you are
to make us all
so very different.
– All
different shapes,
and colours,
and sizes.

Susan Hardwick

547 – All
with a
special
part to play
in your world.
– All
with a
special
place

Continued overleaf

in your heart
and in your love.
Thank you
for making me
the way
I am.

Susan Hardwick

548 Thank you, loving God,
for showing us the way to love
and giving us opportunities to give,
to take second place,
to accept people as they are,
to forgive them when they annoy us,
and look for their needs before our own.

Susan Sayers

549 Father God,
thank you
that the world
is full of wonderful colours
and not just made
in black and white.
Thank you
that you made people
to be colourful too:
black
white
brown
yellow
red
faces;
blue
brown
green
grey
eyes;
black
brown
ginger
blond
hair.
So many different colours
for us to see
and enjoy.

Tony Bower

550 Dear Father God,
sometimes I act as if the world
revolves
around me,
but there are lots and lots of
people
I don't even see
in this big wide world.
Please help me to see
that everyone is just as
important
as me.

Tony Bower

551 Father God,
thank you
that you made this world
full of lots of different people.
Some of them look like me,
some of them don't,
some of them talk like me,
some of them don't,
some of them live near me,
some of them don't,
but all of them,
every single one of them,
is special to you.

Tony Bower

552 Thank you, God,
for making each of us special.
Thank you for the infinite variety
of the people you create.
Help us to value each other
as the unique beings we are.

Michael Forster

553 Loving God,
thank you for showing us
how important we are to you.
Please bless all the people who get left out
because they don't seem special enough.

Michael Forster

554 We pray for people who are unhappy
because they think they're not good enough
for you to love them.
Please help them to know
that you love them just as they are.

Michael Forster

555 I sometimes think, Lord,
that we should value 'ordinary' people more.
You know – the ones we bump into
in our daily lives.
Forgive us for always looking elsewhere
for 'special' people.

Michael Forster

556 Thank, you, God,
for what's 'special' in each of us.
Thank you for making 'ordinary' people
with 'extraordinary' qualities!
Please help us appreciate one another more.

Michael Forster

557 Sometimes, people challenge us, don't they?
They do unexpectedly good things,
or make surprisingly intelligent conversation.
Thank you, God, for good and interesting people
who give us wonderful surprises.

Michael Forster

558 Dear God –
thank you
for making me
me.
I wouldn't
want to be
anyone else.
Being me
is best,
so far as
I'm concerned.

Susan Hardwick

559 Lord,
I suppose I don't like to think about it too much,
you know,
all those annoying ways that other people
behave, act, speak and just, well, you know, live.
Why can't they all be like me?

It would make things so simple.
Just imagine,
no hassles over language,
no arguments over how or what to eat,
no disputes over borders or land,
no complicated debates about nationality,
no violent confrontations about race
or ethnic origins.
No pointing fingers
about the way people look, their skin tone –
in fact, no problems whatsoever.
But, there again,
I suppose,
knowing the human race to be what it is,
sooner or later
we'd find something to argue about,
and someone, somewhere,
would claim to be superior to other people,
even though
we all bleed when we're cut,
we all cry when we're sad,
we all crumble to dust
when death stakes its claim.
Lord,
I'm just so thankful
that, despite who we are
or what we may claim to be,
you love us unconditionally,
with no cultural filters
to weed out the undesirable elements
who you'd rather not have anything to do with.
Your love knows no boundaries,
nor skin tones,
or anything else for that matter.
You love us, full stop, period, without end,
for ever and ever.
Amen to that!

Pete Townsend

560 Dear God,
you love every one of us, different though we are.
Help us to care for each other,
regardless of how we look or what we can do, and in particular
to look after children less fortunate than ourselves.
Amen.

John Wright

561 Father God,
you love us all.
Let us share that love with you
and with everyone we meet.
Amen.

Denis O'Gorman

Including people

562 We're thinking about people
who just can't believe in that kind of love;
people who think they have to be good to be loved,
and blame themselves for not being good enough.
Help them to know that you love them
just as they are.

Michael Forster

563 Something tells us, God,
that an awful lot of people get left out,
because we're all too frantic to notice them.
Please forgive us, and make us more aware.

Michael Forster

564 Dear God,
thank you for not leaving anyone
outside your love.
Thank you for loving
every single one!
Amen.

Susan Sayers

565 You know, God, it's well impressive
how some folk always have time.
It's not that they're lazy,
they just always seem to have time for others.
Thank you for people like that.

Michael Forster

566 It must be horrible to be left out, Lord,
always to be the one no one notices,
or has time for.
Help us to be like Jesus for them,
always to notice – and to have time.

Michael Forster

567 Some people seem to spend all their time
on the outskirts of life.
Please help us all to notice,
and find ways of including them.

Michael Forster

568 Some people are always taken for granted
– never seem to be valued.
Please God, help us and others
to find ways of showing them
a bit of appreciation.

Michael Forster

569 Dear Jesus,
I would like to be like salt
and help people
to enjoy being themselves.
Amen.

Susan Sayers

570 Help us, Lord,
to be salt in the world,
bringing out the best in people
by our love and respect for them.
And help us to be light in the world,
shining with your truth and goodness.
Amen.

Susan Sayers

571 Lord God,
let us not just hear and talk about
being salt and light;
help us to be salt and light
so that we make a difference.
Amen.

Susan Sayers

572 Jesus, this loving you talk about
is HUGE!
I know I don't always want to do it
but I can see it's a good idea.
Please help me to be better at it.
Amen.

Susan Sayers

573 Give me understanding, Lord,
that I may keep your law of love
with my whole life and energy and will.
I pray now for those I dislike
and find it hard to get on with.
Teach me how to treat them with love.
Amen.

Susan Sayers

574 Jesus,
there are so many people
who are ignored
or forgotten.
So many people
who need help.
Sometimes
I'm one of them
and it's horrible.
Sometimes
I ignore people
and don't help them.
That's horrible, too.
You helped people, Jesus.
You sat with them
and talked with them.
Help me be more like you.
Help me help other people like you did, Jesus.
Amen.

David Gatward

575 Lord God, I rejoice in your love
for me and for all people.
May I learn to reveal your love
in my dealings with others
and so help to bring them to know and love you.
Amen.

David Adam

576 Dear God,
thank you that everyone here
is special to you.
Help us to remember that
in the way we treat others.
Amen.

Caroline Vallance

577 Dear God,
please help us to be humble
and put other people before ourselves today.
Amen.

Caroline Vallance

578 When you are kind to anyone
you're being kind to Jesus.

Susan Sayers

579 Treat other people as you
would like them to treat you.

Susan Sayers

580 Do something kind today
and your loving will grow.
Do something mean today
and your loving will shrink.

Susan Sayers

581 Loving God,
thank you for loving all of us,
whether we're impressive or not.
Help us to value each other
in the same way.

Michael Forster

582 God of love, we bring to you
all people who feel left out:
people who don't feel able
to hold their heads high in the world.
Help us to find ways of showing them
that they belong
and we want them here.

Michael Forster

583 Loving God, we pray for everybody,
because everybody is different,
and at times we all feel left out
or not properly understood.
Help us all to value one another,
and to know that we have a place in your world.

Michael Forster

584 Dear Jesus,
you loved everyone
and never excluded anyone because they were different.
You were not supposed to speak to a woman, but you did.

Continued overleaf

You were not supposed to speak to a foreigner, but you did.
Your loving kindness is a great example to us.
May we never exclude people, never be unkind.
Amen.

Tony Castle

585 Dear Lord,
you have said that when we welcome people,
we welcome you;
if we are discourteous to people,
we are discourteous to you.
May we always show respect to everyone
for you love them and expect us to do the same.
Amen.

Tony Castle

586 Thank you, Lord, that each one here
is special to you and that
you value them so highly.

Ashley Guest

587 Lord,
being without friends
is like being alone in a desert
with only the sand and wind to keep me company.
Lord,
being without friends
is like a song
without a voice to sing.
Lord,
being without friends
is like a book
which has no words.
Help me to be your voice
to those who need to hear
a whisper of hope,
a whisper of love,
a whisper of joy.
Help me to be strong
in the face of doubt
in the dark of night.
Help me to be strong
when others are weak.
Help me to show your love
wherever I can.
Amen.

Pete Townsend

Caring for others

588 My name is . . . .
Thank you, Jesus, that you care for me.
My brothers and sisters are . . . .
Thank you, Jesus, that you care for them.
Help me to care for them too.
My friends are . . . .
Thank you, Jesus, that you care for them.
Help me to care for them too.
Thank you, Jesus, that you care for the people around us, whether they are famous or unloved. Help me to care for them too.
Amen.

Nick Harding

589 Heavenly Father,
sometimes we are selfish
and put our own needs
before the needs of others.
Help us to always try to love others.
Amen.

Denis O'Gorman

590 Lord,
help us to care for those around us
and to help those in need in the same way
that we would like to be cared for.

Ashley Guest

591 Loving Father,
help us to care for other people
not only by not hurting them,
but also by trying to help,
as we know you care for us.
Amen.

John Wright

592 Father God,
you love all people.
Help us to love
and care for those who are in need.
Amen.

Denis O'Gorman

593 Father God,
show us how to love and care for others
in the same way that you love
and care for us.
Amen.

Denis O'Gorman

594 Father God,
you love us and show us how to love others.
Help us to love and care for everybody.
Amen.

Denis O'Gorman

595 Father God,
you love and protect us.
Help us to be loving and caring.
Amen.

Denis O'Gorman

596 Father God,
thank you for our gifts.
Help us always to think of others
who need our help and care.
Amen.

Denis O'Gorman

Thinking of others

597 Dear God,
sometimes I can be selfish. I'm sorry.
Help me be a better person
and always to think of others.
Amen.

Heather Ellis

598 Lord,
please help us to
see the needs of
people and to try
our best to help
them be happy.
Amen.

Denis O'Gorman

599 Father God,
you have asked
us to care for the
poor. Help us to
see the needs of
others.
Amen.

Denis O'Gorman

600 Dear Father,
help us to see
when people need
help and to try to
help them in any
way we can.
Amen.

Denis O'Gorman

601 Dear Lord,
help us to think of
others and make
them feel special.
Amen.

Denis O'Gorman

602 Dear Lord,
help each one of us
to see the needs of others
and to be generous and loving.
Amen.

Denis O'Gorman

603 Lord, I may not have much to offer,
I'm not always sure what I have to give.
There are times when all I can think about is me,
what I want and what would make me feel good.
Lord, it isn't always easy to think what other people need,
especially when there are so many things I want.
But you have promised to watch out for me,
I'm never out of your sight or out of your thinking.
You want the best for me and you gave your best for me,
nothing I can give can match that!
Thank you for your gift of life,
the greatest gift of all.
Amen.

Pete Townsend

604 Lord,
I've got my eyes wide shut.
If I keep them open
I can see so many other needs
that get in the way of mine.
I've so much on my mind
but you keep interrupting!
Can I get a word in edgeways
to inform you about some of the things
that need your attention?
It's all right reminding me about other people
and their needs,
but have you seen my list?
If I spend much more of my time
thinking of others
most of my prayers will have passed
their sell-by date!
Either that,
or by the time I get around to asking you
about some of my needs
I've fallen asleep.
So Lord,
let's make a deal.
I'll pray for me,
if you'll look after other people.
Or should it be,
I'll pray for other people,
while you look after me?
Amen.

Pete Townsend

Helping others

605 Dear God,
thank you for all those who help others.
We thank you for those
who look after the sick and injured, the homeless
and the hungry.
Help us to be good neighbours and to help others.
Amen.

Gill Thorniley

606 Dear God,
thank you for all
the good things
we have. Please
help us to see

when we can
help those who
have nothing.
Amen.

Denis O'Gorman

607 Dear God,
please help us to
try to make other
people happy and
be kind when
others are sad.
Amen.

Denis O'Gorman

608 Dear God,
please help us to
do whatever we
can to help other
people to be
happy.
Amen.

Denis O'Gorman

609 Dear God,
you want
everyone to be
happy and so do
we. When things
don't work out
right, please help
us to keep on
trying to help
others.
Amen.

Denis O'Gorman

610 Heavenly Father,
thank you for everything
that you have given to us.
May we help others who
are less fortunate than us.
Amen.

Denis O'Gorman

611 We give thanks for all the gifts we are given.
Help us to see the needs of others.
Help us to be generous in sharing what we have.
Help us to have courage and to be openhearted
in answering the needs of others.
Amen.

Jill Fuller

612 Lord,
it's a good thing
that we have no idea,
know absolutely zilch,
haven't the faintest hope
of being able to predict
when we will finally wave goodbye
to the human race.
But as I take each breath
(which better not be my last!)
I want to say
thanks for my life to date,
and as each day passes
may there be many, many more of them.
Although life may have
its ups and downs,
I would prefer
more of the ups and less of the downs.
And that goes for those people
who may be inclined to think
that their life is going downhill big time.
Give me the courage, Lord,
to make a difference,
to give a helping hand
whenever it's needed,
even at those times
when it feels as if
I'm sitting in a pit
waiting for a rain cloud
to take its juice somewhere else.
Help me, help us,
to be the difference
between a smile and a frown.
Amen.

Pete Townsend

Enjoying life

613 Lord God,
help us to be
happy and enjoy
all the good things
you give to us.
Amen.

Denis O'Gorman

614 Father God,
thank you for all the good things
you give us now
and for the joy and happiness
you have planned for us in the future.
Amen.

Denis O'Gorman

615 Father God,
you love each one of us
and want us to be happy.
Help us to use the gifts
you have given to us to
make the world a happier place.
Amen.

Denis O'Gorman

616 Father God,
you love us.
Thank you for your love
and for the care we give
and get from others.
Help us to see that this is
more precious than all the things we
think will make us happy.
Amen.

Denis O'Gorman

617 Father God,
when we are unhappy,
help us to remember that you love us
and want us to be happy.
Amen.

Denis O'Gorman

618 Father God,
you love us and give us everything we need.
Help us to be happy with what we have.
Amen.

Denis O'Gorman

Honesty

619 Dear God,
when I hurt people with my lies,
please forgive me
and help me to put things right.
Help me always to tell the truth.
Amen.

Heather Ellis

620 Dear God,
when I take things
that do not belong to me
I am so sorry. Help me to give them back.
Amen.

Heather Ellis

621 Dear Lord,
at some time,
most of us tell
lies, either to get
out of trouble or
to boast. Please
help us to tell the
truth, even when
we know that it
will get us into
trouble.
Amen.

Denis O'Gorman

622 Dear God,
please help us to
be honest and
fair in everything
we do.
Amen.

Denis O'Gorman

623 Almighty God,
we know that
some people lie
and cheat. Please

help us to be
truthful and
honest in everything
we do.
Amen.

Denis O'Gorman

624 Dear Lord,
help us to own up
when we have
done something
wrong.
Amen.

Denis O'Gorman

625 Heavenly Father,
it is so easy to do things
that are wrong.
Please help us
to be honest and sorry.
Thank you for loving us
and forgiving us.
Amen.

Denis O'Gorman

Being kind

626 Lord,
help us to be
kind and gentle
with everyone we
meet. Help us to
be patient with
little ones and
encourage all
their efforts.
Amen.

Denis O'Gorman

627 Lord,
help us to be
kind and
generous and to
see the needs of
those around us.
Amen.

Denis O'Gorman

628 Dear God,
help us to love
you with all our
hearts and minds
and to prove it by
being kind to
everyone we
meet.
Amen.

Denis O'Gorman

629 Dear God,
you love us and
give us everything
we need. Please
help us to be like
you and kind to
others who
cannot give us
anything back –
except their
friendship.
Amen.

Denis O'Gorman

630 God our Father,
you love all your
children – those
who are small or
sick and those
who are strong
and healthy –
those who look
lovely and those
who do not.
Please help us
to be kind to
them all.
Amen.

Denis O'Gorman

631 Dear God,
please help us to
be kind. Help us
to think before
we speak, so that
our words do not
hurt people.
Amen.

Denis O'Gorman

632 Dear Lord,
thank you for all
the gifts you give
us. Please help us
to be understanding
and kind to people
who upset us.
Amen.

Denis O'Gorman

633 Dear God,
help us to watch
out for people
who are lonely
and have no
friends and be
kind to them.
Amen.

Denis O'Gorman

634 Dear Lord,
please help me
not to spread
gossip, but to try
to say things that
are kind and
helpful.
Amen.

Denis O'Gorman

635 Dear Lord,
it is easy to love
our friends. Please
help us to be kind
to everyone.
Amen.

Denis O'Gorman

636 Dear Lord,
let us always be
kind and care for
others.
Amen.

Denis O'Gorman

637 Loving God,
help us to be kind and caring
to anybody we meet who is in need.
Amen.

Denis O'Gorman

638 Dear Jesus.
You are loving and kind.
Help us to share
your love and kindness
with others.
Amen.

Denis O'Gorman

639 Lord God,
you love all your children,
even when we have done wrong.
Please help us to be sorry.
Help us to be kind
and not talk about others
with unkind words.
Amen.

Denis O'Gorman

640 Dear God,
we are ALL your children
and you love everyone.
Help us to be kind and caring
to everyone we meet
and never hurt their feelings.
Amen.

Denis O'Gorman

641 God our Father,
you love us and care for us.
Help us to be kind and loving
to everybody we meet today.
Amen.

Denis O'Gorman

642 Father God,
you love all your children
and it makes you happy when
we share what we have with others.
Help us to be kind and caring
to all your children.
Amen.

Denis O'Gorman

643 Dear Lord,
it is easy for us to be kind
to people who are like us,
but help us to see
that you love everybody
and you want us
to love them too.
Amen.

Denis O'Gorman

644 Lord,come on, it's not easy you know,
trying to ignore those things
which get on your nerves and generally drive you mad.
How can some people be so irritating?
(Do they use some kind of anti-social deodorant?)
How can some people live with themselves?
(Have they got rhinoceros skin or what?)
How can other people put up with them?
(Or are all their mates the same?)
Can you imagine having breakfast with them?
(Weetabix, pickled onions and Marmite!)
Can you imagine having to spend time with them?
(It would be like watching stones grow.)
You can?
How do you do it?
What do you mean, 'love'?
Do you mean ignoring the irritations
and all those really awful habits that people have?
Do you mean looking for the best in someone
even though it could take some time?
You mean it, don't you,
that idea about love?
Being kind and watching out for each other
sounds OK, but I'll need some help.
How are you fixed?
Amen.

Pete Townsend

645 Lord, it's difficult enough
trying to cope with myself
without having to understand,
appreciate, care and become friends
with all those people who really
get up my nose, irritate and generally
make me feel as if I've eaten
a few too many jam doughnuts.
Your idea of that funny word,
you know, that thingy word,
the one you talk about so much
(I don't want to say the word,
because if I do
you just might make me behave
like I know the word
and want to act
like that thingy word).
Why should I go out of my way
to be thingy
to everyone whom you thingy?
Thingy makes me feel funny
as if I've done something
odd, different, not normal,
something out of the ordinary
and definitely not the way to behave
if you want street-cred
with all those other people
who don't use that thingy word.
But just suppose,
not for real you understand,
just pretend that I knew what thingy
really meant,
I suppose it might, just might
make a difference.
Amen.

Pete Townsend

646 Father God,
you love us and give us everything we need.
Help us to be grateful for
what we have and to be kind
to those who are not as lucky as us.
Amen.

Denis O'Gorman

647 God our Father,
you know each one of us
and you love us.
Help us to be kind and loving
to everyone.
Amen.

Denis O'Gorman

648 Father God,
please help me to be kind
and loving to everybody.
Amen.

Denis O'Gorman

649 Father God,
help us to be kind to everyone,
even when it's hard to be so.
Amen.

Denis O'Gorman

650 Father God,
help us to see the good in others
and be kind to everyone we meet.
Amen.

Denis O'Gorman

Being patient

651 Lord,
help us to be
patient when
things go wrong.
Amen.

Denis O'Gorman

Saying sorry

652 Lord,
we hate being
wrong. Please help
us to see our
mistakes and to
say, 'Sorry'.
Amen.

Denis O'Gorman

653 Lord God,
we know that you love and care for us
and we know that when we say sorry
you will take us in your arms
and make us better.
Amen.

Denis O'Gorman

654 Lord, sorry!
I don't have to list all the things I'm sorry for,
do I?
I'm just sorry, OK?
I'm not proud of my behaviour,
or the way I speak, or don't speak!
It's not easy, you know,
going out of my way to pass the time of day
with people I'd rather not know;
or stopping to help people who wouldn't stop for me.
How can I spend time with people
who don't like the same things as me?
Who don't watch the same TV programmes?
Who don't dress as they should?
Who don't listen to the music that's good for their ears?
What's that you're saying?
Sorry, I can't quite hear you,
I think I've got selective hearing.
Speak up, Lord,
what's that . . . you love me?
Thanks, I really appreciate that.
Pardon? Could you repeat that?
Love who?
Oh! Sorry!
Amen.

Pete Townsend

655 Lord,
here I am,
saying sorry, again,
for behaving like a cranky gorilla
at a toddlers' tea party.
I didn't mean to make anyone feel
as if they belonged
on another planet –
or even suggest that they should
see a vet.
You know how it is,
one thing leads to another
and before you know it,

bang! I've shot my mouth off,
again.
I wouldn't mind so much,
but I always feel so guilty
afterwards.
As if I've stolen something.
Maybe I have –
stolen something –
like another person's
happiness,
or their confidence.
As if I've screwed it up
and tossed it away like garbage.
I'm sorry, please help me.
Can we start again, like I know we should?
Amen.

Pete Townsend

Forgiveness

656 Dear God,
thank you that I can speak to you
and that you have time to listen.
Please forgive the wrongs that I do.
Help me to get along with others
and always to do good.
God, you forgive us every time,
help me to do the same with others.
Amen.

Heather Ellis

657 Dear God,
you are loving, kind and forgiving.
Help us to be just like you.
Amen.

Heather Ellis

658 Dear God,
thank you that you are so forgiving.
Help me to forgive others,
just as you forgave us.
Amen.

Heather Ellis

659 Lord God,
help us to have
forgiving hearts,
even when it
might be really
hard for us to do so.
Amen.
Denis O'Gorman

660 Dear God,
thank you that even when we make big mistakes you still love us and want us to be your friends.
Help us to be able to forgive our friends when they hurt us, and to give them a second chance.
Amen.
Gill Thorniley

661 Dear God,
at times we all
do things that are
wrong. Please
forgive us for the
times when we
have thought or
said untrue things
about anyone.
Amen.
Denis O'Gorman

662 Dear Lord,
when we have
done something
good, please let it
last for ever. When
we do things that
are bad, please
forgive us.
Amen.
Denis O'Gorman

663 God our Father,
we all do wrong
sometimes. Please
help us to forgive
others who do
wrong as well.
Amen.
Denis O'Gorman

664 Father,
help us to admit our mistakes
and wrongdoing in order that
your forgiveness might flow towards us.
Ashley Guest

665 Thank you, Lord,
for your incredible love for us,
that allowed you to send your
Son Jesus to live and to die for us.
Ashley Guest

666 God, thank you that you love me always.
When I am sorry
you forgive me what I have done wrong
and you welcome me with love.
God, help me to do
what you would like me to do
and to be the person you would like me to be.
Amen.
David Adam

667 Father, thank you for your love for me
and for giving me life.
Thank you for all who love me
and care for me
even when I do wrong.
Help me to be loving and caring
and to forgive from my heart
those who have upset or hurt me.
Amen.
David Adam

668 Forgiveness is too easy to talk about, Jesus,
and too hard to do!
Sometimes we say it but don't mean it,
and sometimes we expect it
just to get ourselves off the hook!
Help us to care for one another,
with all our faults.
Michael Forster

669 When you think about it, God,
we've all been forgiven lots of times.
We must have been,
or we wouldn't have any friends left!
Thank you for friends and family
who love us enough to go on forgiving us!
Michael Forster

670 You know, God, it seems to us
that if we hold grudges against people,
the ones who really suffer are ourselves!
We can be so unhappy, always remembering
the bad things people have done.
So we pray for people who struggle to forgive,
so that they can find happiness.

Michael Forster

671 Almighty God,
we admit our many failures before you, Lord,
and before each other.
You know the difference between failure without trying
and failure despite trying hard.
We know you are a forgiving God. Forgive our
shortcomings and help us to learn from the things
we do wrong or do badly.
We ask this through Jesus Christ, our Lord.
Amen.

Rupert Bristow

672 Almighty God,
bring us to realise our faults and our failures, we pray.
In a moment of quiet let us think of one thing we have
done wrong and for which we are very sorry . . . . . .
Give us and our families and friends a new spirit of
support, love and forgiveness.
Help us not to be selfish and to respect others, however
difficult that sometimes seems.
We ask this through Jesus Christ, our Lord.
Amen.

Rupert Bristow

673 Jesus,
I don't like it
when I get into trouble.
Sometimes
I upset people
and everything feels horrible.
I even cry sometimes.
And, Jesus,
it's not nice
when people upset me,
because I can get angry.
But when things
have calmed down,
and we forgive each other
it is better.

Everything is forgiven,
forgotten.
You taught us this, Jesus.
Thank you.
Amen.

David Gatward

674 Dear God,
help us to be the sort of people
who are prepared to forgive others.
Amen.

Caroline Vallance

675 Please forgive us, loving God,
when we don't love your creation enough.
Help us to value everything you have made,
and to take care of it all.

Michael Forster

676 God will help you learn
to be forgiving by giving
you lots of practice!

Susan Sayers

677 Please forgive us, Jesus,
for the things we do that hurt you.
Please help us to know
how much you love us, even then,
and help us to change.

Michael Forster

678 Please forgive us, Lord Jesus,
when we get impatient
and want to do things in our own time
rather than yours.
Help us to know when to wait, and learn,
and when to get going!

Michael Forster

679 We've all done it, Lord,
and if we haven't yet, we probably will, sometime!
Please forgive us when we get angry and stubborn
and fight against the truth you are trying to reveal.
Please don't give up, Lord;
please keep on prodding!

Michael Forster

680 When we have said bad things
have mercy on us.
When we have done wrong things
have mercy on us.
When we have been rude
have mercy on us.
When we have been greedy
have mercy on us.
When we have been selfish
have mercy on us.
And please help us
to forgive others
as you
have forgiven us.

Tony Bower

681 Holy and ever-loving God,
thank you for the forgiveness of sins
and the opportunity to start anew.
I pray that you will fill my heart
with your goodness
and my mind with your love.
Amen.

David Adam

682 God, thank you for the forgiveness of sins
and the opportunity to start again.
I am sorry for when I have done wrong
and gone against your love.
Forgive me and help me to do better.
Amen.

David Adam

683 Lord God, you forgive me
when I stray away from you
and you seek me with love.
Lord, I turn to you
and give my love to you this day.
Amen.

David Adam

684 Lord Jesus, please forgive us
if ever we treat anybody
as if they don't matter.
Help us to show your love to others,
especially to those who seem least special to us.

Michael Forster

685 Lord,
help us to forgive and
to keep on offering forgiveness,
and help us to receive
your and others' forgiveness
when we need it.

Ashley Guest

686 In quietness we remember the day which has passed.
We give thanks for times of joy, fulfilment and peace.
We ask forgiveness for those words,
thoughts or actions which we regret.
We place our past, our present, our future
into the loving hands of God.
Amen.

Jill Fuller

687 Lord,
you know I used to be so sure
that it wasn't ever my fault,
but now I'm not so sure.
Things seem so complicated,
so confusing
that I feel as if I'm on a roundabout,
can't remember where it started
and don't know if it's ever going to end.
I know this can't continue,
life is being wasted
going around in circles
getting dizzy.
Help me, Lord,
to forgive
and be forgiven.
Help me,
be with me
especially when I screw up with such finesse.
Amen.

Pete Townsend

688 Father God,
you love us and help us
when we make mistakes.
Help us to love and forgive others
when they make mistakes.
Amen.

Denis O'Gorman

689 Father God,
you know we all do things
that hurt other people.
Help us to forgive and
forget the hurts
and be kind to everybody.
Amen.

Denis O'Gorman

Compassion

690 Take my hands, Lord Jesus,
let them work for you.
Let me share in helping
and in caring for others.
Let my hands show your love,
Jesus, Friend and Healer.
Amen.

David Adam

691 God, I want to give my whole life to you.
I am sorry for when I have done wrong
and ask you to forgive me.
I will try to live a good life
and to do what you would have me do,
so that your kingdom may come on earth
as it is in heaven.
Amen.

David Adam

692 Loving Heavenly Father,
thank you
for my family
for my home
for my food
for my friends
for my school.
Please help me
to remember
the children
who have no family
no home
no food
no friends
no school.
It's so very hard
to imagine
what it must be like

to have so little
or nothing at all.
Please help
the children today.
Please show us
what we can do
to show your love.
Please show us
how we can be
your hands and your feet
giving help
showing kindness
showing that we care.

Tony Bower

693 Jesus,
when I'm upset
and someone asks how I am,
it makes me feel cared for
and loved.
And when I see
someone who is upset
and I try to help them,
I want them to know
that I care
and love them, too.
Perhaps, Jesus,
if everyone cared a little more
about each other,
and gave each other help
when upset,
then everyone would be happier.
Wouldn't the world
be wonderful?
Help us
try to make it like that.
Amen.

David Gatward

Sharing

694 God,
you have given me lots of lovely things.
Teach me to share with those who have none.
Help me to be kind and generous towards others.
Amen.

David Adam

695 We often don't appreciate
the things you give us.
Please, God, help us to be more appreciative
of your love and goodness.

Michael Forster

696 Dear God,
sometimes I don't share my things, I'm sorry.
Help me be generous and willing to share.
Help me to be glad to do this all the time.
Amen.

Heather Ellis

697 Thank you God,
when it comes to sharing
you give me very good advice.
Amen.

Heather Ellis

698 Father God,
I like being kind and sharing my things.
Here, you can have the biggest piece!
Amen.

Heather Ellis

699 Heavenly Father,
you give us all the
things we need.
Help us to spend
time with those
who need our
love.
Amen.

Denis O' Gorman

700 God our Father,
you give us
everything we
have. Please help
us to be
generous and
share our things.
Amen.

Denis O'Gorman

701 Dear Lord,
you give us so
many good things.
Please help us to
be grateful and
give generously to
those who are
poor.
Amen.

Denis O'Gorman

702 Dear Lord,
you give us so
much. Please help
us to share with
others who have
less.
Amen.

Denis O'Gorman

703 Dear Lord,
thank you for all
the good things
we have. Please
show us how to
be generous with
them.
Amen.

Denis O'Gorman

704 God our Father,
give us just what we need.
Help us not to be greedy and selfish,
but to share with others.
Amen.

Denis O'Gorman

705 Dear God,
thank you for everything
you give us
and please help us
to share your gifts with others.
Amen.

Denis O'Gorman

706 Dear Lord,
help us to be generous
with what we have
and to be kind and caring
to everybody.
Amen.

Denis O'Gorman

707 Dear Lord,
please help us to be generous
and care for those
who have less than us.
Amen.

Denis O'Gorman

Trust

708 Jesus,
Son of God,
Saviour,
I put my trust in you
and in your almighty power.
You are able to bring light
to my darkness
and rescue me
when I cannot help myself.
Jesus, help me
to know you better
and to love you more.
Amen.

David Adam

709 Holy and strong God, I trust in you.
Help me to stand against all evil
and to seek to tell others of your goodness.
Give me courage in troubles
but, above all, help me to know
you are always with me.
I ask this in the name of Jesus
who died and rose again.
Amen.

David Adam

710 Lord, I come in darkness to your light.
I come in weakness to your strength.
I come in sadness to your joy.
I come in trouble to your peace.
I come in weariness to be renewed.
Lord, change me and I shall be changed.
Amen.

David Adam

711 Dear God,
you are the
maker of all
things and
wonders beyond
our understanding.
Please
help us to trust
and believe in
your promise that
we shall be happy
with you for ever.
Amen.

Denis O'Gorman

712 Dear Lord,
you know
everything we
need, so we put all
our trust in you.
Amen.

Denis O'Gorman

713 Sorry for not trusting you enough, God.
Just that sometimes it really does feel
as if we're all alone in the world.
Then we start feeling sorry for ourselves.
Please help us remember
that you never let things get that bad.

Michael Forster

714 Please forgive us, Jesus,
when we don't really trust you enough,
when we get into a state about things
and act as if you're not around.
Help us to be more trusting.

Michael Forster

715 Some people trust you, Jesus,
so much that they really change things.
Thank you for that kind of faith!

Michael Forster

716 Lord, bless all the people
who are struggling.
Help them to let go of their prejudices,
and to trust you with their fears,
and then to know the greatness of your love.

Michael Forster

717 Sometimes, God, we do wrong things
because they're easier than right things.
When following you is difficult
we look for easy ways out.
Please forgive us
and help us to trust you more.

Michael Forster

718 Loving God,
please encourage all people
who have difficult choices to make.
Help them to trust you
and to do what is right.

Michael Forster

719 We're sorry for not always trusting you:
for trying to tie you down
and thinking you can only work
in ways we expect.
Please, Lord God,
blow our minds open to your greatness!

Michael Forster

720 Sometimes, Lord, we don't trust you enough:
we give up hope too easily;
perhaps we even discourage others.
Please forgive us for doing that,
and help us to be your signs of hope,
like Simeon.

Michael Forster

721 We're sorry for not always trusting you enough,
for sometimes expecting the worst of you,
and being afraid of you.
Help us to remember that whatever we've done,
we can always come to you,
say sorry, and start again, without fear.

Michael Forster

722 Dear God,
please help us to trust you
with things in our lives we don't understand.
Thank you that you care about us
and everything that happens to us.
Amen.

Caroline Vallance

723 God, thank you
that you have many hidden surprises in life
and in my own life.
I trust in you
and I believe that you will keep me safe
for ever.
Amen.

David Adam

724 We're sorry, God,
for not trusting you.
Deep down, we know you love us,
whether we succeed or not,
but we don't always act on that.
Help us to trust you more.

Tony Bower

725 Father God,
in a world
full of broken promises
we can
trust you.

Tony Bower

726 In a world
with big problems
we can trust in you.

Tony Bower

727 Heavenly Father,
thank you
that all your words are true,
all of them are honest,
you never tell a lie,
not even a small one,
or what we might call
'a white one',
you never bend the truth
or try to deceive,
but always speak with honesty
and it's wonderful to know
that we can trust
in your truth.
Please help us
to be honest
with you and
with one another too.

Tony Bower

728 God never tells lies
and so you can trust him.

Susan Sayers

729 We pray for people
who are beginning to give up hope.
Please help them to trust you,
and show us practical ways
in which we can encourage them.

Michael Forster

730 Lord,
Mary, your mother, believed
that you could do something
about an impossible situation
when you turned water into wine.
Help us to trust you
when things in our lives
seem impossible.

Ashley Guest

731 Lord,
I've heard that
Jesus said if you had faith
the size of a mustard seed
then you could do amazing things.
Well, Lord,
I'm not sure

how big a mustard seed is exactly,
but I think that my sort of faith
doesn't compare with that of the seed.
My faith is, well, sort of,
precisely, or thereabouts,
about as big
as a speck of dust
or even smaller.
It might be better
to look at my faith through a microscope,
and then, just possibly,
you might see a tiny,
or even smaller,
speck in the distance.
I'm not quite proud of this fact, Lord,
I'm even a bit embarrassed really.
But at least I'm not going to shout my mouth off
about something I know very little about.
So, I think we've got a bit of work to do,
you know, me and you, Lord,
because there's not a lot I can do
to change the situation,
but I've heard that you can do
sort of amazing things,
out of nothing, nowhere,
in the blink of an eye, sort of.
And I was wondering,
if we can get together on this one,
and maybe, just maybe,
I might be able to see a difference
in the way I trust you.
And that really would be a miracle.
Amen.

Pete Townsend

732 Lord, I know,
no matter how I feel right now,
whether it's a dustbin or a toilet,
you see us for who we really are –
precious people who you care for, every day.
It's difficult, I mean really difficult,
to see above the mess and clutter
that surrounds us.
I'm glad that you can see through the rubbish
and look at my life with love.
Help me
to trust,
to see,
to feel
your love,
no matter what I feel like.
Amen.

Pete Townsend

733 Lord,
can I trust you?
You know, when things get hard,
out of hand
and just a bit messy?
Can I trust you
when my head thumps
from the millions of hassles
that cloud my day?
Can I trust you
when my eyes are tired and my brain aches
and my feet want to give up and go home?
Can I trust you
when I feel cold, lonely,
unlovely, hurt and scared?
Can I trust you
when everything I try to do
and everything I try to say
just make things worse?
Lord, can I trust you
to keep me safe,
to protect me from harm,
to sort out the hassle and the grief?
Lord, be with me.
Amen.

Pete Townsend

734 Lord,
we know you love us and will look after us.
Teach us to trust you,
and that, whatever happens, you will be with us.
Amen.

John Wright

735 Help us, Lord,
to trust you to take us through life and to be there for us
whenever we need you.
In the name of Jesus.
Amen.

John Wright

Emotions

736 When you have to walk
through pain or sadness, stay
close to God and God will give
you strength for the journey.

Susan Sayers

737 Thank you, loving God,
for comfort and sympathy,
reassurance and practical caring
when we are ill or sad.
Make us all more aware
of the needs of those around us
and let our loving show in action.

Susan Sayers

738 Whisper your pain and sadness
into the listening ear of God
and let God's compassion
and comfort enfold you.

Susan Sayers

739 We pray for people who are sad,
so sad that they can't think of anything to do
except get away from the pain.
Please help them to know you are with them,
and give them the strength,
when the time is right,
to face the pain and find hope.

Michael Forster

740 Please, God,
help people who are sad
because they don't like themselves very much
to know that you love them,
and that they are important in your creation.
Help people who have made terrible mistakes
to know they can turn to you
and be forgiven.

Michael Forster

741 In this time of quiet we remember.
We think of those who are sad right now.
We think of those who are despairing.
We think of those who see no hope.
In this time of quiet we remember.
We think of God who knows pain.
We think of God who loves.
We think of God who comforts.
In this time of quiet we remember.

Nick Harding

742 Yesterday was a good day.
Tomorrow could be a happy day
but today is a sad day.
Today is a cloudy and dull day
inside us.
Today is a dark and lonely day
inside us.
Today is a heavy, hurting day
inside us.
Yesterday was a good day.
Tomorrow could be a happy day
but today is a sad day.

Nick Harding

743 In our sadness we don't know what to do.
Lord, hear us and help us.
In our sadness we don't know what to say.
Lord, hear us and help us.
In our sadness we don't know who to blame.
Lord, hear us and help us.
In our sadness we don't know how to look forward.
Lord, hear us and help us

Nick Harding

744 Caring God,
you made life to be a journey.
A journey of fun and amazement
and a journey of hope and purpose.
You made life to be a journey.
A journey of choices and turnings
and a journey of ups and downs.
Help us all on our journey
as we walk through a dark time today.

Nick Harding

745 Loving God,
we think of . . . . and his/her family.
We think of the sadness they are feeling.
We think of the darkness inside them.
We think of the pain they have inside.
We think of . . . . and his/her family
and we offer them to your care.

Nick Harding

746 We don't understand why people die
when they are young and so full of life.
We don't understand why people die
when they have so much yet to give.
We don't understand why people die
when they have brought smiles to so many.
We don't understand. Help us.

Nick Harding

747 Dear God,
please help us to control our anger today
and to walk away if we get wound up.
Amen.

Caroline Vallance

748 You know, God, it really makes us sad
– in fact it makes us cross, too –
that the world is sometimes so unfair!
Please help us not to add to that
in the way we treat one another.

Michael Forster

749 Far too many people have been taught
to feel guilty about being happy!
Please help all people to know your love,
and that you want them to have
the best possible life!

Michael Forster

750 Jesus,
sometimes
when I'm out and about,
I want to run around
and jump,
and dance,
because I feel so happy!
But I know that others
will look at me
as though there is something wrong.
And sometimes,
I want to roll around in the grass
and jump on my bed
or yell and laugh really loudly,
even though my parents
might not want me to!
You don't mind,
do you, Jesus?
I'm just being happy,
and sometimes I need to show it.
Perhaps we should all
show our happiness
a little more?
Help us to, Jesus.
Amen.

David Gatward

751 I'm
so
so
HAPPY!
Thank you!
Thank you
for all the people,
and creatures,
and things,
that make me
feel
like this.

Susan Hardwick

752 Wonderful
God!
Most ace
Jesus!
Beautiful
world!
I'm SO happy,
that I want
to dance –
and sing –
and shout –
and laugh
and laugh –
with all that
I feel inside.
I think
I'll burst
if
I don't!

Susan Hardwick

753 Jesus –
I was feeling sad.
Really ever so sad.
But then
I asked you
to make me better.
Now
I feel
like a light's
been switched on
deep inside
of me,
and it's chased
the sadness away.
Thank you
for
happiness!!
Thank you
for showing
your love
in this way.

Susan Hardwick

754 Happiness is a gift
to pass on
to others,
not just for me
to keep to myself.
And so I pray
you will lead me
to those who need it:
those who are
feeling sad,
for one reason
or another.
Make me a channel
of joy to them.

Susan Hardwick

755 Jesus and God –
we've been
counting blessings –
of all the things
that make us
happy.
There were
millions
and trillions
and
zillions
of them!
Thank you
for them all,
every one.
We want
to pray that
all the whole
wide world
will be happy,
and not sad,
any
any
more.

Susan Hardwick

756 Oh, Jesus! –
I'm really sad.
I don't like
feeling this way.
What is wrong?
Is it me?
Please will you
make me
happy again.
And please,
will you show me
what I must do
as well,
to help you
do this for me.

Susan Hardwick

757 God –
even mighty lions
can feel depressed.
But just talking
to you
and telling you
all about it
helps so much.
Now,
help me
to see why
I'm feeling like this.
Then,
help me
to see
what I need
to do to help
make myself feel better.

Susan Hardwick

758 Lord,
Some days
I feel like singing,
some days
I feel like crying;
some days
I feel like dancing,
some days
I feel like curling up
into a ball
and hiding away;

Continued overleaf

some days
I want to play
forever,
some days
I want everything
to go away
forever;
some days
are great,
some days
I just hate.
But I thank you
that on each and every day
you promise
to be with me
and help me
because
you love me.

Tony Bower

759 Dear God,
sometimes people may have more than others.
Sometimes I get jealous, I'm sorry.
Help me to be happy with what I have.
Amen.

Heather Ellis

760 Dear Lord,
you give us
everything we
need. Teach us to
be happy with
what we have.
Amen.

Denis O'Gorman

761 Dear God,
sometimes people can be so unkind.
Help me not to hate them,
but always to be kind and loving.
Amen.

Heather Ellis

762 Dear God,
when I laugh, I know you laugh with me.
Thank you God for making laughter.
Thank you for making me so happy.
Amen.

Heather Ellis

763 Dear Lord,
thank you for
always being near
to us, especially
when we feel
lonely and sad.
Amen.

Denis O'Gorman

764 Dear Lord,
may we always
thank you,
whether we are
happy or sad.
Amen.

Denis O'Gorman

765 Lord,
we know you love us
and are always waiting
to hear from us.
Whether we are sad
or whether we are happy,
you want to hear our voices.
We can tell you anything.
Let us call upon you
sometime, every day.
Amen.

Denis O'Gorman

766 Dear God,
thank you for exciting times like *(whatever is seasonally appropriate)*
when we are happy and excited.
Help us to share our joy with others.
Amen.

Gill Thorniley

767 Heavenly Father,
thank you for your love and care.
Please help us to trust in you.
Amen.

Denis O'Gorman

768 Lord, if I think too much
there are so many things
which make me really, really angry.
So angry that they make my head feel
crowded, heavy, too full to think.
I can't help looking at everything else
through angry eyes.
I don't want to feel like this,
as if my life is one long angry statement.
Lord, take this anger from me,
help me to do what is right in your eyes.
Help me to look beyond the anger
and see someone whom you love,
even though they really get under my skin at times!
Amen.

Pete Townsend

769 Lord,
I've gone through every emotion in the dictionary.
I've shouted until my throat hurts.
My head aches with the thoughts
of senseless violence,
of mindless actions
that have robbed people
of their hopes, their dreams, their lives.
I can't pretend to understand
or find an answer
to the jigsaw of events
that froze a moment in time
for ever.
Tears sometimes say more
than mere words can express.
A cry from the heart
speaks more wisdom
than a thousand wise men.

But all I can say is
I don't understand, Lord.
All I can pray is that somehow,
for all those involved,
you would bring peace
and understanding,
while I place my life
in your hands.
Keep me safe, keep me willing
to hear your voice and your heart.
Amen.

Pete Townsend

When we struggle

770 Lord,
when trouble comes
we often want to run
to the hills,
head for cover,
hide away
and hope that the troubles
will go away,
but often they don't
and won't
if we do nothing
about them.

Tony Bower

771 Lord,
when troubles come
please help us
to look to the hills
and to the one
who made them,
the one who never sleeps
nor slumbers
but watches
over us.

Tony Bower

772 Father God,
we thank you,
that you know
everything.
Sometimes
things happen
that we don't understand,
things happen
that we don't like,
and we wonder why.
And we don't know why.
Please help us
in our times of being in the
dark
to know that you,
the true light of the world,
are with us
and can help us.
Please help us
to see your light
in a dark, dark situation
and in a dark, dark world.
Please help us
to let your light
SHINE.

Tony Bower

773 Lord,
help us to keep going when
life is challenging
and we face difficulties.
Amen.

Ashley Guest

774 Lord,
help us when the pressure is on
to remember to cast our burdens onto you,
because you care for us.

Ashley Guest

775 Lord,
help us to remember you
and your care for us
when we face times of
difficulty or crisis.

Ashley Guest

776 Lord,
well, it's kind of difficult.
I suppose with all your omniscience
you know what's going on or what's supposed to be happening
but it isn't turning out according to plan.
I thought everything was fine
until everything fell apart
like the proverbial pack of cards.
And now here I am, wanting to know
what on earth you were doing
which took your mind off my situation?
Am I so inconsequential?
Or were things wrong from the beginning?
I really did think that I knew what I was doing
even though I hadn't got a clue
what was going on, down and along
until I started to go under.
So, here I am.
Better late than never I always say.
I would have chatted sooner
but I was so busy doing this, that and the other,
and thought you might be a touch busy
dealing with all those things
that occupy the creator of all things.
And now, having realised
that I've put my foot in it big time,
I thought I'd better get around to asking
how we're going to sort this mess out.
I know it might seem a cheek
to ask for your help after the event,
but, as I said earlier, better late than never.
I can't promise I'll do things any different
the next time,
but it's good to know that you're a very forgiving sort,
which is just as well because,
although I don't mean to,
I somehow always forget
to check things out with you first,
but still, I get around to it, eventually.
And as I always say,
better late than never.
Amen.

Pete Townsend

777 Lord,
you know I've been having a few problems lately.
But there's nothing to worry about,
I'm only up to my ankles
in the emotional swamp.
I could mention others
who are not so lucky.
I only hope
that you've taught them how to swim.
If I'm honest,
things have been tough for a while.
You know how it is,
one thing leads to another and . . .
whoops, it's up to my waist.
There's still nothing to worry about.
I've dealt with this before.
Not too successfully though,
as you know.
Oh, I seem to have sunk up to my armpits.
Look, this isn't funny.
I'm really trying, you know,
to keep up appearances
but it doesn't seem to help.
In fact, it makes matters worse,
because everyone thinks I'm all right,
and I'm not.
So, if you've got a moment,
could you lift me out?
And it would help a lot
if there was someone else about.
Amen.

Pete Townsend

778 Lord,
you may understand –
but I certainly don't –
why things happen to me
the way they do.
At times I feel like a magnet
that attracts problems looking for a home.
Sometimes
I go to sleep feeling on top of the world
and wake up the next morning
with a head
that feels as if it's just been trampled on
by a herd of cattle.
Also, you may have noticed,
I've developed a bit of a stoop when I walk.

Having the weight of the world
on one's shoulders
is a bit much for anyone to bear.
I've been let down, put down,
ignored and rejected.
But rather
than place my trust
in anyone
or any system
that will only make me feel
more screwed up than I am already,
I'm turning to you,
with all my baggage
and dodgy ways –
because you don't seem to care
that I'm not a neat, sorted, top-notch
kind of person –
you love me just the way I am.
Amen.

Pete Townsend

779 Sometimes, God,
I want to scream and shout . . .
at YOU.
It's like I've been walking for so long,
my feet ache, I'm hungry,
and I'm desperate for something to drink.
I feel like just falling down
flat, horizontal,
and not getting up again,
at least not for a while.
Do you understand what I'm trying to say?
I'm tired, God.
All this,
everything,
everybody,
just seem far too much to cope with.
At times I feel as if I've got a problem
for every letter of the alphabet,
and some more!
When times are tough,
when I'm hurting,
crying with frustration,
angry at the world and everybody in it,
it would be really neat
to be able to snap my fingers
and say: 'Job done!'
But you know, and I know,

Continued overleaf

that if that was all there was to it,
I'd probably find myself in the same mess,
the same hassle,
feeling the same hurt, frustration and anger,
as I did the time before,
and the time before that, and the time before that,
etc., etc., etc., for ever, amen.
Whenever I feel like this, God,
just give me a hug,
a smile and a nudge,
and tell me that I'm not on my own.
That together we're a team,
me and you.
Amen.

Pete Townsend

780 Lord, I need a hug.
Sometimes I feel so lonely,
and at times I feel it's me against the world.
I'm not sure I can carry that weight,
I'm not the muscle-mad type!
Walking the extra mile and going the distance,
is it really worth the effort?
You tell me it is,
but you've been there before.
I don't like the sound of going through the pain barrier,
is it worth getting to the other side?
So when you hug,
don't hug too tightly, you might crumple my ego!
Only joking, or maybe I'm not.
If I make a move, will you move with me?
I'm not sure I can do this, I know that you can.
So, be with me each step of the way –
hold me gently, don't let me go.
Amen.

Pete Townsend

781 Lord,
was that really necessary?
What on earth were you doing
while I was trying to deal
with a truck-load of garbage?
How could this have happened to me?
Why me? Isn't there someone else
more deserving and better able
to deal with this emotional sewer material?
I can't believe you let this happen.
One moment I was quietly minding my own business –

well, that and the occasional verbal assessment
of someone else's predicament –
when, all of a sudden,
I'm up to my neck,
drowning, slipping, going under,
sliding and generally
having the sort of day
that I'm sure someone else
would appreciate more than me!
Hey! Don't interrupt.
I only paused for a breath.
Excuse me?
But, but . . .
oh, yeah, I do remember
how you helped me
the last time
to defy gravity, walk on water
and turn pigswill into a picnic.
Any chance of a repeat performance?
Sincerely yours . . .
Amen.

Pete Townsend

782 Lord,
I often feel as if I'm standing
in the middle of a football crowd.
The deafening roar
hurts my ears
and makes my head ache.
Sometimes it seems as if I'm in a dark tunnel
without a light.
I can't see where I've been
or where I should go.
I'm not too sure
about putting my feet down
when I can't see
what I might be stepping in.
And then there are the really bad times
when the football crowd
have joined me in the tunnel
and now I can't hear a thing
or see anything,
and no one can hear me shout.
But you, Lord,
can perform miracles.

Continued overleaf

You can make yourself heard
above the deafening noise,
be seen in the darkest night,
and can hear me when I whisper.
Be with me,
teach me,
listen to me
as my heart beats to the rhythm
of the Creator of the universe.
Amen.

Pete Townsend

Doing our best

783 Dear God,
we are always
happy when we
do well and often
sad when we get
things wrong.
Please help us to
know that
whatever we do
you always love
us and are happy
that we have
done our best.
Amen.

Denis O'Gorman

Being worried

784 Loving Father,
you know how my mind
works
and how sometimes
it works in overdrive,
how I worry
about all sorts of things,
about almost everything;
I worry about
so much stuff
I feel like my mind's
going to blow
with all the overload.
Please help me to offload
all my cares,
all my concerns
onto you,

because you
care for me
and are concerned about
every part
of my life;
thank you.

Tony Bower

785 Father God,
thank you
that I can give you
whatever is bothering me,
whatever is worrying me,
whatever is troubling me;
thank you
that it is no trouble to you
and you can help me through;
thank you.

Tony Bower

786 Lord,
you know I get worried about things.
They might seem really daft to some people,
but to me they are worse than
a face full of spots.
I don't go out of my way to worry,
it sort of stomps around my head,
making itself known,
just in case I try to ignore it.
Hiding my face in my hands doesn't seem to change things,
I can't blink and make things go away.
I can't turn my back and hope they'll go away.
It never seems long
before the finger of despair
taps me on the shoulder
and I'm faced with the reality
of sinking under the ocean of my worry.
Help me, shield me,
so that I can feel secure
in your love.
I don't want to go it alone,
or drown in anxiety.
I want to put my trust in you,
I want to feel at peace
with you.
Amen.

Pete Townsend

787 Father God,
please help me
to know
that worry can never add
anything
but it can take away.
It can take away my peace,
leave me in pieces,
make me feel nervous,
fearful and tearful.
It can take away
my fun,
my happiness,
my love of life.

Tony Bower

788 Please help me
to know
that the hours I waste
worrying
can never be replaced.

Tony Bower

789 Please help
replace
my worries
with the knowledge
that you are there
and that you care
for me.

Tony Bower

790 Jesus,
sometimes
when I'm scared,
or feel unsure,
it's not all that nice.
It's like walking
in the dark
without a torch.
I can't see
where I'm going.
Help me, Jesus,
to trust you.
To know that you will help me,
even if I think it all looks
a bit scary.
Amen.

David Gatward

791 Thank you, Jesus, that you called yourself
the Good Shepherd.
You look after us all, even when we feel ....
Help us to ask you for help when we are worried about things.
Amen.

Nick Harding

792 Lord,
when I am anxious
or scared or unhappy,
bring to me your life,
peace and joy.

Ashley Guest

Being afraid

793 Dear Lord,
new things can be
frightening. Please
help us to know
that you are with
us and will always
help us.
Amen.

Denis O'Gorman

794 Dear Lord,
sometimes we
feel frightened.
Thank you for
always being with
us so that we need
not be afraid.
Amen.

Denis O'Gorman

795 Jesus, thank you that you stilled the storm
and saved the disciples.
You are with me always.
Help me when I am afraid.
Amen.

David Adam

796 Lord Jesus,
when I am afraid or in trouble
help me to know you are with me
and that you love me always.
Amen.

David Adam

797 God, help me to know
that you are always with me;
you love me and protect me.
Keep me and those I love safe
and in your peace.
Amen.

David Adam

798 Dear God,
please help us when we are frightened.
Please help us when we have to do something difficult,
or we have a hard choice to make.
Give us wisdom to make right choices.
Amen.

Gill Thorniley

799 You, Lord, are my shelter and my strength.
You are always ready to hear me.
In time of trouble you are with me.
So I will not be afraid.
Amen.

Jill Fuller

800 Lord, we are often afraid when we find
ourselves in frightening situations.
We sometimes fear that we will sink
beneath the problems we face.
We sometimes wonder if you hear our cries
for help.
Help us to be brave and to trust the power
of your love.
Teach us to listen for your calm reassurance
above the sounds of our storm: Peace be still.
Amen.

Jill Fuller

801 Lord,
I realise it sounds daft,
possibly really stupid
in the warm light of the day,
but I just can't help
looking behind me
whenever I walk upstairs to bed.
Now, please don't laugh,
I know it's irrational,
that there's nothing there,
but you never know,
one day there just might be

something which will throw my life
into confusion, disarray,
and make it seem like
the sun's gone to sleep.
You see,
the stairs
are my life.
It's my journey
from birth to the future.
And I really need to know
that you're there,
right behind me,
beside me, in front of me,
watching my feet
so that I don't trip over my own shadow.
Amen.

Pete Townsend

802 Lord,
you are the light of my life.
But sometimes,
just sometimes,
it seems very dark.
Dark enough to make me feel cold,
lonely,
isolated from the warmth of your love.
It feels as if the long fingers of fear
creep around me, over me, swallowing the light.
I want to run,
hide, cover my face with my hands.
But they just make it seem even darker.
Lord, remind me
that you are my strong tower
where I can run to.
And, Lord,
remind me that putting my hands in front of my face
only makes things worse,
like trusting my own senses
to get me through the darkness.
Lord, light my life,
light my way as I walk each day with you.
Amen.

Pete Townsend

803 Father God,
we are often frightened.
Help us to know that we are
always safe in your hands.
Amen.

Denis O'Gorman

Trying new things

804 I tried something new today
and you were there to help.
I wasn't scared because God,
you were with me.
Thank you God for your patient love.
Amen.

Heather Ellis

805 This is fun!
When I try things for the first time
I will think of you God.
I will never be scared
because you are right by my side.
Amen.

Heather Ellis

806 Lord, give us enthusiasm to try new tasks.
Help us to continue when we meet
difficulties.
Guide us to understand when we need help.
Grant us joy and satisfaction in the
completion of a task.
Amen.

Jill Fuller

807 Lord, sometimes I am afraid of
using my gifts and tackling a new task.
I fear people will laugh at my efforts.
I fear people will think I am being
too big for my boots.
I fear failure and sometimes I fear
success.
Help me to approach new tasks
trusting that you want me to use
all my gifts.
Reassure me, encourage me,
calm my fears.
Amen.

Jill Fuller

Listening

808 Dear God,
sometimes we
talk so much that
we don't hear
what others have
to say. Please help
us to listen to our
parents, teachers
and those who
teach us about
you.
Amen.

Denis O'Gorman

809 Dear Lord,
help us to listen to
others and give
them what they
really like.
Amen.

Denis O'Gorman

810 Lord, I know listening is important.
I can help others if I listen attentively.
Sometimes people need to share sorrows or joys.
Taking time to listen is a sign of friendship.
Encouraging others to talk can help them with problems.
Nobody wants to feel their voice isn't heard.
Interconnecting our lives we share our stories and tales.
New chances come to listen every day.
Glory be to God for the gift of listening.

Jill Fuller

811 OK, Lord
so what's going on?
Why do I feel this way?
It can't be all my fault, can it?
Well, see it my way:
if I spend all my time
wondering what other people think or feel,
how will I ever get
to where I want to go?
How will I ever get what I want?
Although I have to admit
that at times I feel like I'm chewing sand,
or walking through treacle.

Continued overleaf

Perhaps I shouldn't struggle
and keep yelling in your ear.
Perhaps I should listen,
take the time to see and hear
just how much you love me,
and him and her.
Amen.

Pete Townsend

812 Lord,
at times there seem so many voices,
so many people
shouting, calling, pointing,
I can't hear myself think.
What am I expected to do?
Whose voice should I listen to?
Where can I look?
Then, in the middle of the noise,
the confusion, the chaos,
I think I can just hear
a small, persistent voice
whispering, calling, comforting.
It's a voice I recognise,
a voice that I've come to appreciate;
always there, always speaking
with a love that's awesome;
a love that's there for me.
Everything else becomes distant,
as I turn my ear towards the voice,
and hear you speak my name.
You're here for me, I'm listening.
Amen.

Pete Townsend

Death

813 Lord Jesus,
you know what it's like
to lose a friend.
You know what it's like
to see your friends crying
because someone they love
has died.
Lord Jesus,
you wept
when Lazarus, your friend,
died.

You wept
when you saw his sisters,
and you shed your tears
for someone you loved,
even though you brought
Lazarus
back to life.
Lord Jesus,
thank you
that you understand how we
feel
and even though we believe
in life after death,
we know it's OK
to cry
because
you wept.

Tony Bower

814 Father God,
thank you,
that you are a God
who comforts,
like the warmth of the
summer sun,
like the voice of our favourite
friend,
like the person and the place
we love the most,
you comfort us and are all of
these things
and much, much more.
You bring us comfort
when we are upset,
you care for us
when we cry,
and you carry our burdens
when we can't carry them any
more,
and you carry us
when we can't go on any more.
Thank you.

Tony Bower

815 Heavenly Father,
when the ones
we love
have gone,
passed on,
it can feel like they've left
a great big hole
in our lives
that no one can ever fill
and we don't know how
we're going to cope.
Thank you,
that because of you
we do have hope,
hope for our loved ones,
that we will see them again,
one day,
in heaven;
hope for our lives,
as our journey goes on,
and the thoughts
and special memories
of the ones we love
we will take with us
and carry them safely in our
hearts
for ever.

Tony Bower

816 Father God,
we pray
for those today
who are sad and upset,
who are grieving
for the ones they love.
We want to wrap
our thoughts and prayers
around them,
comfort and protect them.
Father God,
please help them to know
how much we care,
how much we feel for their loss,
for their heartache and pain,
and as we pray
our hearts
go out to them.

Tony Bower

817 Grieving for loved ones
can never be rushed or avoided.
It is precious
and all part of our love.

Susan Sayers

818 It's very sad when people die, Jesus,
but then you know that already. . .
Thank you for knowing how I feel,
and for all the lovely memories that are left;
and thank you for giving me hope.
Amen.

Michael Forster

819 Dear God,
our friends who have died
are with you in heaven.
They still love us
and we still love them,
so let's be happy together,
for ever.
Amen.

Denis O'Gorman

820 Father God,
we are very sad
when someone we love dies.
Help us to know that they
are happy with you
and waiting to welcome us.
Amen.

Denis O'Gorman

Our family and friends

Home

821 Loving God, thank you for people who care for us,
whether relations and friends
or professional carers like doctors and nurses,
police and home helps.
Help them to know that they are making
your whole world new.

Michael Forster

822 God, thank you for this day,
for my home
and for all the people who love me
and care for me.
Amen.

David Adam

823 Thank you, God, for my home.
Thank you for food to eat.
Thank you that I can rest.
Thank you for all who love me.
Thank you that you are with me always.
Amen.

David Adam

824 God, I thank you
because you love me always.
Thank you for my home and family
and all who love me.
Amen.

David Adam

825 Lord God,
thank you that Jesus lived in a house
and was loved by Mary and Joseph.
Be with me and my family in our home
and keep us in your love always.
Amen.

David Adam

826 Father God,
thank you
for houses
for bungalows
for flats
for cottages
for igloos
for huts
for tents
for caravans
for farms
for ranches
for boats
for barges
for all the different places
that we can call
home.

Tony Bower

Parents and guardians

827 Dear God,
thank you for my mum and dad.
I love them with all my heart.
Help me always to do good.
Amen.

Heather Ellis

828 I love my mum and dad.
I love their special cuddles and kisses.
They look after me.
Thank you God for my mum and dad.
Amen.

Heather Ellis

829 I love my mum and dad.
They love and care for me.
Thank you God for my mum and dad.
Amen.

Heather Ellis

830 Dear God,
help us not to be too proud to look after one another.
Thank you for all those who look after us, and bless them.
Amen.

Gill Thorniley

831 Dear God,
thank you for people who look after us
and prepare our meals.
Thank you for things to do and thank you
for quiet times too.
Amen.

Gill Thorniley

832 Lord God,
thank you for all
the people who
care for us and
help us to be
happy and good.
Please help us to
remember to say
thank you.
Amen.

Denis O'Gorman

833 Father God, we thank you for all who look after us.
We thank you for our fathers.
We ask you to help them be better ones.
Amen.

Nick Harding

834 Dear God,
we know you love us
and all your children.
Help us to be kind
and try to help everyone
we meet today.
Amen.

Denis O'Gorman

835 Father God,
you love us as your children
for what we are and
not just how we look.
Without you, we have nothing.
Take us in your loving arms
and give us all we need.
Amen.

Denis O'Gorman

836 Heavenly Father,
thank you for letting us
be called your children –
for that is what we are.
May we give back to you
some of the joy and happiness
you have given to us.
Amen.

Denis O'Gorman

837 God, our heavenly Father,
whether we are young or old,
we are all your children.
May we always care for each other
and share your love with everyone.
Amen.

Denis O'Gorman

838 God, you love me.
God, I love you.
I love my parents.
Help us to love each other.
Amen.

David Adam

839 Thank you that you
are always nearby.
You watched over me
when I was in my
mummy's tummy
and brought me safely
into the world.

George and Angie Allen

840 When I was a little baby
I know you helped
Mummy and Daddy
to love me
and keep me safe
from all that would harm.

George and Angie Allen

841 Dearest Jesus
and God –
thank you for
mums and dads
and families.

Susan Hardwick

842 Dear God,
I'm glad you love me.
I like being one of your children!
Amen.

Susan Sayers

843 We're grateful for people
who do the little things for us.
who remind us when we forget,
or who make sure there's toothpaste in the bathroom.
Thank you, God,
for people who care.

Michael Forster

844 What an amazing way to love!
Are you like our father, God?
Do you wait patiently
for us to come to our senses?
And then celebrate when we do?
Now, isn't that something!

Michael Forster

845 Loving God,
I ask your special blessing
on my very special mum.
Your love shines
through her laughing eyes
and gentle smile.
Your kindness
through her tender care.
So bless her, Lord,
and keep her safe.
She taught me how to love.
Amen.

846 There is nothing you can do
that would stop God loving you.
You are always his precious child.

Susan Sayers

847 Father God,
we are your children.
We believe in you.
We trust in you.
We love you.
Make all the world one happy family,
loving you and caring for one another.
Amen.

Denis O'Gorman

848 Father God,
you love us and want us to be safe and happy.
Help us to obey those who care for us.
Amen.

Denis O'Gorman

Brothers and sisters

849 Heavenly Father,
as we celebrate the arrival of a new brother/sister
for . . . .
we pray for all new-born babies around the world.
In these early weeks of life, bring renewed efforts to all who care and protect the new-born.
May love combine with nursing and medical care to safeguard their health.
May adequate nourishment be available wherever it is needed and not just where it is wanted.
May hope overcome adversity.
We ask this in Jesus' name.
Amen.

Rupert Bristow

850 We thank you, loving God,
for giving us one another to enjoy,
to laugh and cry with, to learn to live with.
May even our conflicts and arguments be used
in helping us to grow up in your love.

Susan Sayers

851 O most merciful Redeemer,
friend and brother,
may I know you more clearly,
love you more dearly,
and follow you more nearly
day by day.
Amen.

(The prayer of Richard of Chichester)

852 Everybody will want to share
in the good news,
that my beautiful baby brother is here at last.
He will brighten up everyone's day!
Thank you, God, for this little boy.
Amen.

Anon

853 Everybody will want to share
in the good news,
that my beautiful baby sister is here at last.
She will brighten up everyone's day!
Thank you, God, for this little girl.
Amen.

Anon

854 God bless this baby,
newly born,
with all the gentle love of heaven.
A miracle,
wrapped up and fast asleep,
reminding us again
of human hope and innocence.
Amen.

Anon

855 All the other people in the world
are your sisters and brothers
because God made
and loves all of us.

Susan Sayers

856 Dear Jesus,
we know that everyone we meet
is your brother or your sister.
What we do to them,
we do to you,
because you love them.
Help us to be kind
to everyone we meet.
Amen.

Denis O'Gorman

Family

857 Jesus,
I'm a part of a huge family,
aren't I?
You know,
not just here with my family,
or me
and my friends,
but everyone
around the world!
We are one BIG family!
That's amazing!
I wish we could all get on well, though.
There is so much sadness in the world,
but there is a lot of happiness, too.
Help us, Jesus,
to spread the happiness around a bit.
Maybe then,
we can be a worldwide
happy family!
I hope so.
Amen.

David Gatward

858 Lord, you know the need and pain
of those we love and worry about.
As you look after them,
give them the sense of your caring presence
to uphold and sustain them.

Susan Sayers

859 God bless my family.
Look after us all.
Help us look after each other.
In life and death
keep us safe for ever.
Amen.

Susan Sayers

860 Thank you, God, for all the people we know
who make life good for us.
Thank you for all those
who show us your love
and help us to celebrate it.

Michael Forster

861 Please, God, bless all families,
especially the unhappy ones
where people damage one another.
Please bless us, too,
and help us to be truly loving.

Michael Forster

862 Lord Jesus,
we're sorry for the times we hurt each other
because we're jealous or angry.
We know it hurts you, too.
Please forgive us.

Michael Forster

863 Thank you, Jesus, for loving us
and for wanting us to have a really good life.
Thank you for all the things you give us,
especially each other.

Michael Forster

864 Thank you, Jesus,
for friends, for family, for freedom,
for blue skies and glistening raindrops.
Thank you for all the important things in life.

Michael Forster

865 Please, God, comfort people who are sad
because they've been separated from someone.
Help us always to be honest about our feelings,
and at the same time to trust you.

Michael Forster

866 We want to pray for each other, God:
for the people who are really special to us,
and who also happen to be very close to us!
Help us to know how important we are
to one another.

Michael Forster

867 Thank you, God, for our families,
for people who put up with us
when it's difficult,
and who love us
even when we're not very lovable.
Thank you for people
who are so like you!

Michael Forster

868 Father, we thank you
for the personal and affectionate way you care for us
and provide for all our needs;
may we spread the good news of your love
by the way we respond to you and to one another.

Susan Sayers

869 Our Father God,
thank you
for our families,
the people we live with,
share a home with,
share our food with,
share our lives with,
have fun with,
fall out with, and
make up with.
Please help
my family
to see the good
in one another,
to be patient
with each other,
to remember
that families
are special
and come in all shapes
and sizes.

Tony Bower

870 I know I'm young
and that it will be
a very long time
before I fall in love,
or get married,
but can we talk about it anyway?
I think it's amazing
that you can love someone
so much
that you want
to spend the rest of your life
with them!
It's brilliant!
I know that it must be hard,
and at times you may argue
or disagree,

but if you love each other
it's probably even better
than having a best friend!
Jesus,
I hope that if I get married
you will help me
make it a brilliant one.
Amen.

David Gatward

871 Loving God, we pray for each other
– because we love each other!
Help us all to know each other's needs
and try to make each other happy.

Michael Forster

872 Lord,
thank you for all
the people in our
families who
make us happy.
Help us to be
kind and
considerate so
that we make
others happy too.
Amen.

Denis O'Gorman

873 Lord,
thank you for all
the love that
comes to us from
our parents, our
friends and family.
Keep them all
safe and help us
to love others as
you have loved
us.
Amen.

Denis O'Gorman

874 God our heavenly
Father,
thank you for our
families and all
the things they do
for us. Please help
us to be kind and
loving to
everyone.
Amen.

Denis O'Gorman

875 Dear God,
thank you for all the people we can communicate with.
Help us to keep communicating with our friends,
our families,
and those we care about.
Amen.

Nick Harding

876 Dear God,
you love us
and in your eyes
we are all valuable.
We thank you for everything
you have given us.
Help us to be kind
and care for our families
and other people.
Amen.

Denis O'Gorman

877 God, our loving Father,
you gave us Jesus,
who taught us to love
and respect one another.
Help us never to forget
that we are all members of your family;
we need to help and support one another,
in love, at all times.
May our hands be always
used in friendship and love,
to the glory of your name.
Amen.

Tony Castle

878 Father God,
Thank you for our families.
Help us to be loving and caring children.
Amen.

Denis O'Gorman

Friends

879 Dear God,
your love cares for others.
Help me to show this when friends
feel upset or sad.
Amen.

Heather Ellis

880 Thank you that I can have fun times
with my friends.
The best friend of all is you, God.
I want to grow closer to you every day.
Thank you for being you.
Amen.

Heather Ellis

881 Thank you God for being my best friend.
You are helpful, loving and kind,
just like best friends should be.
Our friendship will go on for ever.
Amen.

Heather Ellis

882 Dear God,
thank you for friends. Thank you that you want to be our friend, even when we get things wrong.
We pray for the lonely, that you will bless them and that they might find friends.
Amen.

Gill Thorniley

883 Dear Lord,
we all make
mistakes and
sometimes end
up quarrelling.
Please help us to
make friends again.
Amen.

Denis O'Gorman

884 Dear Lord,
may we become
true friends with
others, even
though they may
have nothing to
give us in return.
Amen.

Denis O'Gorman

885 Lord,
everything we
have comes from
you, so there is
nothing we can
give to you but
our love and
friendship.
Amen.

Denis O'Gorman

886 Thank you, Jesus, that you know everyone
and you love us all.
Thank you, Jesus, that you know me and love me.
Thank you, Jesus, that you have given me friends.
Help me to be a good friend.
Amen.

Nick Harding

887 Father God,
your love and our friendship with Jesus
are more precious than any treasure
we could find.
Thank you for letting us find
this wonderful treasure –
Jesus, your Son
and our dearest friend.
Amen.

Denis O'Gorman

888 Thank you for
friends
and sharing
and playing.

Susan Hardwick

889 Dear Jesus, God –
please bless
and take care of
all my bestest people.
But, specially,
please will you
help my friend …
they're feeling sad.
Make them happy
once again.

Susan Hardwick

890 Lord God, we thank you for all those
who have directed us to know you better,
and for the way you are drawing us closer
into friendship with you.

Susan Sayers

891 Jesus, I want my friend . . .
to meet you and find out how good it is
to live in your company.
Amen.

Susan Sayers

892 Isn't it great, God,
when we meet really caring people
– the kind who stick with us
through thick and thin?
Thank you for giving us such signs of your love.

Michael Forster

893 Please, God, help people in trouble
to know you're with them,
even when they find it hard to see you.
And help us to be the kind of friends
that make you more visible.

Michael Forster

894 We're sorry, God,
if we've ever let our friends down
because we were afraid to be pushy!
Help us to know when it's time
to be a nuisance
for the good of someone else.

Michael Forster

895 Thank you, God,
for all my friends
and for the fun
I share with them
every time we meet.
Amen.

Anon

896 A friend is like a tower strong;
a friend is like a joyous song
that helps us on our way.
When golden ties
of friendship bind
the heart to heart,
the mind to mind,
how lucky we are!

Michael Forster

897 Thank you, God, for all our friends,
all the people who love us.
Thank you for the chances we have
to show your love
by being kind to others.

Michael Forster

898 Isn't it strange, God,
how we often don't really appreciate people
until we have to separate from them?
Please help us to appreciate all our friends.

Michael Forster

899 Thank you for friends, Lord,
and thank you for your promise of new life.
Thank you for showing us that every ending
paves the way for a new beginning.

Michael Forster

900 The more love we give,
the more love there is!
Help us to spread your love around
so there's lots and lots and lots!
Amen.

Susan Sayers

901 Loving God,
thank you
for friends –
people who like us,

care about us,
play with us,
share with us,
stay with us.
When we're sad,
when we're bad,
when we're mad
and angry,
thank you
for friends
who love us
at all times.
Please help us
to be good friends
to others.

Tony Bower

902 Father God,
thank you for friends.
Friends are special,
friends are fun,
friends are great,
friends are neat.
Yet . . . sometimes
we fall out.
We break up our friendships
by unkind words,
by doing selfish things.
Please help us
to make up
with our friends,
to say sorry
and to forgive,
so we can be friends . . .
. . . again.

Tony Bower

903 Lord,
thank you
for the joy of talking,
sharing our secrets
with our friends,
laughing and joking
with our mates,
answering questions
in our class,
having conversations
about our favourite things,

Continued overleaf

deep discussions
on various topics,
shouting for our team
to win,
or whispering the words
'I love you'
to our family.
We thank you
for the words
we can say
to express
whatever we are feeling
every single day.

Tony Bower

904 What must it be like
to have no friends at all?
I don't think I'd like that.
Jesus,
I pray for all those
who don't have any friends
or who are finding it hard
to make new friends.
Be a friend to them, Jesus.
Amen.

David Gatward

905 Jesus,
some people just can't seem to understand each other,
even though they speak the same language.
We pray for people whose friendships are spoilt
by misunderstandings.
Please, loving God, send them your Holy Spirit
and help them understand each other better.

Michael Forster

906 Father God,
we know that
we do things that
are wrong. Please
help us to say
sorry and to be
friends again.
Amen.

Denis O'Gorman

907 Lord,
we all need to ask for help from time to time.
Thank you for those around us
who can help us out
and also thank you that you
are always there for us
when we are in need.

Ashley Guest

908 We give thanks for the meaning which
ordinary things have in our lives.
We give thanks for memories and friendships
which can make everyday objects special for us.
Help us to treasure these special things.
Amen.

Jill Fuller

909 Father God,
you know that at times I could scream,
at other times I feel numb.
I'm not sure if some of my friends are enemies
or if some of my enemies are friends!
It all gets a bit confusing.
You know that the best way to spread gossip
is to tell your friend not to say a word!
Trouble is,
if you don't share your thoughts with a friend,
they get angry
and accuse you of not being open with them.
Don't get me wrong,
I want friends around me,
it's just that sometimes
I'm not sure who I can trust.
There's only one thing for it . . .
If I tell you what's on my mind
will you tell me what's on yours?
Amen.

Pete Townsend

910 Lord God,
help us to get to know you better
and to learn to trust you
as our friend.
Amen.

John Wright

911 May God's peace fill our lives
and make us friends with each other.
Amen.

John Wright

912 Lord God, be our friend and help
us to know you better and better.
Amen.

John Wright

913 Father God,
you want us all to be friends,
but sometimes that is difficult.
Help me to be kind and caring
to everyone.
Amen.

Denis O'Gorman

914 Father God,
thank you for all my friends.
Help me to be loving and kind to everybody.
Amen.

Denis O'Gorman

915 Father God,
you love and care for us.
May we your children enjoy our friendship
here together and be happy with you
for ever in heaven.
Amen.

Denis O'Gorman

916 Father God,
everything we have comes from you.
Let us care for all your children,
share their joys when all goes well
and still love them when all goes wrong
and they need our friendship.
Amen.

Denis O'Gorman

Our world

Environment

917 Dear God,
thank you for making this beautiful world.
Sometimes we forget to look after it.
Please forgive us.
Help us to care for and not to spoil
what you have made.
Amen.

Heather Ellis

918 Dear God,
thank you for this world.
Thank you for its beauty and preciousness.
Thank you for the light and the dark, the sea and the land.
Thank you for animals, fish and birds.
Thank you that we share it.
Help us to look after our world.
Amen.

Nick Harding

919 Lord of all,
help us to see the
wonderful world
you have created
for us and take
care of it.
Amen.

Denis O'Gorman

920 Thank you, God,
for making us such a lovely world to live in.
Help us to look after it
and the other people who live here.
Amen.

Susan Sayers

921 Heavenly Father,
thank you
for the world
we live in,
our big, beautiful blue
planet,
full of oceans,
tall mountains,
green fields
and so much stunning scenery.

Continued overleaf

Please help us
to look after our planet
and keep it clean,
please help us
to recycle our waste
and not to waste
this wonderful world
that you have created.

Tony Bower

922 Jesus,
I'd just like to say
that I think
this world
is brilliant!
It is so full
of surprises,
and sights,
and smells,
and tastes,
and experiences,
and much, much more!
And I live here!
That's brilliant, too!
I know, Jesus,
that the world
is not being looked after very well.
But I will do my best
to help.
I love it here, Jesus!
Thank you!
Amen.

David Gatward

923 Lord God, thank you for the world
and all that is in it.
Teach me to care for it
and for all your creatures.
Let me not be responsible for the hurt
or spoiling of anything,
but let me help to make your world
a good place to live in.
Amen.

David Adam

924 God, thank you for this wonderful world
and for our marvellous lives.
Help me to help keep your world clean
and free from evil,
and to enjoy living and working for you.
Amen.

David Adam

925 God, thank you for the sounds of birds
and that I am able to hear.
Help me to listen carefully
and to be quiet in my prayers.
Amen.

David Adam

926 God, you made the world and all that is in it.
You sent your Son Jesus Christ
to show your love and to be our Saviour.
Help me to be careful and respectful
in how I use your world
and to give thanks and worship you.
Amen.

David Adam

927 God, you have made all things
out of your love and for your love.
Help me to show my love to you
in the way I care for the world.
Amen.

David Adam

928 God, help me to love the world
the way you do.
Teach me to respect all creatures
and not to make any suffer
through my greed or neglect.
May I know at all times
that you love me.
Amen.

David Adam

929 God, thank you for our good
and beautiful world.
You have made all things for us to enjoy
and to care for.
May I always do what you want me to do
and be kind and good to others.
Amen.

David Adam

930 God, thank you for a wonderful
and beautiful world.
Thank you for the love and care of my parents.
Help me to care for the world
and make sure that I do not spoil it for others.
Amen.

David Adam

931 Lord God, as you give freely to me,
teach me to be free in my giving.
I pray that the resources of the world
may not be hoarded or squandered
but used for the benefit of all.
Amen.

David Adam

932 Creator God,
thank you for the wonder of creation.
I pray that I may use the resources of the world
to the benefit of others
and in the care of our planet.
Make me sensitive and caring
in my dealings with others,
that we may learn through each other
of your great love.
Amen.

David Adam

933 Lord God, you have created a world
where there is enough for everyone's needs
but not for everyone's greed.
Help me not to damage
or squander your creation
but to share with others.
Amen.

David Adam

934 God bless the air.
Help us not to spoil it.
God bless the sea.
Help us not to poison it.
God bless the earth.
Help us not to trample it.
God bless the planet.
Help us not to ruin it.
God bless here.
Help us to look after it.

Ray Simpson

935 When we eat our food,
may we think of the earth who gives it.
When we have rides in a car,
may we think of the oil that moves it.
When we buy something in a shop,
may we think of the people who made it.
When we go to sleep,
may we think of God who creates us.

Ray Simpson

936 Thank you, Lord God, for a wonderful world.
Forgive us when we spoil it, and help us to use it well so that we can all enjoy the best of it.
In Jesus' name we pray.
Amen.

John Wright

Rich and poor

937 We pray for people who suffer
because others are greedy:
especially the victims of crime,
and those who are taken advantage of
by more powerful people and organisations.
Loving God, please help your world
to be rich in justice, as well as other things.

Michael Forster

938 Lord, you have given us a rich world
where there is enough for everyone.
Help us who have received plenty
to be generous with others
and so express your care for all.
Amen.

David Adam

939 God, you have given me lots of lovely things.
Teach me to share with those who have none.
Help me to be kind and generous towards others.
Amen.

David Adam

940 Please, Lord, bless all the people
who are rich in money
but poor in friends.
Help them to know that they are lovable,
and to treasure the things
that you know are real wealth.

Michael Forster

941 Loving God, you want us to have life,
but some people never get the chance to enjoy it
because of poverty, or illness, or fear.
It's as though they're not really fully alive.
Please help them, Lord Jesus:
offer them real life!

Michael Forster

942 We pray for people who have turned gold into god,
whose lives are ruled by things they want
but that can't truly satisfy them.
Please, God, set us all free
when we find ourselves getting into that.

Michael Forster

943 We've got so much,
compared with some other people!
Please forgive us, God, if sometimes
we're unkind or selfish.
Help us to remember how much
we need each other.

Michael Forster

944 Sorry, God!
Not that we've got enough to eat
– we're not sorry about that!
We're sorry that sometimes
we tend to blame other people
as if poverty were their fault.
Please help us to be more caring.

Michael Forster

945 Jesus,
sometimes
I can be greedy.
I put too much on my plate
at teatime and then end up
not being able to finish it.
Then someone says,
'Your eyes are too big
for your stomach!'
Being greedy can even
make me feel
a bit sick.
Like when I eat
too many sweets.
It makes me think about all those
who never have a chance

to put a little extra on their plate.
They have little to eat
and we have so much.
It's not fair, Jesus.
We should share our food
so that everyone
has something
to eat.
Help us to do that, Jesus.
Amen.

946 God, there are lots of hungry and poor people
in our world.
Show me how to help them
and not to be greedy with what I have.
Let me learn to share and to care
as you care for me.
Amen.

David Adam

947 Jesus, I know that you love me
and care for me.
I pray for all the hungry people in the world.
Show me how I can help them
to know of your love and care.
Amen.

David Adam

948 Dear loving Father,
we believe that you care for everyone:
people with money
and people without money,
people with homes
and people without homes,
people with jobs
and people without jobs.
May we, who live in a country
where most people
have money, homes and jobs,
really try to give a hand-up to the people
who are struggling to live a happier life.
Amen.

Tony Castle

949 We live such comfortable lives, Lord,
that we forget how hard life is
for millions of our brothers and sisters in other lands.
Today we pray for all the people like Delwar,
who work so hard and get so little
to feed and support their families.
Help us to not to forget them,
and help other people
to come to know and understand their problems.
Amen.

Tony Castle

950 We pray, Almighty God,
for the people in developing countries
who have skills and work so hard,
but do not earn enough money
to have a happy and secure life.
May we, who enjoy a very comfortable life
and have money to spare for all kinds of extra luxuries,
remember the poor.
May we use every opportunity to help them
and show our gratitude to you, Lord,
for your generosity to us, by our generosity to them.
Amen.

Tony Castle

951 Heavenly Father,
there are many very poor people in the world.
We believe that you have always shown a special love
and concern for them;
may we show the same love and concern.
We believe that you have blessed us
with the privilege of living in a wealthy country;
we enjoy so many good things in our lives.
May we be always grateful to you and show our gratitude
in a loving care for the poor, who are your special concern.
Amen.

Tony Castle

Charity

952 We pray for people who are really poor,
people who are so hungry it hurts.
We pray for charities like Christian Aid
and all who try to find real, permanent answers
to the problem of poverty.
Please help us to do our part
in supporting them.

Michael Forster

953 Thank you, God, for all those good people
who are standing up for truth and for goodness
even when the things going on around us
lead us to forget them.
Thank you for loving, caring people.

Michael Forster

954 Some of those good people
are in very dangerous places,
because they choose to be there.
Thank you for people who take aid to war zones,
or face danger to rescue people in trouble.
Please bless all unselfish people
and let them know that they're appreciated.

Michael Forster

955 Even though it's unfair, though,
this is your world.
And that means there's always lots of good in it, too.
Help us to see the signs of your goodness,
and to celebrate them.

Michael Forster

956 Father God,
please help us
to make poverty
history,
a thing of the past,
something that will not last
another lifetime.
Please help us
to be a lifeline
to those who are drowning
in a sea of poverty,
overwhelmed
by wave upon wave
of calamity,

Continued overleaf

causing poverty so bad
it's like a tidal wave,
all consuming,
a debt
that is never ending,
please help us
to put an end
to this worldwide
problem.

Tony Bower

957 Father God,
thank you
for 'Children In Need'
and the chance
to do what we can
and give what we're able.
Thank you
that you are able
to take small offerings
like a few fish
and some loaves of bread
and feed multitudes.
Please help our small offerings
make a world of difference.

Tony Bower

958 Father God,
thank you
that every child
is precious
in your sight
and every need
is known
by you.
Please help us
to see the need
and do all we can
to help.

Tony Bower

959 Father God,
thank you
for charity,
the opportunities
provided
to think of others
and to give to others.

Please help us
to be charitable
constantly
and not just
once or twice a year,
but every day
in some small way
to give
something,
do
anything
we can
to help,
be kind,
be generous,
to others.

Tony Bower

960 Father God,
in some way or another
we all need
charity:
people being generous
to us,
giving us their time,
the gift of a smile,
passing on a kind word,
helping us with a problem.
In some small way
help us
to brighten up someone's day
today.

Tony Bower

961 Father God,
thank you
for events
that help raise
the profile
of charities,
that help raise
awareness
of issues
that we need
to deal with.
Please help us
to have wisdom
in how to be as effective

Continued overleaf

as we can
in helping,
in understanding,
in caring
for others.

Tony Bower

962 Dear Lord,
we have so much
to say, 'Thank you'
for; help us to
remember that
there are people
who have no
homes or food.
Please show us
how to be
generous and
send them help.
Amen.

Denis O'Gorman

963 God our Father,
help the world to
share the vast
riches you have
given for us all, so
that there will be
no more hunger
and all may live in
peace.
Amen.

Denis O'Gorman

964 Dear Lord,
there are many people
in the world who
are hungry and
cannot help
themselves – show
us how to help
them.
Amen.

Denis O'Gorman

965 Almighty Father,
it must be terrible to have no proper home;
to live on the streets,
under lorries or in big cardboard boxes.
Yet many thousands of children,
who are our age, do live like that.
What can we ask you, Lord?
Can you help us to be
really grateful for our own homes?
Can you send those children
adults who will help them?
Can you get governments
to take some real action?
Can you help us to be
more generous when we are asked
to support agencies that help street children?
Father, may we have a loving concern
and do what we can.
Amen.

Tony Castle

966 Lord God, whose son Jesus taught us to love one another, help us to care about people in faraway places who have nothing, and be prepared to help them.
Amen.

John Wright

967 Father God,
help us to care for and love
the poor and the lonely.
Amen.

Denis O'Gorman

Suffering

968 We pray for people who suffer
because of lawlessness,
where evil appears to rule
and the only law seems to be survival.
Please, God, help people who try to transform such places
with your law of love.

Michael Forster

969 Almighty God,
help us to understand what has happened, Lord.
Give strength to those who are still suffering –
the homeless,

Continued overleaf

the hungry, those who have lost loved ones,
those who have lost the will to live.
Show your love to them, give them hope and show us the way to help.
We ask this through Jesus Christ, our Lord.
Amen.

Rupert Bristow

970 Almighty God,
we do not know why this disaster has struck . . . . . .
You know all those who have been hurt. You know all those who have been killed. You know all those who are still missing. We pray especially for anyone we know who has been affected; give us the insight to find the ways in which our school can be of assistance.
Meanwhile we pray for the rescue services and we hope for speedy recovery.
We ask this through Jesus Christ, our Lord.
Amen.

Rupert Bristow

971 Right now, in lots of places,
there are people who are feeling guilty,
or hurt, or frightened,
and are afraid to say so.
Please, God, find them a friend to help.

Michael Forster

972 We remember all who are forced to escape
from their homes, and live without security;
we think particularly of those with young children
who are homeless or in danger.

Susan Sayers

973 Dear, dearest Jesus –
this is a prayer
for all the lonely,
and sad,
and hurting people
in the
whole wide world.
Please
may they know
you are
there for them
always,
and that you are
their very best friend.

So –
they don't need
to be lonely,
or sad,
or hurting,
any more –
because
you are
always
there
FOR
EVERYONE.

Susan Hardwick

974 Lord Jesus, you love everyone
and are concerned when anyone suffers.
Help me to care for all who are
in need or in trouble.
Amen.

David Adam

975 Jesus, thank you for your love
and your power to heal.
I ask your blessing
upon all who are ill or suffering
at this time.
Amen.

David Adam

976 Lord Jesus, thank you for healing people
and making them well.
Help me to keep in touch with you
through my prayers.
Amen.

David Adam

977 God, I pray for all children who are ill
and away from home.
May they remember that you are with them
and that you love them always.
Amen.

David Adam

978 Lord, let there be peace on earth and let it begin with me.
Amen.

John Wright

979 Dear Jesus,
many of your followers
have to suffer a lot
because they believe in you.
Help us to be brave
like them and you.
Amen.

Denis O'Gorman

980 Father God,
may our worship of you
be respectful, worthy and simple,
but never without care, concern
and an awareness of your children
who might be poor and suffering.
Amen.

Denis O'Gorman

981 Dear loving Father,
we find it hard to believe
that such terrible things can happen
to women and children.
We would be so unhappy
if anything dreadful happened
to the people we love.
Father, you love those people;
please protect them from harm.
May they find happiness;
may they find freedom.
Amen.

Tony Castle

982 Heavenly Father,
we are all your children, wherever we live in the world.
Some of us never have terrifying earthquakes
or tidal waves,
or terrible flooding that washes away our homes.
We thank you for that.
Today we pray for the people
who do suffer such dreadful tragedies;
especially the poor who have no money
and rely on the help we can provide.
May we always be kind, understanding and generous.
Amen.

Tony Castle

People

983 Father God,
thank you for the letters that
the postman brings.
The rattling of the milk
bottles as the dawn chorus sings.
The pilot who flies the planes
with big, big wings.
The food in the shops that the
lorry brings.
The emergency rescuers as
the siren rings.
We thank you
for all the
different jobs,
for all the
different people
and for all the differences
they make to our lives.

Tony Bower

984 Lord Jesus, teach me to love the world
with the love that you have for the world.
May I learn to care for others
and help any who are in need,
for as much as I do it to the least
I do it to you.
Amen.

David Adam

985 Please, God, give all people
the insight to see your glory in the world.

Michael Forster

986 You know, God,
there are lots of people
who could change the world for us
if only we'd give them a chance.
Help us to appreciate them more.

Michael Forster

987 Father God,
all the people in the world
are our brothers and sisters,
because you made and love all of us.
Amen.

Susan Sayers

988 If the world is ever to see real hope,
then purify and transform our lives
and stretch out our arms in loving forgiveness,
with no exceptions and no small print,
so that we shine as lights in the darkness.

Susan Sayers

989 Father God,
thank you
that out of a world
of six billion people
not one of them
is the same
and each one of them
is known by name
by you;
thank you
that you care for us
and love each one of us
the same.

Tony Bower

990 Lord,
thank you
for cars, planes and trains,
for bicycles, buses and balloons.
Thank you
for so many different ways
in which we can travel today.
Thank you
for the people
who invented them.
Thank you
for the people
who drive the vehicles.
Thank you
for the journeys
that we can go on.

Tony Bower

991 Loving God,
thank you
for our government,
thank you
for people willing to take big
responsibilities.
Please help them
to listen well
and decide wisely
for everyone in our country.

Tony Bower

992 Father God,
thank you
for the royal family,
thank you
for all the things they do
for our country.
Please protect them,
please bless them
and please grant them
wisdom.

Tony Bower

993 Dear Jesus –
I think there must be
lots and lots
AND LOTS
of people who need you
to take care of them –
just like
you take care of me.
So –
please – will you
look after them as well?

Susan Hardwick

994 Jesus –
I wish
that your love
will spill out
to fill
everyone's
hearts,
and the
whole world.

Continued overleaf

Then,
heaven
will live on
earth
and fill it
all over.
Then,
there will be
no place
where you are not.

Susan Hardwick

995 Jesus, thank you for your love
towards all people.
I pray to you for all who are ill or troubled
at this time.
May they know you are with them
and want to help them always.
Amen.

David Adam

996 God, thank you for the bravery
of all who work in the rescue services.
Thank you that Jesus came
to rescue us from death
and to bring us to eternal life.
Amen.

David Adam

997 God, thank you for doctors and nurses
and all who help to make people well again.
Amen.

David Adam

998 Lord Jesus,
as you love everyone
help me to be loving and caring
to all who are in need.
Amen.

David Adam

999 Lord Jesus, thank you
for healing the woman with the bent back.
I know that you care
for all who are ill or in trouble.
Amen.

David Adam

1000 We pray for people who are falsely accused of crimes,
who lose their jobs, their families,
their faith in human nature,
their faith in you.
Please, loving God,
help them to remember that you are always fair,
and that you are able to create new hope.

Michael Forster

1001 Loving God, we give you thanks
for people of vision,
and for people who have the sense to listen to them.
Thank you for helping people to understand the signs,
and to make provision for the future.

Michael Forster

1002 We ask your blessing on planners;
people who have to try to see future needs
and find ways of providing for them.
That's everybody really – but especially governments
and people who manage companies,
and have a lot of people depending on them.
Help them to listen, and to learn,
even from the most unlikely people.

Michael Forster

1003 All over the world, there are people
whom you are calling to do great things
or to do little things.
Please help them to trust you
and to answer, 'Yes',
and to keep trusting you
and saying, 'Yes',
until the job is done.

Michael Forster

1004 Thank you, God,
for people of faith.
Thank you for people who step into the unknown –
without being certain how things will work out –
to benefit the human race.

Michael Forster

1005 Thank you, God, for wise people.
And thank you that some of them
are powerful as well!
Help them to make a difference to your world,
and help us to learn
the wisdom of your love.

Michael Forster

1006 Please, God, bless all people
who have power:
teachers, politicians, parents,
and us – because we all have some power.
Help us to use it wisely.

Michael Forster

1007 Thank you, Lord Jesus,
for being the kind of king
who rules by love, not fear.

Michael Forster

1008 Everyone gets just a little bit
power-mad at times,
even though we're not quite as bad as old Herod!
Sometimes we want our own way,
or we're determined to win an argument
and other people get hurt.
Please forgive us, Lord Jesus.

Michael Forster

1009 Please, God, bless people in power:
help them to use their power
to benefit other people.
And we pray for people who suffer
because others abuse their power.
Help them to find good ways
of changing their situation.

Michael Forster

1010 Please, Lord Jesus,
help people who enforce rules –
like judges and police,
and parents and teachers –
always to do so with love.

Michael Forster

1011 We pray for people
who are frightened about the future,
because they do not know what it holds.
Help them to put all their trust in you,
for whom nothing is impossible.

Michael Forster

1012 Thank you, God,
for making such different people.
Thank you for a world full of variety!

Michael Forster

1013 Heavenly Father,
you love all children in the world.
May we love them too,
by using kind words
and helping them as best we can,
without asking for anything in return.
Amen.

Denis O'Gorman

1014 God our heavenly Father,
there are many people
who are poor, homeless and cold.
Help us to see their needs
and try to help them.
May we see the face of Jesus
In everyone we meet today.
Amen.

Denis O'Gorman

1015 Lord Jesus Christ, you taught us to love each other.
Help us to live that way and to understand that the world
works better when we do.
Amen.

John Wright

As a creation

1016 Lord, may our world become sensitised
to hear the whispered voice
of your love;
may we honour your creation
and value one another
as you value us.

Susan Sayers

1017 *Throw a ball which is designed to look like the earth, as you sing:*
You've got the whole world in your hand,
you've got the whole wide world in your hand,
you've got the whole world in your hand,
you've got the whole world in your hand.

Susan Sayers

1018 Thank you, loving God,
for the world we live in,
for the colours and shapes,
the sounds and textures in it.
Thank you for giving us minds and emotions
and help us to reverence the whole of creation.

Susan Sayers

1019 Life-giving God,
the universe we live in
you created.
The planet we play upon
you created.
The stars in space
you created.
The hot, burning sun
you created.
The bright, shining moon
you created.
The person that I am
you created.

Tony Bower

1020 Lord God, all power and strength belongs to you
for you have created the heavens and the earth
and all that is in them.
May I give my love to you each day
and care for the world that you have given us.
Amen.

David Adam

1021 God, you have chosen to make this wonderful world
and to give us life.
As you love me and give me so many things,
help me to show my love to you
by doing what you want me to do.
Amen.

David Adam

1022 God, thank you for life and health.
Thank you for the world in which we live
and for all my loved ones.
Each day may I give you thanks and praise
for all that you have done for me.
Amen.

David Adam

1023 Lord, the earth is yours and all that is in it.
All things come from you.
Help me to love the world
with the love that you have for the world
and to give glory to you
for all that I have each day.
Amen.

David Adam

1024 God, you are the Creator of all things.
You give us life and this world to live in.
Help me to use all to your glory
and to the benefit of your creation.
Amen.

David Adam

1025 Lord God, thank you
that you have made the world
and all that is in it.
I rejoice in your love and protection.
Help me to trust in you
and to know you are with me always.
Amen.

David Adam

1026 Father God,
thank you for the lovely world,
which you made.
Help me to know you made everything
out of your love.
Amen.

David Adam

1027 Please forgive us for the times we spoil things,
and help us to take care of your creation,
to love and value each other,
and to make your creation even more beautiful.

Michael Forster

1028 Creator God,
you have given us all the ability
to make beautiful things.
Help us to remember
that nothing we can make
is as wonderful as the world
you have created.
Amen.

Denis O'Gorman

1029 Lord God of
space and time,
so many people
give glory to
themselves and
not to you, help
us all to
understand that
everything we are
comes from you.
Amen.

Denis O'Gorman

1030 God, our Father,
you have made
so many
wonderful things
and we have still
not seen them all.
Please help us to
see that we
cannot
understand
everything.
Amen.

Denis O'Gorman

1031 We give thanks for the wonder of
the earth.
We stand in awe of the vastness of
time during which the rocks and
stones, mountains and hills were
formed.
We give thanks
for the ground beneath our feet
which we take for granted each
day,
for the vast variety of stones and
pebbles on the beach,
for the grandeur of towering hills
and mountains,
for deep mines hiding treasures of
coal, and precious rocks.
Open our eyes to see and our minds
to understand.
Amen.

Jill Fuller

1032 Lord,
I can appreciate the colours
in a field full of flowers.
I can smell the richness
of the differing scents
as the breeze blows across every plant.
I can hear an orchestra
of sounds in the air,
with each whisper of life
giving an identity,
a unique expression
of living
in a world of variety.
I appreciate the difference
in everything that surrounds me.
Each building, tree, flower or person
combines to make
a tapestry of existence.
Lord,
thank you for being
the Creator of all things,
the giver of life
and a Father to humanity
in a world of variety.
Amen.

Pete Townsend

1033 Lord God,
help us to see you in everything you have made,
in obvious things like food and water,
and the less obvious things such as materials we turn into products for our use.
Teach us to use all we have unselfishly,
so that others may benefit as well,
and most of all, give us thankful hearts.
Amen.

John Wright

1034 Father God,
we are your children.
We believe in you.
Open our eyes to see the wonderful things
you have created in our world.
Amen.

Denis O'Gorman

1035 Father God,
you have filled our world with beautiful things.
Help us to protect and care for your creation.
Amen.

Denis O'Gorman

1036 Father God,
you made the world
and all its wonders just for us,
so that we could be
happy for ever.
Help us to see your love
in the world today.
Amen.

Denis O'Gorman

1037 Father God,
thank you for all you have made.
Let us sing your praise for ever.
Amen.

Denis O'Gorman

Jobs

1038 Dear God,
we pray for all those who look after babies. Help them to care for the babies and to love them. Please bless all babies, because every baby is special to you.
Amen.

Gill Thorniley

1039 Dear God,
we pray for all those at work. We pray especially for all those who help to provide our food: for farmers, fishers, cooks, factory workers and lorry drivers. We ask your blessing on them and on all those who work to provide for us.
Amen.

Gill Thorniley

1040 Dear, caring Father,
you have given us hands, that we may feed ourselves,
help ourselves, make things and play.
We have been thinking of your children,
who have to spend all day, every day, working in factories,
unable to help themselves and unable to play, as we do.
It is very unfair, Lord, and we ask that one day
there may be more fairness and more happiness
for the children and teenagers of the countries
that make the clothes.
Amen.

Tony Castle

Animals

1041 Dear God,
help us to be kind to animals.
We are sorry when we do wrong.
Help us to look after them, Lord.
Amen.

Heather Ellis

1042 Dear God,
you show us the wonder of your love
through all the animals and plants
you have made.
Help me to love and appreciate them, Lord.
Amen.

Heather Ellis

Seasons

Spring

1043 Thank you for the
spring. The rain
brings new flowers
and plants.
Thank you, Jesus,
for new things
in my life.

George and Angie Allen

1044 God, spring is here
and we are excited by all the signs.
We are excited by the new growth
and flowers blossoming.
We are excited by the change in the weather
and the warm sun.
We are excited by the signs of summer
and the hope of the future.
God, spring is here
and we are excited
and may we be like them.

Nick Harding

1045 God, we like the things we see
green and growing.
We like the tiny plants and shoots
peeping out of the soil.
We like the new leaves just beginning
to sprout on the branches and trees.
God, we like the things we see
green and growing.

Nick Harding

1046 There are beautiful things at springtime.
There are baby lambs and chickens,
fresh leaves on bushes and trees.
There are crops beginning to grow,
and new shoots of bulbs and flowers.
There are skies of fresh blue
with light, white clouds.

Nick Harding

1047 You are the Lord of the seasons,
and a new season is here.
You are the Lord of the spring,
of fresh mornings and signs of life.
You are the Lord of the spring,
with time to work, and time to rest.
You are the Lord of the seasons.

Nick Harding

1048 Lord God, you have brought us safely through.
Through the cold chill of winter.
Lord God, you have brought us safely through.
Through the sadness and darkness.
Lord God, you have brought us safely through.
To see signs of hope all around.
Lord God, you have brought us safely through.

Nick Harding

1049 We thank you for heroes who spring into action,
for saints we remember at this time of year.
We thank you for heroes who hear your words,
and act to serve you with their lives.
We thank you for saints in our own lives,
who are there to listen, to help, to smile.
We thank you for heroes who spring into action.
May we be heroes for you.

Nick Harding

1050 From the smallest bud to the tiny chick
we see your glory, Lord of all.
From the morning dew to the warming sun
we see your glory, Lord of all.
From the death on that cross to the living Lord
we see your glory, Lord of all.

Nick Harding

1051 Creator God, you renew all things.
You renew the world as the sun rises each day.
Creator God, you renew all things.
You renew the land with flowers and green leaves.
Creator God, you renew all things.
You renew us with your love.
Creator God, you renew all things.

Nick Harding

1052 Life springs at spring.
Life in new animals, bulbs and shoots.
Jesus defeated death at spring.
Jesus lives now, thank you God.

Nick Harding

1053 Father God,
Thank you for the springtime,
for the first sight of new life.
Buds beginning to open,
flowers starting to wake up out of the sleepy earth.
Thank you for the colours, for the flowers. . .
for those sun-coloured daffodils
swaying gently in the breeze.
Thank you for the lambs racing through the grass,
bleating and baaing now that spring has been sprung.
Amen.

Tony Bower

Summer

1054 Thank you for the
bright summer sun
and the long
warm days.
I know you are
always smiling
warmly at me.

George and Angie Allen

1055 Summer is a time to rest.
Summer is a time to play.
Summer is a time to enjoy.
Summer is a time to think back.
Summer is a time to look forward.
Summer is a time to be warm.
Summer is a time to be happy.

Nick Harding

1056 Thank you, God, that you made it possible
for us all to stop, rest and be refreshed.
Thank you, God, that you made the weather
to help us feel good and relaxed.
Thank you, God, that you made a world
which is full of great places to visit.
Thank you, God, for summer.

Nick Harding

1057 God who made everything, we thank you for summer.
We thank you that we have time to get away from school.
We thank you that we have good places to go.
We thank you that we have good weather to enjoy.
We thank you that we have a good time.
God who made everything, we thank you for summer.

Nick Harding

1058 You are the Lord of the seasons,
and a new season is here.
You are the Lord of the summer,
of bright sunshine and holidays.
You are the Lord of the summer,
with time to work, and time to rest.
You are the Lord of the seasons.

Nick Harding

1059 The summer reaches our senses –
we taste ice cream and salads,
we hear people playing and laughing,
we speak of happy times of rest.
We see suntans and smiles.
We feel warmth in the air,
we touch the sand as it runs through our fingers.
The summer reaches our senses.

Nick Harding

1060 Thank you, God, for this special time.
Special holidays with special people.
Special resting and refreshing.
Special memories and hopes for the future.
Special hope, from our special God.
Thank you, God, for this special time.

Nick Harding

1061 Refresh us, Lord, through your Spirit.
Refresh us, Lord, through peace and calm.
Refresh us, Lord, through sunshine.
Refresh us, Lord, through others.
Refresh us, Lord, through summer.

Nick Harding

1062 Keep us safe through this summer we pray.
Keep us safe so we may meet again.
Keep us safe so we can be stronger.
Keep us safe so we can be happy.
Keep us safe through summer we pray.

Nick Harding

1063 Father God,
thank you for summer days,
never-ending light,
sunny outdoor plays.
Thank you for sun and sea,
big blue sky and sandcastles for me.
Thank you for the summer holidays
that stretch as far as the horizon
and seem to last forever.
Amen.

Tony Bower

Autumn

1064 In autumn
when leaves blow
in the wind,
I know your love
will never fall
to the ground
like a leaf.

George and Angie Allen

1065 Thank you God for leaves.
I like the crunchy sound they make
when I walk on them.
I love throwing them up into the air!
Thank you God for autumn.
Amen.

Heather Ellis

1066 There is damp in the air,
and the mist takes time to clear.
There are leaves underfoot,
and trees are becoming brown and red.
There is cold all around,
and the wind blows hard and strong.
There is autumn all around us,
and a special time of year.

Nick Harding

1067 We see the leaves changing colour
and we know that you are good.
We see the nights getting darker
and we know that you are good.
We see the breeze move the branches
and we know that you are good.
We see the seasons come and go
and we know that you are God.

Nick Harding

1068 Thank you, Creator God,
that you made us.
Thank you, Creator God,
that you made our world.
Thank you, Creator God,
for this autumn time.
Thank you, Creator God,
for the golds and browns we see.
Thank you, Creator God,
for all that this says to us.
Thank you, Creator God,
that you made me.

Nick Harding

1069 The trees tell the tale,
the leaves are beginning to fall.
The air is getting colder,
the nights are starting sooner.
The autumn is upon us,
and change is in the air.
Help us through this season,
Lord, we pray.

Nick Harding

1070 Thank you, God, for the colours of the season.
Thank you for the golds, reds and browns of trees and bushes.
Thank you for the greens and greys of fields and paths.
Thank you, God, for the colours of the season.

Nick Harding

1071 In the dark we see lights,
we hear bangs and whizzes,
we see showers of red, yellow, blue.
We smell smoke and light burning.
In the dark we see lights,
and we are really thankful!

Nick Harding

1072 You are the Lord of the seasons,
and a new season is here.
You are the Lord of the autumn,
of leaves falling and winds chilling.
You are the Lord of the autumn,
with time to work, and time to rest.
You are the Lord of the seasons.

Nick Harding

1073 Why do we want to stamp in leaves,
kick them all over and hear them crunch?
Why do we want to jump in puddles,
splashing water and wetting our socks?
Why do we want to swing on branches
with damp bark and few leaves?
Thank you that we can do all these things –
to celebrate your creation.

Nick Harding

1074 Lord God,
thank you for
the burning fiery leaves,
the golden colours
as the season mellows
and autumn changes
the window dressing
of the trees.
Amen.

Tony Bower

Winter

1075 Winter's chill
may be cold
but your love
keeps me warm.
You are never
hidden away
like the grass
under the snow.

George and Angie Allen

1076 Caring God, who cares for all,
we pray for those who suffer in winter.
We pray for the old who have seen many winters,
and we pray for the homeless with nowhere to be warm.
We pray for the poor without warm clothes,
and we pray for those in frozen lands.
Caring God, who cares for all,
we pray for those who suffer this winter.

Nick Harding

1077 The cold in the air and the power of the wind
remind us of you, God.
The crisp soil underfoot and white frost
remind us of you, God.
The dark of the night and the bright, winter sun
remind us of you, God.
All the joys and challenges of the winter season
remind us of you, God.

Nick Harding

1078 Thank you for the snow that falls.
Thank you for the frost and fog.
Thank you for the warmth of home.
Thank you for the lights of night.
Thank you for the winter time.

Nick Harding

1079 Winter is a time when things die down
and then they grow stronger.
Winter is a time when we stay inside
and then we look forward to spring.
Winter is a time to be cosy and warm
and then be stronger.

Nick Harding

1080 You are the Lord of the seasons,
and a new season is here.
You are the Lord of the winter,
of howling winds and frosty mornings.
You are the Lord of the winter,
with time to work, and time to rest.
You are the Lord of the seasons.

Nick Harding

1081 We celebrate the snow!
We celebrate each flake with its unique pattern.
We celebrate the buzz of excitement in our school.
We celebrate the clean white look over everything.
We celebrate the crunch of snow under our feet.
We celebrate the fun of snowball fights.
We celebrate the snow!

Nick Harding

1082 You speak to us in winter, Lord,
through the low sun on a fresh day.
You speak to us, Lord,
through the frozen webs on bushes.
You speak to us, Lord,
through the strong storms and whining winds.
You speak to us, Lord,
through the rain which seems to go on forever.
You speak to us in all these ways, Lord.

Nick Harding

1083 In the darkness of winter bring us your light.
The light of morning, and sunny clear skies.
The light of your Son, Jesus born in winter.
In the darkness of winter bring us your light.

Nick Harding

1084 May we be warm
despite the cold outside.
May we be warm as we
learn and take in
new things.
May we be warm as we
feel your Spirit with us.
May we be warm
despite the cold outside.

Nick Harding

1085 Father God,
thank you for snow and ice,
white frosted paths
and the frozen duckponds.
Thank you for the crimson sky,
the early golden sunsets,
for seeing our breath
hanging in the air,
telling us that winter is here.
Amen.

Tony Bower

Christian seasons

Advent

1086 Dear God,
the world is full of your love. *(trace big circle)*
Help us to listen out for it. *(cup ears)*
Help us to watch out for it. *(shade eyes and look around)*
Thank you for all the goodness and love
that we can hear and see.
Amen.

Susan Sayers

1087 May we all be given a new enthusiasm
for walking God's way,
clothed in the armour of light.

Susan Sayers

1088 As we prepare ourselves
for the time when Christ comes again in glory,
we pray for the grace and honesty
to see what needs transforming
in our lives as individuals
and as members of the Church of God.

Susan Sayers

1089 Lord, help us to see
the signs of your love today
in the world around us
and in the people we meet.
Train us to be ready to see you
and recognise you
when you come in glory.
Amen.

Susan Sayers

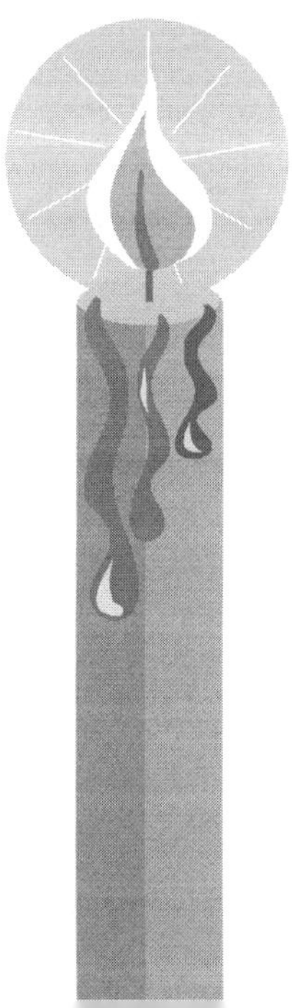

1090 Lord our God,
make us watchful and keep us faithful
as we wait for the coming of your Son our Lord;
that, when he appears,
he may not find us sleeping in sin
but active in his service
and joyful in his praise.
Amen.

Susan Sayers

1091 Heavenly Father,
we thank you for helping us
to get ourselves ready to receive you.

Susan Sayers

1092 Dear Jesus,
when I open today's window
in my Advent calendar
I remember the present
I am getting ready to give you.
Please help me to do it well.
Amen.

Susan Sayers

1093 Lord God,
help us to get ourselves ready
to welcome you
into our lives.
Amen.

Susan Sayers

1094 Lord God of Israel, we praise you.
Only you can work miracles.
We will always praise your glorious name.
Let your glory be seen everywhere on earth.
Amen.

(From Psalm 72)
Susan Sayers

1095 Lord, awaken us to expect you with joy;
we give you thanks for your tender parenting
and your unfailing patience with us.

Susan Sayers

1096 Our God is so big,
so strong and so mighty,
there's nothing our God cannot do!
Amen.

Susan Sayers

1097 Lord,
help me
to recognise you today.
Amen.

Susan Sayers

1098 My soul glorifies the Lord
and my spirit rejoices
in God my Saviour . . .
for the Mighty One has done
great things for me –
holy is his Name!

(From Mary's song)
Susan Sayers

1099 Dear God,
when you want someone to help,
ask me.
I don't want to say 'No!' *(thumbs down)*
I want to say 'Yes!' *(thumbs up)*
Amen.

Susan Sayers

1100 Here I am, Lord,
ready to work with you
however you like.
Lead on and I'll follow!
Amen.

Susan Sayers

1101 Lord Jesus Christ,
you have no body on earth but ours,
no hands but ours,
no feet but ours.
Ours are the eyes through which
your compassion must look out on the world.
Ours are the feet by which
you may still go about doing good.
Ours are the hands with which
you bless people now.
Bless our minds and bodies,
that we may be a blessing to others.

(Based on a prayer of St Teresa of Avila)
Susan Sayers

1102 Almighty God,
as we begin to prepare for the wonder and mystery of Christmas, we remember the special role of Mary, the mother of Jesus.
You showed her the way through the Angel Gabriel and she responded obediently and joyfully.
Help us to be obedient and joyful in our preparation for Christmas.

Continued overleaf

Let darkness turn to light as we share the expectation of the season ahead.
We ask this through Jesus Christ, our Lord.
Amen.

Rupert Bristow

1103 Almighty God,
we thank you for the special people who helped to prepare the way for Christmas.
For Moses and the patriarchs of ancient Israel; for the prophets who foretold the news of Christ's coming; for John the Baptist, who paved the way for Jesus; and for Mary who accepted your call to bring your Son into the world.
Come, Lord Jesus, for we await the arrival of the Light of the World.
We ask this through Jesus Christ, our Lord.
Amen.

Rupert Bristow

1104 Father God,
thank you
for this time of Advent,
this time of preparing,
this time of thinking
what Christmas is all about.
Why you sent your Son,
why the wise men wandered,
why the star shone brightly,
why the angels sang
beautifully,
why the shepherds ran
delightedly,
why the world was waiting
expectantly.

Tony Bower

1105 Father God,
at this time of year
when we think about
what we want,
please help us
to think about
what we can give.

Tony Bower

1106 In Advent, Father God, help us to be quiet.
In Advent, Father God, help us to think
about what it meant to send Jesus to us.
In Advent, Father God, help us to listen.
Help us to hear you speaking to us
and helping us grow in faith.
In Advent, Father God, help us to be quiet.

Nick Harding

1107 Jesus is coming, and we
want to be ready.
Jesus is coming, and we
want to pray.
Jesus is coming, and we
want to have fun.
Jesus is coming, and we
want to sing.
Jesus is coming, and we
want to remember.
Jesus is coming, and we
want to be ready.

Nick Harding

Christmas

1108 Dear God,
when I give someone a gift,
help me to give with love in my heart
and to do this all the time.
Amen.

Heather Ellis

1109 Dear God,
thank you for sending Jesus,
who taught us how to love one another.
Help me to tell other people
about your love.
Amen.

Heather Ellis

1110 God our Father,
you sent your Son Jesus
to be the light of the world.
Help us to share the light
and love of Jesus
with everyone we meet.
Amen.

Denis O'Gorman

1111 Father God,
you sent Jesus to show us
the way to heaven
and he is our guide.
May we follow him
all our lives
until he brings us all to you.
Amen.

Denis O'Gorman

1112 Lord Jesus,
thank you that you were willing
to leave the glory of heaven
and limit yourself to the form of a baby.
All that power in such a tiny form.

Ashley Guest

1113 Lord,
thank you for Christmas
and thank you for coming.
Help us to remember you
this Christmas in the middle
of all the fun and games.

Ashley Guest

1114 Jesus,
you came into the world
to be our Saviour.
Thank you that you became
a child of the earth
so that I may become
a child of God.
Amen.

David Adam

1115 Glory to you, O God,
in sending your Son into the world.
Help me to see your glory
as revealed in Jesus
and to seek to show
your glory to others.
Amen.

David Adam

1116 God, thank you
for sending Jesus your Son
to be a shining light
in the darkness of the world.
Amen.

David Adam

1117 Lord God, thank you for sending Jesus
to show your love and brightness.
Help me to know you are always with me.
Amen.

David Adam

1118 God, thank you for the birth of Jesus.
Help me to love him as he loves me.
Amen.

David Adam

1119 God, thank you
that you sent the angel messenger to Mary
and that she let Jesus be born into the world.
I will try to do what you want me to do
because I know that you love me.
Amen.

David Adam

1120 God, thank you for the love and obedience
of Joseph and Mary.
Thank you for my home and family.
Keep me in your love always.
Amen.

David Adam

1121 Father God,
help me to get ready for Jesus
and for Christmas Day.
Amen.

David Adam

1122 God, thank you for the donkey
that carried Mary to Bethlehem
and that Jesus was born there in a stable.
Amen.

David Adam

1123 Lord Jesus,
thank you for being born
and for the stable.
I pray for all the people
who do not have a home.
Amen.

David Adam

1124 Lord God, thank you
for all who watch and work
while I am asleep.
As the shepherds came to Jesus,
may I come to him
and give him my love.
Amen.

David Adam

1125 Lord God,
thank you for sheep and shepherds
and for telling us that Jesus is born for us.
Amen.

David Adam

1126 God, thank you
for the angels and the shepherds.
May I show my love for Jesus.
Amen.

David Adam

1127 O God, you are always with me,
even in the dark.
As you told the shepherds about Jesus,
help me to learn about his coming
and his love for me.
Amen.

David Adam

1128 God, thank you
for the coming of Jesus into the world
and for loving us all.
Amen.

David Adam

1129 Lord,
awaken me to your love.
Make me aware that you come to me
today and every day.
Help me to rejoice
in your coming
and in your abiding presence.
Amen.

David Adam

1130 Thank you, Lord God,
that what was secret for many ages
has been made known to all.
I give you thanks
for the Word made flesh,
that Jesus has been born in Bethlehem
and told us of your love.
Amen.

David Adam

1131 God,
I rejoice in your greatness
for you are wonderful.
I give thanks that you sent your Son
to be our Saviour.
May I be prepared for his coming.
Amen.

David Adam

1132 Lord God,
as Mary and Joseph said 'Yes'
to you and did your will,
help me to work
for the coming of your kingdom
and to serve you.
Amen.

David Adam

1133 God,
thank you that you have revealed
your love for all people,
in all places and at all times.
I can find you wherever I am
and know that you are with me
and that you care for me.
Amen.

David Adam

1134 Awaken me, O God, to your coming.
Open my eyes that I may see you.
Open my ears that I may hear you.
Open my lips that I may talk about you.
Touch my heart that I may love you.
Come, Lord, come.
Amen.

David Adam

1135 Jesus, I am getting ready
to celebrate your birthday.
Let me make sure I make room for you that day.
As you come to me in love,
may I come to you
and give you my love.
Amen.

David Adam

1136 God, thank you for Joseph
and that he cared for Mary.
I am glad he did what you asked him to do.
Help me to do what you want me to do.
Amen.

David Adam

1137 Father, thank you
that Jesus was born in the city of David
and that he came to be our Saviour.
As the shepherds came to see the baby Jesus
may I rejoice in his birth.
Amen.

David Adam

1138 God, thank you that you sent Jesus
to be our Saviour,
to heal the ill
and to bring joy to the world.
I pray that I may be ready to celebrate
his coming into the world.
Amen.

David Adam

1139 Lord Jesus, thank you
for the wise men and their gifts.
I love you as my King, my God
and my Saviour.
Amen.

David Adam

1140 God, thank you
for the escape of Jesus into Egypt.
I pray for all refugees
and those whose lives are in danger at this time.
Amen.

David Adam

1141 God, thank you for my parents,
for all the love and care they give me,
and thank you for the love and care
that Mary and Joseph gave to the baby Jesus.
Amen.

David Adam

1142 Lord Jesus, thank you
for coming to live among us.
You come to share in our lives
and to give us your love.
May I give my love to you
and know that you are with me.
Amen.

David Adam

1143 Glory to you, O God,
in sending your Son into the world.
Help me to see your glory as revealed in Jesus
and to seek to show your glory to others.
Amen.

David Adam

1144 God, who by the leading of a star
brought the wise men to Jesus,
guide me in my life
and bring me to give my love to you.
Amen.

David Adam

1145 Jesus, you came into the world
to be our Saviour.
Thank you that you became a child of earth
so that I may become a child of God.
Amen.

David Adam

1146 The bells and lights and presents and decorations
in church and in our homes
express our thanks to you, Lord,
for coming into the world in person.

Susan Sayers

1147 The world Jesus was born into
was the world we know.
Thank you for being prepared
to face the dangers and risks
of human mistakes and sin
in order to save us.

Susan Sayers

1148 Many of us will be celebrating
with our families and friends.
We invite you to join us in all the festivities,
and ask you to teach us true loving.

Susan Sayers

1149 For all the many blessings of this past year
and for all the good that you have enabled us to do;
for the experiences that have taught us
humility and patience,
we thank you.

Susan Sayers

1150 As we celebrate Christmas,
when the Word of God became flesh,
we pray for the Church, the Body of Christ.
May we be so filled with God's loving life
that our actions touch the world with hope
which lasts even when Christmas decorations
are put away.

Susan Sayers

1151 Thank you, Lord God,
for coming to save us.

Susan Sayers

1152 As Christmas brings together
family members and friends,
and we make contact with those
we seldom meet,
may all our relationships be nourished
with love and forgiveness,
and may we value one another more.

Susan Sayers

1153 Lord, we recognise our great need of your grace,
and give you thanks and praise
for making possible what would otherwise
be impossible.

Susan Sayers

1154 Thank you, Lord Jesus,
for coming to share our human lives.
Dying, you destroyed our death.
Rising, you restored our life.
Lord Jesus, come again in glory.

Susan Sayers

1155 Thank you, Jesus,
for being born
into our world.
Thank you for showing us
God's love.
Amen.

Susan Sayers

1156 Lord, to whom else could we go?
You alone have the words of eternal life!

Susan Sayers

1157 Word of the Father,
now in flesh appearing.
O come, let us adore him,
Christ the Lord.
Amen.

Susan Sayers

1158 We offer our thanks and praise
for the way you see us when we are still far off
and welcome us home.

Susan Sayers

1159 Jesus,
the best present
I can give you
is myself!

Susan Sayers

1160 Heavenly Father,
we thank you for all the wonderful things that happen at Christmas; the gifts that we give each other, the love that is shown for those in need.
But, above all, Lord, as the star shone out above Bethlehem on that first Christmas, we thank you for the gift of your Son, the Light of the World.
As Christmas comes, let us join with people down the ages who have celebrated this event and rejoice.
We thank you, Lord.
Amen.

Rupert Bristow

1161 Heavenly Father,
make this Christmas special for all here today.
Even if we are unable to give presents, help us to give greetings; even if we do not receive what we want,
help us to let people know that we are grateful that they thought of us.
Help us to remember what it was like in that stable in Bethlehem, where the baby Jesus spent his first days with Mary, Joseph and the animals gathered round, shepherds assembled outside and the bright star showing the way to this place, your Son's first home.
We ask this in Jesus' name.
Amen.

Rupert Bristow

1162 Father God,
thank you
for this special season,
please help us
to remember the reason:
your Son,
our Saviour
Jesus Christ.

Tony Bower

1163 Heavenly Father,
at this time of year
we pray for peace
to remove our fear.
Peace in our hearts
peace in our minds
peace in our lives
peace in our homes
peace in our school
peace in our land
peace in our world.
May we find
true peace
real lasting peace
with you.

Tony Bower

1164 Father God,
thank you
for Christmas
for snow and ice
for parties and presents
for cards and tinsel
for holidays and good food
for so many things.
We want to say
THANK YOU,
but most of all
we want to thank you
for the greatest gift
you gave the world – Jesus.

Tony Bower

1165 Our Father God,
thank you
for gifts,
for presents,
for things we don't have to
buy.
Thank you
for grace,
your loving kindness,
a gift from you,
that we can never afford,
but we can receive.

Tony Bower

1166 God our Father, and Father of Jesus,
help us get ready for Christmas.
Help us remember the journey of Mary and Joseph.
Help us remember the journey of the wise men.
Help us remember the hillside of the shepherds.
Help us remember the stable of the birth.
God our Father, and Father of Jesus,
help us get ready for Christmas.

Nick Harding

1167 Oh God, you didn't need to send Jesus . . . but you did.
You didn't need to have him born in a stable . . . but you did.
You didn't need to make him poor . . . but you did.
You didn't need to place him in a manger . . . but you did.
Oh God, you didn't need to send Jesus
. . . but we are glad you did.

Nick Harding

1168 There in the manger the baby lies.
Thank you, Jesus, for coming to us.
There in the stable the shepherds kneel.
Thank you, Jesus, for coming to us.
There in the sky the star shines.
Thank you, Jesus, for coming to us.
There in the heavens the angels sing.
Thank you, Jesus, for coming to us.

Nick Harding

1169 Kind and loving God,
we are excited about Christmas.
We are excited about presents and parties;
we are excited about feasts and fun.
Kind and loving God,
we are excited about Christmas.
Help us enjoy it all.

Nick Harding

1170 May God who sent his son to die
help us understand his great kindness.
May God who gave new life to Jesus
help us to understand this joy.

Nick Harding

1171 God, thank you for this special time.
Thank you for the special decorations.
Thank you for the big celebrations.
Thank you for the family times.
Thank you for the exciting moments.
God, thank you for this special time.

Nick Harding

1172 God, who made us and sent your Son,
help us to remember the reason for the season.
Help us to remember the first Christmas
that took place two thousand years ago.
Help us to remember the little child
who was and is the Son of God.
God, who made us and sent your Son,
help us to remember the reason for the season.

Nick Harding

1173 Thank you, God,
for the gift of your Son,
we pray that we might
receive his gift with thankfulness.

Ashley Guest

1174 Thank you, Lord,
for all the good gifts that we take for granted.
Thank you for *(list things that the children have suggested).*

Ashley Guest

1175 Jesus is the reason for the season!
Lord, help us to remember you this Christmas.

Ashley Guest

1176 God, your forgiveness is wonderful
and it's amazing how big it is.
Help us to forgive others as a result of it.

Ashley Guest

1177 The sleigh bells ring,
but they don't bring Jesus.
The pop songs play,
but they don't bring Jesus.
The presents pile up,
but they don't bring Jesus.
The banks give out more cash,
but they don't bring Jesus.
Thank you, God, that you gave
Jesus.

Nick Harding

1178 As we get ready for the Son of God,
be with us, Generous God.
As we get ready to worship him,
be with us, Generous God.
As we get ready to celebrate,
be with us, generous God.
As we get ready to meet Jesus again,
be with us, Generous God.

Nick Harding

1179 God, you know what we have done
to the special time of Christmas.
We have filled it with shopping and stress,
doing too much, spending too much.
We have filled it with parties and feasts,
rushing too much, eating too much.
God, remind us of the first time,
the first special time of Christmas.
The first journeys, moving slowly to Bethlehem.
The first party attended by kings and shepherds.
The first celebration . . . in a cold stable.
God, help us to remember
The real, special time of Christmas.

Nick Harding

1180 As the December wind blows
so may your Spirit blow into our hearts.
As the lights shine in the streets
so may your light shine in us.
As the Christmas season brings joy
so may your joy fill us.

Nick Harding

1181 We think about Jesus coming to the world at Christmas.
We think about Jesus, born in a stable instead of a palace.
We think of Jesus, laid on a bed of rough straw.
We think of Jesus, his poor birth and suffering for us.
We think of Jesus, coming to the world at Christmas.

Nick Harding

1182 God our Father,
you sent Jesus to live among us and to teach us your ways;
help us to know you better because of Jesus
and to live as you would want.
Amen.

John Wright

1183 Dear God,
thank you for making our world and for sending us Jesus
to love us and care for us.
Teach us that the best way to thank you
is to look after your world and the people on it.
For Jesus' sake.
Amen.

John Wright

1184 Father God,
we thank you for the first and best Christmas present ever,
your Son Jesus Christ.
As we enjoy Christmas,
may we remember those who will not,
and try to help those less lucky than us,
because Jesus came for us all.
Amen.

John Wright

1185 Father God,
once a year we celebrate the birth of Jesus, your Son;
help us to see that his is the best way for every day,
and to know and trust him all year long.
Amen.

John Wright

1186 Lord Jesus, you were a baby like us, a child like us,
and an adult as we will be one day.
Teach us that, because you knew what it is like to be human, you can understand our problems and help us with them.
Amen.

John Wright

1187 Father God, at Christmas we remember the birth of your son, Jesus; help us to see he is worth knowing every day of the year.
Amen.

John Wright

1188 Lord God, we know you are with us now.
We know you are with us wherever we go.
We know you love us whatever we do.
Help us when we need it, and look after us and those we love always.
Amen.

John Wright

1189 Father God,
thank you for sending Jesus into the world.
Help us to live our lives the way he told us to.
Amen.

Denis O'Gorman

Epiphany

1190 *This is a prayer the wise men might have said. We have all been invited to find Jesus as well, so we can say it with them.*
Thank you, Jesus,
for inviting me
to come and look for you.
I am glad I have found you!
Amen.

Susan Sayers

1191 *Gold*
The wise men brought gold to Jesus.
Jesus, we bring you the gold of our obedience.
Help us to live as you want us to. Amen.
Frankincense
The wise men brought frankincense to Jesus.
Jesus, we bring you the incense of our worship.
You are God and we worship you. Amen.
Myrrh
The wise men brought myrrh to Jesus.
Jesus, we bring you the myrrh of the world's sadness.
Help us to look after one another better. Amen.

Susan Sayers

1192 Jesus, I believe and trust
that you are God's Son,
the promised Saviour,
the Christ, the Messiah of God.
Amen.

Susan Sayers

1193 Take my life and let it be
consecrated, Lord, to thee.
Take my moments and my days,
let them flow in endless praise.
Amen.

Susan Sayers

1194 Holy God, we thank you
for making yourself known to us
in the many blessings of life,
and most of all in the person of Jesus, the Christ.

Susan Sayers

1195 Jesus, we can't see God,
but you show us what God is like.
Help us to be kind and loving
as you are kind and loving.
Amen.

Susan Sayers

1196 Almighty God,
as wise men came travelling, we pray for travellers at this time of year, joining or leaving family and friends.
Help us to follow the wise men's example to make special efforts to reach out to things that are important, to go the extra mile to do the right thing.
Let us share the special times of Epiphany by honouring the presence of your Son in our lives, just as the wise men honoured the arrival of Jesus in their world so many years ago.
We ask this through Jesus Christ, our Lord.
Amen.

Rupert Bristow

1197 Almighty God,
just as the star brought the Magi to Bethlehem, create in us the desire
– to travel far to find the truth
– to bring gifts without expecting any in return
– to be open to wonder at your marvellous creation
– to hold on to the power of the Christian story in our daily lives.
Bring us, Lord, closer to you, as your Son's birth brought the wise men to Bethlehem.
We ask this through Jesus Christ, our Lord.
Amen.

Rupert Bristow

1198 God, thank you for the star
to guide the wise men.
Be with me always
and bring me to love you.
Amen.

David Adam

1199 *(You can sing this to the tune of 'Twinkle, twinkle, little star'.)*
Guide us, guide us, little star,
we have travelled very far.
We have seen your lovely light
as we journey through the night.
Now we come to Christ our King
and our love to him we bring.

David Adam

1200 Father, thank you that the wise men found Jesus
and that the wicked King Herod did not.
I would like to give Jesus my love this day.
Amen.

David Adam

1201 God, thank you
that Jesus escaped the wicked Herod.
I ask you to look after all children
who are in danger.
Amen.

David Adam

1202 God,
who by the leading of a star
brought the wise men to Jesus,
guide me in my life
and bring me to give
my love to you.
Amen.

David Adam

1203 Lord, sometimes we feel we must follow
our star on a special journey.
Sometimes the way is difficult and the
journey long and hard.
Sometimes the journey is full of surprises.
Sometimes the ending is unexpected.
Help us always to be ready, like the wise
men, to continue travelling, to lay our
gifts at the manger and worship the
new-born King.
Amen.

Jill Fuller

Lent

1204 As we begin this season of Lent
we ask you to remind us of what is important
and what is not;
of where we are wandering away
and what we need to change;
so that by Easter
we will be renewed and strengthened
for your service in the world.

Susan Sayers

1205 Lord, we give you thanks and praise
for the hope we have in Jesus;
for the strength to resist temptation
and the joy and relief of forgiveness when we fall.

Susan Sayers

1206 Jesus, you want us to be loving each day
and we say, 'OK!'
Jesus, you want us to do as you say
and we say, 'OK!'

Susan Sayers

1207 Lord Jesus,
when I am tempted to do what is wrong
and unloving and selfish,
make me brave
and keep me strong.
Amen.

Susan Sayers

1208 As we call to mind the guidance and help
you give us each moment of every day,
we thank you and praise you, Holy God,
for you alone have the words of eternal life.

Susan Sayers

1209 Holy God, breathe your life into us now
as we offer you here our thanks and praise
for your life laid down out of love for us.
May our words be worked out
in fresh commitment to you.

Susan Sayers

1210 God be in my head and in my thinking.
(hold head with both hands)
God be in my hands and in my doing.
(hold out hands)
God be in my heart and in my loving. Amen.
(hands on heart, then arms and hands stretched out)

Susan Sayers

1211 Lord Jesus, bring us all to life
by the power of your love.
Bring us all to live
in the life of your kingdom.
Amen.

Susan Sayers

1212 Out of the depths have I called to you, O Lord:
Lord, hear my voice.
If you, Lord, should note what we do wrong:
who then, O Lord, could stand?
But there is forgiveness with you:
so that you shall be revered.
I wait for the Lord, my soul waits for him:
and in his word is my hope.
Amen.

From Psalm 130

1213 Father, if we
are truly to be the body of Christ,
then let us stand at the foot of the cross
and learn what it means to love
and keep on loving;
to serve and keep on serving.

Susan Sayers

1214 Father, through the life-giving death of Jesus,
may the dying turn to you
and know your merciful love;
may the grieving be comforted,
and may we all one day share
with those who have died
the eternal joy of your heaven.

Susan Sayers

1215 Father God,
thank you
for pancakes
with sugar and syrup
or chocolate and lemon
or any kind of combination.
Please help us
to remember the reason
why we have pancake day,
a start of a new season,
the beginning of Lent,
a feast before the famish,
a time when people make
sacrifices,
a time when we remember
Jesus,
and what he sacrificed for us.

Tony Bower

1216 God, our Father,
we know we do things we should not do,
and forget to do good things we could do:
encourage us in the weeks before Easter
to become better people, by giving up bad habits
and taking up good ones.
In the name of Jesus.
Amen.

John Wright

1217 Lord God, we offer you our promises for Lent.
Help us to keep them in Lent and, because they are
the right thing to do, after Lent as well.

John Wright

1218 Jesus, help me when I am ill or in trouble. And help me to become a better person, a little more like you.
Amen.

John Wright

1219 Lord God, help us to feel the special something the
disciples felt with Jesus on the first Maundy Thursday
and be ready to follow him and to live his way.
Amen.

John Wright

Palm Sunday

1220 Clip, clop, clip, clop!
Hosanna! Hosanna!
Hooray for Jesus,
the king on a donkey!
Hosanna! Hosanna!
Clip, clop, clip, clop!

Susan Sayers

1221 What a challenge that was,
to walk the road into Jerusalem.
What a horror that was,
to hear the crowd calling for your death.
What a sacrifice that was,
to give your life for all people.
What a miracle that was,
to come alive and meet with so many.
What a love that is,
to love all people, including me.

Nick Harding

1222 Lord,
trouble seems to have a habit of getting under my skin.
It itches and aggravates,
and the more I scratch it, the more it itches.
How does trouble find me?
I certainly don't go looking for it,
it seems to find me wherever I am.
It's not always my fault,
well, sometimes maybe, but not every time!
Please help me to see things your way,
because my way sometimes misses the point
or makes the trouble worse!
I need to see things your way,
because I have the knack
of sometimes missing the obvious
or making up my mind
without knowing all the facts.
You seemed to know what you were doing
on the way into Jerusalem.
Even though others thought it odd
that a king should ride a donkey.
But you had other thoughts in mind,
beyond what could be imagined
by your closest friends.
Prince of Peace, take my troubles
and bring your peace instead.
Amen.

Pete Townsend

Easter

1223 Dear God,
you died on the cross
to forgive all the things we've done wrong.
Thank you for doing that for me.
Amen.

Heather Ellis

1224 Dear God,
thank you for happy surprises.
Thank you that Jesus' story does not end on the cross.
Thank you for the joy of Easter.
Amen.

Gill Thorniley

1225 Heavenly Father,
Jesus your Son
died upon the cross
to make up for
the bad things
people have done.
Help us to praise
and thank him
for ever and ever.
Amen.

Denis O'Gorman

1226 Lord God, we pray that our school
may proclaim with joy your message of hope
for the world;
may our lives, as well as our worship,
testify to the truth of the Resurrection;
broaden our vision of what is possible
through new life in you.

Susan Sayers

1227 Lord God, we thank you
for the precious gift of new life;
may we never again take it for granted,
but live each moment in the fullness of life
that Jesus has gained for us.

Susan Sayers

1228 Jesus, you died for me.
(arms out like a cross)
Jesus, you came to life for me!
(arms up)
Jesus, you are alive for ever and ever and ever!
(clap, clap, clap during the 'evers')

Susan Sayers

1229 Christ has died. *(arms out)*
Christ has risen. *(arms up)*
Christ will come again! *(kneel on one knee, arms down, palms up)*

Susan Sayers

1230 We bring to you, Lord,
the love of our hearts
as we recall the extent of your love for us
which understands our frailty
and reaches out to us where we are.

Susan Sayers

1231 Who cares if I can't see you?
(shrug shoulders with hands open)
I certainly know that you're here!
(nod)
Who cares if I can't touch you?
(shrug shoulders with hands open)
I certainly know that you're here!
(nod)
You love me.
(hands on heart)
You listen to me.
(touch ears)
You see me
(point to eyes)
and you talk to me.
(fingers to mouth then out from it)
So who cares if I can't see you?
(shrug shoulders with hands open)
I certainly know you're here!
(nod)

Susan Sayers

1232 Lord, we thank you for walking with us
wherever we travel.
We thank you that you are indeed
real and alive every step of the way!

Susan Sayers

1233 Walk with me, Jesus,
today and every day.
I want to walk with you, Jesus,
right through my life!
Amen.

Rupert Bristow

1234 Father God,
thank you
for Jesus
your Son
who died a death
so horrible
so painful
so brutal
that we might be
forgiven.

Tony Bower

1235 Creator God,
thank you for Easter.
At this time of year
we think about new life,
we see it in the fields
with the tiny newborn lambs,
we see it in the trees
with the sprouting of tiny
new buds,
we see it on the earth
with the daffodils springing
out of their beds.
We see new life everywhere
and remember an empty tomb,
frightened, startled disciples,
confused, bewildered soldiers
all struggling to understand
the new life that had begun
in Jesus.

Tony Bower

1236 Father God,
thank you
for your Son,
Jesus,
who gave his life,
so that we may have
freedom
in our lives
today.

Tony Bower

1237 Loving Heavenly Father,
before the world was made
you loved us.
Before we were born
you loved us.
When we do wrong things
you love us.
When Jesus died on the cross
he showed
you love us.

Tony Bower

1238 Jesus, we welcome you with joy
and with shouts of Hosanna
for you are our King and the Prince of Peace.
Through you, may we have peace
in our hearts, in our homes and in the world.
Amen.

David Adam

1239 Lord Jesus,
you gave your life in obedience to the Father
that we might live in the fullness
of your kingdom.
Keep me faithful and true to you
and help me to resist all temptation.
Amen.

David Adam

1240 Lord Jesus, risen from the dead,
I believe in you,
I trust in you,
I love you.
You are my Lord and my God.
Amen.

David Adam

1241 Lord Jesus, I rejoice today in your resurrection.
I am pleased that you appeared
to Mary Magdalene
and you showed her that you were alive.
May I trust in you as my risen Lord,
for you are always with me and ready to help me.
Amen.

David Adam

1242 Father, thank you for Jesus
and that he offered his life for us.
He died on the cross for us all
and rose again
that we might share in life eternal.
Thank you for Jesus.
Amen.

David Adam

1243 Jesus, I am so happy
that you rose again from the dead.
You are alive and with me wherever I go.
Help me to keep in contact with you
through my prayers
and so know that you are my friend and Saviour.
Amen.

David Adam

1244 God our Father, thank you
for the resurrection of Jesus,
that he is alive and is my friend.
Jesus, I know that you are alive
and I am happy to say,
'Jesus is risen. Alleluia.'
Amen.

David Adam

1245 Lord Jesus, risen from the dead,
help me to know you are alive,
you are with me
and you love me.
Through my prayers
may I make you one of my friends
and know that you are with me to help me.
Amen.

David Adam

1246 God,
thank you that seeds and bulbs grow in secret
without me seeing them.
I trust they will rise out of the earth.
Thank you for Jesus who,
though crucified, dead and buried,
rose again for us all.
Amen.

David Adam

1247 Lord Jesus, you are unseen yet always near.
I believe in you.
I trust you.
I love you.
Help me to tell others of you
and of your resurrection.
Amen.

David Adam

1248 God, thank you for those who have told me
the Good News of your love
and that Jesus is risen from the dead.
As I know the risen Christ,
let me tell others about this wonderful miracle.
Amen.

David Adam

1249 Jesus, my Lord and my God,
let me rejoice in the Resurrection;
let me know you now by faith.
Jesus, I give thanks to you
for life and life eternal.
Amen.

David Adam

1250 Lord God, to you be praise
for through your Son Jesus Christ
you have conquered death
and opened the way to eternal life.
I rejoice in your love
and in the resurrection of your Son.
Alleluia.
Amen.

David Adam

1251 Jesus, thank you
for the power of the Resurrection
and the courage you give to your people.
Help me to know I am never alone
but that you are with me always
as my friend and Saviour.
Amen.

David Adam

1252 Lord Jesus, in you is life
and life eternal.
I put my trust and my hope in you
for with you is life and love.
To you be glory and praise
for ever and ever.
Amen.

David Adam

1253 I give you praise and glory, Lord God,
for you give us the seasons:
a time for sowing and a time for reaping,
a time for burying seeds
and a time for watching them rise.
Help me to understand the power
of the death and resurrection of Jesus.
Amen.

David Adam

1254 Lord Jesus, who in a wonderful sacrament
has left us a memorial of your life offered
and of your death and passion,
help me to understand and respect
this wonderful mystery
and to know the joy of your resurrection
and your presence with us.
Amen.

David Adam

1255 Jesus, you died on the cross.
Jesus, you were buried.
Jesus, you rose again.
Alleluia!

David Adam

1256 Jesus, as the people of Jerusalem welcomed you,
may I welcome you in my home and my life
as my King.
Amen.

David Adam

1257 God, thank you for all things that grow;
that buried seeds rise again.
Thank you for the love of Jesus.
Amen.

David Adam

1258 Thank you, God,
that Jesus is alive and is my friend.
He is with me always.
Alleluia!

David Adam

1259 Jesus, you are alive
and always ready to help me.
You rose from the dead
and make those who follow you happy.
Amen.

David Adam

1260 Jesus, help me to remember you each day
and to give my love to you.
Amen.

David Adam

1261 Jesus, I am happy
that you are alive
and you want to be my friend.
Amen.

David Adam

1262 God, thank you for Easter.
Thank you that Jesus rose again from the dead.
I know that Jesus is alive and loves me.
Alleluia.
Amen.

David Adam

1263 Dear God,
please help us to find out the truth
of the Easter story for ourselves.
Amen.

Caroline Vallance

1264 Thank you, God,
for raising Jesus to life,
and showing that there is nothing greater
than your love.

Michael Forster

1265 Please forgive us, Lord,
for not always being open to your surprises.
We get used to expecting you
to act in certain ways,
and then we're not ready
when you do something new.
Help us to have more faith.

Michael Forster

1266 Easter eggs and Easter bunnies,
Easter chicks and Easter bonnets.
Easter Jesus going to die.
Easter Jesus, coming to life again.
Easter time, a time to celebrate
new birth, new life, new hope.

Nick Harding

1267 New life comes in spring.
New life of little animals, birds and fish.
New life comes in spring.
New life of plants, crops and bushes.
New life comes in spring.
New life of Jesus, who came alive again.
New life comes in spring.

Nick Harding

1268 Father God, for you Easter must have been a sad time.
A sad time as Jesus went up that hill
and was put on a cross.
A sad time as Jesus died in such pain.
Father God, you made Easter a good time.
A good time when Jesus was not defeated by death.
A good time when Jesus breathed again after three days.
Father God, for us Easter can be a special time.
A special time to remember you, and to remember Jesus.
There are beautiful things at springtime.

Nick Harding

1269 Thank you, Lord Jesus,
that you were willing to give your life for us.

Ashley Guest

1270 We remember Simon of Cyrene who carried
the cross for Jesus.
Help us to be ready to carry each other's burdens.
Amen.

Jill Fuller

1271 Lord Jesus,
some people hated you enough to kill you.
You gave yourself
out of love for all people.
You have the power to change lives.
Amen.

Ashley Guest

1272 Father God, why did Jesus have to come down
to earth as a boy and man?
Was that your plan?
Father God, why did Jesus have to be hurt
by whips and thorny crown
to bring him down?
Father God, why did Jesus have to die
on wood chopped from a tree?
Is it true he died for me?

Nick Harding

1273 Lord Jesus,
you know the pain of disappointment and sadness.
Grant us courage when we feel defeated.
Renew our vision when we feel dispirited.
Refresh our hope when we feel without energy.
Lead us always in your ways of resurrection.
Amen.

Jill Fuller

1274 Jesus, remember me and all those for whom we have prayed.
May we be ready to carry each other's crosses and to stretch out our arms in love and care for each other.
So may we travel onwards on our life's journey.
Amen.

Jill Fuller

1275 Lord God, whose Son Jesus suffered pain on the cross of the tree at Calvary,
look mercifully on our prayers for those we know are in pain.
Help us to bring comfort to those who suffer.
Give them courage and strength to trust in your love.
Amen.

Jill Fuller

1276 Be gentle when you touch bread.
Let it not lie uncared for – unwanted.
So often bread is taken for granted.
There is so much beauty in bread –
beauty of sun and soil
beauty of patient toil.
Winds and rains have caressed it,
Christ often blessed it.
Be gentle when you touch bread.
Amen.

Jill Fuller

1277 Lord,
if you ask me,
this sacrifice thing is a bit much.
What's the point?
How can giving something away
mean so much?
Can you tell me
how my actions
can change the way other people
behave, or think or believe?
I'm not so sure
that the best thing to do
isn't to keep everything I've got
and to look after myself,
just so that other people can see
how good you are to me.
And, just think,
you could give me even more good things,
just to make the point, OK?
But there is one thing that niggles me.
Somewhere along the way,
didn't you do something for me
that changed everything,
and made it possible to get to know
God the Father, like a friend, a dad,
someone you like to have around?
And, when I think about it a little more,
didn't Jesus make all this a reality
by giving up everything he had,
everything he could be,
everything everybody wanted him to be,
just so that me and you could get to know each other?
I'm not saying I understand this sacrifice thing,
but however it works,
it's made a difference to me,
and I suppose that's the point of it all.
Lord, help me to make a difference
to those people around me.
And, just a final thing,
do you know anybody
who might like
half a packet of custard cream biscuits?
Amen.

Pete Townsend

1278 Jesus, at times it's really difficult,
really difficult to understand what you mean.
It's even more difficult to do what you say,
even when we understand.
It's not easy.
I know it's about faith, it's about trust.
Easy to say, but not easy to put into practice.
As I lift my eyes
allow me to see what you meant
by dying to live;
by giving to receive.
Thank you for my choice.
Help me to use my choice,
rather than ignore it.
You died for me to live.
What more can I say?
Amen.

Pete Townsend

1279 Lord, thank you.
Although thank you doesn't really seem enough,
considering that you didn't trust your lucky rabbit's paw,
or keep your fingers crossed, just in case.
When you touched wood it wasn't for luck,
or even to make sure that everything would work out
all right.
You touched wood,
the wood of the cross,
to turn harm into good;
to bring life where there was death;
to give hope where there was doubt.
Lord, thank you.
Amen.

Pete Townsend

1280 Lord, it is easy to think that it gets dark too quickly,
that clouds obscure the sun.
When it's night, someone somewhere else is enjoying the light.
Our darkness can often seem to last longer than everyone else's.
Help us to see.
Help us to open up the dark areas for your light to shine.
Help us to trust you when dark clouds gather on the horizon.
Be with us as the shadows give way
to the brightness of your Son.
Amen.

Pete Townsend

1281 God our Father,
we find it hard to understand
why Jesus had to die on Good Friday,
when all he said and did was good.
Help us to see that not even death
could end the love and goodness he showed us,
and that the Resurrection is the proof
that he and love and goodness
are with us for ever.
Amen.

John Wright

1282 God our Father,
we thank you for all Jesus said and did,
and for you bringing him back from death;
help us to see that although he left earth,
he is still there for us when we need him.
Amen.

John Wright

1283 Lord God,
we don't fully understand why Jesus had to die as he did,
but we believe it was done for us.
Give us the faith to believe he is with us now and for ever,
to be with us and to help us.
Amen.

John Wright

Ascension Day

1284 Jesus, you were born as a baby.
(rock baby in arms)
You worked as a carpenter, sawing the wood.
(saw wood)
You died on a cross and you rose again.
(arms out, then jump and clap hands)
You are loving and kind and good.
(put up fingers, counting to three)
In heaven and on earth your glory shines.
(point up and down, then trace big circle with fingers stretched out)
You are loving and kind and good.
(count on fingers again)

Susan Sayers

1285 God of glory, we thank you
that through your ascension into heaven
the way was open for us to receive the Holy Spirit.
Prepare our hearts each day to welcome you.

Susan Sayers

1286 Jesus, you are our Lord and Saviour,
reigning in the glory of heaven!
You were sent to love us to freedom
and you did it!
Glory to you for ever.

Susan Sayers

1287 God our Father,
Jesus your Son died upon the cross
and looked broken and in a mess.
Now he is beautiful and lovely in heaven.
We thank you for his promise that
one day we shall be in heaven too –
shining and lovely just like him.
Amen.

Denis O'Gorman

Pentecost

1288 Breathe on me, too, Lord God almighty,
as you breathed on the disciples that day.
Touch me with your fire
and set me ablaze with your love!

Susan Sayers

1289 Almighty God,
bring your Holy Spirit to work in our hearts.
Let the wind and the flames that the disciples felt renew our faith.
Help us to show the Holy Spirit in our lives that others may know your love and learn your way.
We ask this through Jesus Christ, our Lord.
Amen.

Rupert Bristow

1290 Almighty God,
as we celebrate the receiving of the Holy Spirit by the disciples, we ask that we can know the Holy Spirit too.
If we cannot feel this wind in the same way as the disciples, bring us the fruits of the Spirit in other ways.
If we cannot understand or communicate in many tongues, help us to try to communicate God's love in the best way we can.
May Pentecost show, in our lives, that we depend on Jesus even though we do not see him, and feel his presence with the help of the comforter, the Holy Spirit.
We ask this through Jesus Christ, our Lord.
Amen.

Rupert Bristow

1291 Lord, I wait for you.
Come, Holy Spirit.
Lord, take away my fear.
Come, Holy Spirit.
Lord, give me the courage to proclaim your gospel.
Come, Holy Spirit.
Lord, fill my life with your power.
Come, Holy Spirit.
Lord, teach me patience as I wait.
Come, Holy Spirit.
Amen.

David Adam

1292 Come, Holy Spirit of God,
fill my life with your presence,
strengthen me through your power
and guide me in your goodness.
May my life show
that you are with me and within me always.
Amen.

David Adam

1293 Come, Holy Spirit of God, fill me with your love.
Come, Holy Spirit of God, fill me with your power.
Come, Holy Spirit of God, fill me with your light.
Come, Holy Spirit of God,
fill me with your inspiration.
Then may I bring others to know you
and to love you.
Amen.

David Adam

Harvest

1294 Heavenly Father,
as the harvest is gathered in we praise you for all that is growing and picked and eaten at this time of year.
In thanking you, we also remember the hard work of the farmers who planted and fed and tended the crops, transported the food and made it all available to us.
We take this opportunity also, Lord, to pray for areas of the country and the wider world where crops have failed this year and where food is short.
May communities with plenty help those who have little.
We ask this in Jesus' name.
Amen.

Rupert Bristow

1295 God of plenty,
we thank you for the fruits of the earth at this harvest time.
May we always remember the link between the food on our plate and the fields and farms around us.
Help us to choose and use our food wisely.
Bring food and water to the people who need them and restraint and generosity to the people who have more than enough.
We ask this in Jesus' name.
Amen.

Rupert Bristow

1296 Dear Father God,
thank you
for the farmer,
for the fields and the crops
which the combine harvester
goes out and chops.
Thank you
for the food,
the riches on our plate,
delicious tastes, pleasing smells
which we think are great.
Thank you
for the harvest,
the food that helps us live,
please help us to share it and
teach us how to give.

Tony Bower

1297 For all the
food we eat,
for all the
things we drink,
we say:
'Thank you, God.'
For all the
heat for warmth,
for all the
power for light,
we say:
'Thank you, God.'
For all the
world gives,
and all that
people take,
we say:
'Thank you, God.'

Nick Harding

1298 As we think of your great world
we celebrate your gifts.
As we think of food we eat
we celebrate your gifts.
As we think of all we drink
we celebrate your gifts.
As we think of harvest time
we celebrate your gifts.

Nick Harding

1299 There is nothing that grows
that God didn't make for us.
There is nothing that flows
that God didn't pour out for us.
There is nothing that we need
that God doesn't give to us.

Nick Harding

1300 At harvest time we think
of the good things that grow:
we think of plants and trees,
crops and bushes.
We think of fish and animals
and all that provides our food.
At harvest time we think
of good things that grow:
help us all grow into good things.

Nick Harding

1301 God the Maker,
you made great food for us to eat –
great green apples, brilliant bananas,
perfect peaches and marvellous mandarins.
You made great food for us to eat –
wheat for bread, crunchy carrots,
beans for baking and tomatoes for tins.
God the Maker,
you made great food for us to eat.

Nick Harding

1302 We delight in the food we eat,
tangy, spicy, sour or sweet.
We delight in things to drink,
keeps us lively, helps us think.
We delight in all you give
so that all the earth can live.

Nick Harding

1303 At harvest we give thanks.
We give thanks for farmers
who work to feed us.
We give thanks for creation
which provides for all our needs.
We give thanks for the rain
which gives us the water of life.
At harvest time we give thanks.

Nick Harding

1304 You are King of the world
where plants, bushes and trees grow.
You are King of the land
where animals run and walk.
You are King of the oceans
where fish swim and bask.
You are King of the harvest,
when we give thanks for all things.

Nick Harding

1305 God, your world is just amazing!
It's amazing that seeds grow
and provide us with the food we need.
It's amazing that animals and fish live,
providing people with more to eat.
It's amazing that streams and rivers
provide water for life.
God, your world is amazing –
thank you for your amazing world.

Nick Harding

1306 Thank you, God, you made it all.
The chips we eat until we're full,
the apples that crunch and spray with juice.
The sweets we grab that make us smile,
the fizzy drinks that make us burp!
The cheese dippers and yoghurt drinks.
Thank you, God, you made it all.

Nick Harding

All Saints' Day
(1 November)

1307 Almighty God,
today we remember all the saints who have shaped the Christian story.
Those who died for their faith, remembering especially . . . . ;
those who through their lives and works ensured the foundation of our faith, remembering in particular Mary the mother of Jesus; and those from our own communities and families who have made a difference as Christian people.
We thank you for all those saints who are now at peace with you.
Amen.

Rupert Bristow

1308 Almighty God,
you know that we each have our special saints whose lives and works mean a lot to us.
In a moment of silence we remember them now.
Thank you, Lord, for who they were, what they did and what they still mean to us today.
Amen.

Rupert Bristow

All Souls' Day
(2 November)

1309 Heavenly Father,
on the day of All Souls we remember those who have died, and especially those who are known to us and our families and who are now at peace with you.
Create in us not the fear of death, but grateful thanks for their lives.
Keep away the doubts and dangers of those who are disrespectful of the dead.
Show your love to those who have recently lost someone close to them.
We ask this in Jesus' name.
Amen.

Rupert Bristow

1310 Heavenly Father,
help us to remember and celebrate the lives of those who have died.
You have shown us through your Son's death and resurrection at Easter that death is not the end, but a new beginning.
In this world, let us not forget all who went before us,
the famous and the little known, those who died young and those who lived long.
We know you loved them all, Lord, and still love them now.
May we remember and give thanks, may we never forget.
We ask this in Jesus' name.
Amen.

Rupert Bristow

Christian faith

Jesus

1311 Jesus, you are the Light of the World.
Shine in our lives
and make them bright and beautiful.
Amen.

David Adam

1312 Jesus,
help me to shine as a light in your world.
Let me show that I love you
and help others to know of your love.
Amen.

David Adam

1313 Jesus, you are the Light of the World.
Keep me in your light
and let me shine for you.
Amen.

David Adam

1314 Lord Jesus, I am sorry
when I have lost contact with you,
when I have forgotten my prayers
or thought I was too busy.
I seek your presence and your healing power
in my life.
Amen.

David Adam

1315 Jesus,
let your light shine upon me
and my home.
Amen.

David Adam

1316 Lord Jesus,
help me to be still and quiet,
to know you are with me
and that you love me.
You are the Good Shepherd
and I am one of your sheep.
Let me try and do what you want me to do.
Amen.

David Adam

1317 Jesus, you are the Good Shepherd;
you love us all
and seek all who are lost or in trouble.
May I learn to follow you
and to love you always.
Amen.

David Adam

1318 Jesus, you are my King and my God.
Help me to love you as you love me.
I know that you protect me.
You are always with me.
Hurrah, for you are my King.
Amen.

David Adam

1319 Jesus, you are the King of Love.
I love you
and thank you for caring for me.
I will serve you
by loving and caring for others.
Amen.

David Adam

1320 Jesus, you are my King.
Help me to love you
and to do what you want me to do.
I know that you love me and care for me.
Amen.

David Adam

1321 Jesus, you are the King of Love.
Thank you for being so kind and gentle.
Help me to be kind and gentle too.
Amen.

David Adam

1322 Jesus, you are the Light of the World.
When we know you,
you bring brightness and hope to our lives.
I know that you are God's Son
and I love you.
Amen.

David Adam

1323 Lord Jesus, help me to walk in your light
so that I may reflect your love
and so bring others to you
and to the brightness and life
that you offer to all.
Amen.

David Adam

1324 Lord Jesus, it is wonderful to know you.
You are my friend and you are the Light
that chases away the darkness of our world.
Help me to love you every day.
Amen.

David Adam

1325 God our Father, thank you for Jesus
who is the Light of the World.
Thank you that he shows your love for us.
May we learn to love you more and more
every day.
Amen.

David Adam

1326 Jesus, you are the King of kings.
You are the ruler of the whole world.
Yet in love you come to serve us and help us.
You gave your life for us.
Help me to give myself to you
and to serve you by caring for others.
Amen.

David Adam

1327 Jesus, you are the Servant King.
Help me to care for others
and spend time looking after them.
Amen.

David Adam

1328 Jesus, you are my King and my God.
I want to love you and serve you always.
Help me to do your will
and so be part of your kingdom.
Amen.

David Adam

1329 Jesus, my King and my God,
let me work for you,
let me tell of you,
let me love you,
let me obey you
and let me be part of your kingdom.
Amen.

David Adam

1330 Jesus, I welcome you as my King.
Come rule in my heart.
I know that you love me
and you are my Saviour.
Come, Lord Jesus, as King
and help me.
Amen.

David Adam

1331 Lord Jesus, you came
that we should enjoy living
and to give us life that is eternal.
Thank you for your power and presence
with us always.
Amen.

David Adam

1332 Lord Jesus, you are the Good Shepherd.
You seek out the troubled and the lost
to bring them safely home.
Teach me always to be generous
and to care for others as you care for me.
Amen.

David Adam

1333 Jesus, you look after me
as a shepherd would look after his sheep.
I thank you for your love and care
and ask you to protect me in all dangers.
Amen.

David Adam

1334 Come, Jesus,
be known as my companion and friend.
Let me know that you are ever with me
and love me
and help me to work for you.
Amen.

David Adam

1335 Lord Jesus, you are the Prince of Peace.
You stilled the waves, the storm
and the troubled mind of the madman.
Let me live in your peace
and know your power in my life.
Amen.

David Adam

1336 Thank you, God, for water,
for rain, rivers and seas,
for wells, reservoirs and tap water.
Thank you for Jesus, the Water of Life.
Amen.

David Adam

1337 Jesus, help me to know you as my friend
and as my Saviour and my God.
Thank you for all the wonderful things you do.
Help me to know your power and your love.
Amen.

David Adam

1338 Lord Jesus,
thank you for all that you have done for me
and that you love me always.
Amen.

David Adam

1339 Lord Jesus, as the fishermen listened to you
and followed you,
help me to follow you each day
and be part of your team.
Let me show my love for you
and do what you would like me to do.
Amen.

David Adam

1340 Lord Jesus, I would like to be on your team
to fight against evil and to do good.
Help me to be your friend
and to work for you and your kingdom.
Let me not give in to evil but seek to help you.
Amen.

David Adam

1341 Jesus, help me to listen to your word
and seek to do your will.
May I show that I love you
by doing what you want me to do.
Amen.

David Adam

1342 Jesus, you are wonderful.
Help me to tell others of your love
and your saving power.
Show me how to share with my friends
the Good News that I have learnt.
Amen.

David Adam

1343 Lord Jesus, as you gave your life for me
and offer me your friendship,
help me to be your close friend
and to talk with you each day.
May I give my love and my life
to work for you and your glory.
Amen.

David Adam

1344 Jesus, I love you
and want to shine as a light in your world.
Help me to show I love you
by saying my prayers
and by telling others about you.
Amen.

David Adam

1345 Lord Jesus,
help me to know that in obeying you
my life is enriched and changed
into something precious and wonderful.
Amen.

David Adam

1346 Lord Jesus, help me to fight against evil.
Deliver me from temptation
and make me strong to serve you.
Amen.

David Adam

1347 Take my hands, Lord Jesus,
let them work for you.
Let me share in helping
and in caring for others.
Let my hands show your love,
Jesus, Friend and Healer.
Amen.

David Adam

1348 Lord Jesus,
as the fishermen listened to you
and obeyed you,
help me to be ready to do
what you want me to do.
Amen.

David Adam

1349 Lord Jesus,
help me to know you as the Prince of Peace
and to accept your rule in my heart
and in my life.
Teach me to pray and live by the words
'Your will be done'.
Amen.

David Adam

1350 Lord Jesus,
guide me into the way of peace.
I give my hands to work for you.
Let my feet always be on your path.
Let me speak your praises and do your will
this day and for ever.
Amen.

David Adam

1351 Lord Jesus, you are the Son of God,
the Promised One.
You are Christ our Saviour.
As you give yourself for me and to me,
help me to give my life and love to you.
Amen.

David Adam

1352 Jesus, you just need to speak the word
and people are healed.
Thank you for the words of the Bible,
especially the Gospels.
More than anything, thank you
that you are the Word made flesh.
Amen.

David Adam

1353 Jesus Christ, Light of the World,
scatter the darkness from about me
and within me
and help me to walk as a child of the light.
Help me to know that you love me
and are with me always.
Amen.

David Adam

1354 Jesus, Son of God, Saviour,
I put my trust in you
and in your almighty power.
You are able to bring light to my darkness
and rescue me when I cannot help myself.
Jesus, help me to know you better
and to love you more.
Amen.

David Adam

1355 Lord Jesus,
friend of the friendless
and help of the helpless,
I come to you in faith.
I trust in you, in your love and in your power.
Lord Jesus, help me to hear your call
and to follow you.
Amen.

David Adam

1356 Father, thank you for Jesus the Good Shepherd;
through his death he has destroyed death,
and by his rising to life again
he has opened for us the gate of glory.
May I know his love and protection in my life.
I ask this through Jesus Christ my Lord.
Amen.

David Adam

1357 Lord Jesus, you are the Good Shepherd.
You seek and save the lost.
You care for the fallen and restore the sick.
You call each of us by our name
and you offer us eternal life.
Lord, help me to know you
and to follow you day by day.
Amen.

David Adam

1358 Lord Jesus, you bring healing to the ill,
strength to the weak
and love to the lonely.
Help me to care for all who are in need
and be grateful for all that I have.
Amen.

David Adam

1359 Jesus, you are able to change
emptiness into fullness
and to turn lives from wickedness
and wastefulness
into goodness and usefulness.
Bless my life with your presence and power.
Amen.

David Adam

1360 God, thank you for the faithfulness of your word
and for Jesus, the Word made flesh.
May I find in him the way to life eternal.
Amen.

David Adam

1361 Jesus, I welcome you as my King and Saviour.
Take my heart and fill it with your love.
Take my mind and work through it.
Take my will and act through it.
Take my life and make it yours.
As you give yourself to me,
I give myself to you,
Christ my King and my God.
Amen.

David Adam

1362 Jesus, you are the Christ, the Son of God.
You came to our world and became human
so that you could lift us into your kingdom
and let us share in the Divine.
Thank you for your love
and your abiding presence with me.
Amen.

David Adam

1363 Lord Jesus, thank you that you have shown
the love and the forgiveness of the Father.
I think you are great and do wonderful things.
Amen.

David Adam

1364 Lord Jesus, you are my King.
Come and rule in my heart
that your kingdom may come in me.
Lord, I give thanks to you
for you are my Saviour.
Amen.

David Adam

1365 Lord, you are my shepherd,
my protector and my guardian.
You have given your life
that I can have life eternal.
You will lead me into the way of peace
if only I will follow you.
I thank you for your love and sacrifice for me.
Amen.

David Adam

1366 God, I know the sun is there
on the cloudiest of days.
Help me to know that Jesus is always with me.
He is ready to hear my prayers and to help me.
Lord Jesus, thank you for being with me
and for praying for me.
Amen.

David Adam

1367 Abide with me, Lord,
abide with me today and for ever.
Abide with me in my joys and my sorrows.
Abide with me in darkness and light.
Abide with me, and your whole Church.
Abide with me in time and eternity.
Amen.

David Adam

1368 Lord Jesus, thank you for becoming one with us
and sharing our joys and sorrows.
Help me to know you are always with me
and let me not lose my awareness of you
through neglect or busyness.
Amen.

David Adam

1369 Lord Jesus,
I do not know what might happen to me,
I do not know where I might have to go,
but I do know you are with me
and you will guide me
on my journey through life.
Lord Jesus, as you seek to be my friend,
let me welcome you each day.
Amen.

David Adam

1370 Christ is with me, Christ is before me,
Christ is behind me, Christ is within me,
Christ is beneath me, Christ is above me,
Christ on my right and on my left.
Christ all around me and within.

David Adam

1371 Lord Jesus, as you called the fishermen
and they obeyed you,
help me to do what you would have me do
and to seek to be the person you would have me be.
Amen.

David Adam

1372 Jesus, as you came to the disciples,
you come to me.
You want me to be your friend
and to help in the work that you do.
Jesus, I ask that I might be a true friend
and know that you are with me always.
Amen.

David Adam

1373 Lord Jesus,
as you love all and care for all,
may I share in your healing and caring ministry.
Make me aware of those in need
and how I can help.
Amen.

David Adam

1374 Risen Lord, may I know that you are with me
and seek to be my friend.
Help me to give time and attention
to you each day,
that I may share in your mission
and do what you would have me do.
Amen.

David Adam

1375 Lord Jesus, may I know you
and, in knowing you, love you,
and, in loving you, proclaim you,
that it may be known I believe in you
and that you are with me always.
Amen.

David Adam

1376 Lord Jesus,
take my hands and work with them;
take my feet and reach others through them;
take my lips and speak through them;
take my heart and set it on fire
with love for you and for all people.
Amen.

David Adam

1377 Jesus, thank you that you have called me
to know you and to enjoy your presence.
Give me the wisdom and the courage
to proclaim the Good News
and tell of your saving power.
Amen.

David Adam

1378 Lord, you have called me
to share in your ministry of love and care.
You reveal yourself to me in the cry
of the poor and needy.
Help me to be open and generous in my life
and know that when I care for the least of these
I am showing my love for you,
Jesus Christ my Lord.
Amen.

David Adam

1379 Loving Father, help me to listen carefully
to the call of Jesus.
Give me a love for him that sends me out
to tell others of his power and his greatness.
May I share in his mission and in his message
by the way I live and speak.
Amen.

David Adam

1380 God, you made me to love and obey you.
Help me to do what is right
and to stand against evil;
to show my love for you
by the way I care for others
and the world around me.
Amen.

David Adam

1381 Lord Jesus, you have called me
to work for you and with you.
Help me to be faithful to you,
to work against evil
and to seek to do what is right and good.
May I be ready to stand up
for all who strive for goodness and peace.
I ask this in your power and in your name,
Jesus Christ my Lord.
Amen.

David Adam

1382 God, you have called me to work with you
and to do good for the world.
Protect me from all evil
and keep me in the right way
today and always.
Amen.

David Adam

1383 Jesus, help me to shine with love for you
and by my life show that I know you
and love you.
May I share with others
the love that you give to me.
Amen.

David Adam

1384 Lord God, you have called me
to be one of your people,
to give my life to you
and in the service of others.
As you have called me,
strengthen me
and make me worthy of my calling.
Amen.

David Adam

1385 Lord Jesus, you have called me
to be your apostle
and to go out and tell others of you.
Give me strength and wisdom to do this
and help me to know
that you are with me always.
Amen.

David Adam

1386 Lord God, you have called me
to follow you and to belong to you in love.
Help me to show your love to all people.
Send me out to tell of your presence and your kingdom
in the world.
Amen.

David Adam

1387 Lord Jesus, you have called me
to be the salt of the earth.
Help me to fight quietly against evil
and to encourage people to enjoy life.
Let me show I belong to you
and that you give me the gift of life eternal.
Amen.

David Adam

1388 Lord Jesus, there are some people
who are afraid of you because they feel guilty.
Help them to know that you love them so much
that all you want is to be their friend.

Michael Forster

1389 Jesus –
you are
EVERYWHERE.
And,
AND
AND
you are
in each one of us.
That's
very
VERY
clever and amazing
to be able
to do both
AT
THE
VERY
SAME
TIME.
We guess
you can do it
because you're
God
and
Jesus
rolled into one.

Susan Hardwick

1390 Hey, Jesus! –
you are
always saying
that children
are
extra-special.
Then –
that means
you
extra-specially
care
when
children are sad,
or hurt
in any way.
You kiss away
our tears.
And your
extra-special-children-love
hugs us better.

Susan Hardwick

1391 Jesus –
you are always saying
we should
ask you for
everything
we want
or need.
So –
I want to ask
that all
girls and boys,
EVERYWHERE,
will know you
and your love,
just like
I do.
Please
make this wish
come true!

Susan Hardwick

1392 Jesus and God –
my wish is
that
I will grow
in my love
of you,
every single day.
And
that I
will become
more and more
and more like you
as I grow
in body,
and mind,
and soul,
and spirit.

Susan Hardwick

1393 Jesus said,
'Let the little children come to me,
and do not hinder them,
for the kingdom of heaven
belongs to such as these.'
Amen.

Matthew 19:14

1394 Thank you, Jesus,
you are the way,
the truth and the life.
Your way is the right way.
I will follow you always.
Amen.

Anon

1395 Lord Jesus,
help me to know you as the Prince of Peace
and to accept your rule
in my heart and in my life.
Teach me to pray
and live by the words 'Your will be done'.
Amen.

David Adam

1396 Lord Jesus,
you are the Son of God,
the Promised One.
You are Christ our Saviour.
As you give yourself
for me and to me,
help me to give
my life and love to you.
Amen.

David Adam

1397 Jesus,
you just need to speak the word
and people are healed.
Thank you for the words of the Bible,
especially the Gospels.
More than anything,
thank you that you are
the Word made flesh.
Amen.

David Adam

1398 Jesus Christ,
Light of the World,
scatter the darkness
from about me and within me
and help me to walk
as a child of the light.
Help me know that you love me
and are here with me always.
Amen.

David Adam

1399 Father,
thank you for Jesus,
the Good Shepherd;
through his death
he has destroyed death,
and by his rising to life again
he has opened for us
the gate of glory.
May I know his love
and protection of my life.
I ask this through
Jesus Christ my Lord.
Amen.

David Adam

1400 Lord Jesus,
you are the Good Shepherd.
You seek and save the lost.
You care for the fallen
and restore the sick.
You call each of us
by our name
and you offer us
eternal life.
Lord, help me
to know you
and to follow you
day by day.
Amen.

David Adam

1401 Lord Jesus,
you bring healing to the ill,
strength to the weak
and love to the lonely.
Help me to care for all
who are in need
and be grateful
for all that I have.
Amen.

David Adam

1402 Jesus,
you are able
to change emptiness
into fullness
and to turn lives
from wickedness and wastefulness
into goodness and usefulness.
Bless my life
with your presence and power.
Amen.

David Adam

1403 God,
thank you for the faithfulness
of your word and for Jesus,
the Word made flesh.
May I find in him
the way to life eternal.
Amen.

David Adam

1404 Jesus, I welcome you as my King and Saviour.
Take my heart and fill it with your love.
Take my mind and work through it.
Take my will and act through it.
Take my life and make it yours.
As you give yourself to me,
I give myself to you,
Christ my King and my God.
Amen.

David Adam

1405 Thank you for being there, Jesus,
when things are bad for us
– even when we don't realise you were there
until we look back.
Thank you for all the times
that you bring new life out of bad times.

Michael Forster

1406 Lord Jesus,
thank you
that you are good,
good in every way
and good towards us;
every single day
you watch over us
and watch out for us
like a shepherd
watching his flock.
You look and you watch,
watch over us
and watch out for us
in a good, good way,
leading us always
in the right ways.

Tony Bower

1407 Lord Jesus,
thank you
that you are the bread
of life,
the bread that we need,
the bread that will feed
our soul,
make us complete
and whole.
Our daily bread,
not the sliced loaf

that we eat,
but the life-giving Spirit
we can receive
and the love we can know
which helps us grow
more like you
every single day.

Tony Bower

1408 Lord Jesus,
thank you
that you show us the way
to live our lives,
thank you
that you are the way
for us to live our lives
and we thank you
that you open the door
for us to go through,
and to follow you
in your glorious kingdom
of heaven.

Tony Bower

1409 Lord Jesus,
thank you
for fruit,
for delicious apples, pears
and bananas, oranges
and mangoes.
So many kinds of tasty,
healthy fruit
that we can eat,
fruit that grows from fruit trees.
We thank you
for the fruit of your Spirit,
for love, joy, peace, patience,
kindness, goodness,
faithfulness,
gentleness and self-control.
Please help us
to grow in our relationship
with you,
so we can grow more
of your wonderful, healthy
life-enhancing fruit.

Tony Bower

1410 Lord Jesus,
thank you
that you are
the defeater of death,
and have shown us
that breathing our last breath
is not the end of the road.
Our journey over,
it is not a full stop
but a comma,
a pause
for new breath
after death,
a promise of a new chapter
beginning
with you for eternity
where life
is never ending.

Tony Bower

1411 God, thank you for Andrew, Peter,
James and John
who followed Jesus.
May I also follow Jesus
and do what he wants me to do.
Amen.

David Adam

1412 Lord Jesus, I want to follow you.
I want to be a fisher of people.
I want to tell others that you love us all.
Amen.

David Adam

1413 Jesus, friend of the disciples,
be a friend of mine.
Let me know that you love me
and you are with me.
Let me learn to talk to you every day.
Amen.

David Adam

1414 Jesus, I am happy
that you shared a meal with your friends
and helped them to catch fish.
I would like to be your friend
and talk to you each day.
Amen.

David Adam

1415 I'm a friend of Jesus', too.
Jesus, I love you and like being quiet with you.
I like the stories about you
and that you want me to be your disciple.
Amen.

David Adam

1416 Jesus, you want me to help you
by being good and caring for your world.
I will try to be helpful in my home
and be kind to others.
Amen.

David Adam

1417 Lord Jesus,
show me the way I should live
and the things I should do
to please you and to serve God.
Amen.

David Adam

1418 Jesus, I am glad that you are alive
and that you want to be my friend.
Let me remember you every day
and speak to you in my prayers.
Amen.

David Adam

1419 Jesus, you are with me always.
I come to give my love to you
and I want to be your friend.
I cannot see you but I still love you.
Amen.

David Adam

1420 Jesus, I know that you love everyone
and that you love me.
Help me today to love you
and to be kind and generous to others.
Amen.

David Adam

1421 Jesus, you shared your life with us,
you gave us your love.
I love you and want to share with you.
Amen.

David Adam

1422 Jesus, thank you
for all the lovely things you do for me
and that you look after me.
Help me to look after others.
Amen.

David Adam

1423 Jesus, I am happy that you are my friend
and that you never leave me.
Help me to remember you each day
and to speak to you in my prayers.
Amen.

David Adam

1424 Jesus, be my friend.
Bring your love and your light into my life.
Help me to know that you are always with me
and that you look after me.
Amen.

David Adam

1425 Jesus Christ, thank you
for all the wonderful things you have done.
I know that you are alive
and want to be my friend
and to love me.
Jesus, I want to love you
because you are great.
Amen.

David Adam

1426 Lord Jesus,
as you love me,
help me to love you
and to bring my friends to you.
Amen.

David Adam

1427 Jesus, you do wonderful things
when I obey you.
Thank you for making me happy today.
Amen.

David Adam

1428 Lord Jesus, you love me
and do not want me to be sad.
Help me to love you
and make people happy.
Amen.

David Adam

1429 Lord Jesus, help me to listen to you
and to do what you want me to do.
I love you, Lord Jesus,
and want you to be my friend.
Amen.

David Adam

1430 Loving Jesus,
let me be still and quiet, close to you,
learning of your love for me,
giving all my love to you.
Amen.

David Adam

1431 Jesus, thank you for the stories you told
and all that you teach me.
Thank you that you healed people
and wanted them to enjoy living.
Amen.

David Adam

1432 I love singing songs about you, Jesus.
Praising you is what I love best.
Thank you for listening to me.
Amen.

Heather Ellis

1433 Lord Jesus,
please let your
kingdom of love,
justice and peace
rule for ever and
ever.
Amen.

Denis O'Gorman

1434 Thank you, Jesus, that you helped many people.
Thank you, Jesus, that you said many good things.
Thank you, Jesus, that you know me and you love me.
Amen.

Nick Harding

1435 Lord Jesus,
thank you for your presence.
Come to us today.
Amen.

Ashley Guest

1436 Thank you, Lord Jesus,
that you can help to clean us up
when our lives get messy.
Help us, Lord.
Amen.

Ashley Guest

1437 Dear God,
thank you for all the people Jesus walked with and helped.
Thank you that you will walk with us and help us.

Nick Harding

1438 God our Father,
your Son Jesus showed his love for the people he met
by healing them when they needed it.
Teach us that Jesus will still help us if we ask him
because he loves us too.
Amen.

John Wright

1439 Lord God,
Father of Jesus and of each one of us,
give us the desire to want to know more about Jesus and what he said and did, so that as we learn more we can try to live more and more the way he wants us to.
Amen.

John Wright

1440 Teach us, good Lord,
that it is not enough to say we believe,
but that it must be seen in everything we say and do.
Help us to do this, in the way and the name of Jesus.
Amen.

John Wright

1441 God our Father,
you have given us everything we need,
and most of all you gave us Jesus to be our light,
the light of truth.
Help us to be children of light
and to live by the example of Jesus,
so that the world may be as good
as you always meant it to be.
Amen.

John Wright

1442 Lord Jesus,
light up our lives, and as you are light for us in our lives,
may we show that same light to those around us.
In your name.
Amen.

John Wright

1443 Thank you, Jesus,
that you called those fishermen.
Thank you that you did
so many good things.
Amen.

Nick Harding

1444 Lord Jesus, I can't see you – but I can see you in others.
Help me to be such a follower
that people can see you in me.
Amen.

John Wright

1445 Father God,
thank you for sending us Jesus.
Please help us to be as loving and caring
as he was.
Amen.

Denis O'Gorman

Father, Son and Holy Spirit

1446 Father, thank you that you made me
and that you love me.
Jesus, thank you that you came to earth for me
and that you love me.
Spirit, thank you that you are always with me
and that you love me.
Amen.

David Adam

1447 Father God, thank you for making the world.
Jesus, thank you for loving me.
Holy Spirit, thank you for being my friend.
Thank you, Father, Son and Holy Spirit.
Amen.

David Adam

1448 Father, you love me.
Jesus, you love me.
Spirit, you love me.
Help me to love you
and to know you are with me.
Amen.

David Adam

1449 Father, you are always with me.
Jesus, you are always with me.
Spirit, you are always with me.
Thank you, Father, Son and Holy Spirit.
Amen.

David Adam

1450 Father, thank you for the creation of the world
and for giving us life.
Jesus, thank you for living and dying for us,
that we may share in life eternal.
Spirit, thank you for your power
and that you are always ready to guide us.
I give my love to you,
Father, Son and Holy Spirit.
Amen.

David Adam

1451 Father, you are my Creator.
Jesus, you are my Saviour.
Spirit, you are my Guide.
Thank you for your love
and your presence with me
today and always.
Amen.

David Adam

1452 Father God, I love you
and I know you love me.
Jesus, Son of God, I love you
and I know you love me.
Spirit of God, I love you
and I know you love me.
May I do the work that you want me to do always.
Amen.

David Adam

1453 Father, thank you for the world and for loving me.
I give my love to you.
Jesus, thank you for loving me,
for dying and rising again.
I give my love to you.
Spirit, thank you for loving me,
for helping me and guiding me.
I give my love to you.
Amen.

David Adam

1454 Glory be to the Father
and to the Son
and to the Holy Spirit,
as it was in the beginning,
is now
and shall be for ever.
Amen.

David Adam

1455 Glory to you, Father,
for you have created me out of your love.
May I live to your glory.
Glory to you, Jesus, Son of God,
for you have redeemed me by your love.
May I share in your saving work.
Glory to you, Holy Spirit,
for you refresh and restore me
through your love.

Continued overleaf

May I walk before you in newness of life.
Glory for ever to you, Father, Son and Holy Spirit.
Amen.

David Adam

1456 Father, you are here with me and I love you.
Jesus, you are here with me and I love you.
Spirit, you are here with me and I love you.
Amen.

David Adam

1457 Father, Creator and giver of life,
I come to you in love.
I worship and adore you.
Jesus Christ, Saviour and rescuer from death,
I come to you in love.
I worship and adore you.
Holy Spirit, Guide and giver of power,
I come to you in love.
I worship and adore you.
Blessing and praise to you, Holy Three,
glorious Trinity.
Amen.

David Adam

1458 God, Three in One, we are thankful.
We are thankful that you are Father and Creator,
and you are Jesus our friend.
We are thankful that you are the Spirit, who helps us.
God, Three in One, we are thankful.

Nick Harding

1459 Lord,
although I've no real idea
how to understand the concept
of you having three parts,
I can relate to the idea
that you know what it's like
to have someone who
acts as a parent,
telling us what to do,
when to do it,
how to do it,
and that it's for our own good
(although we really don't want to do it,
but who said anything about choice?),
and you know something about being a parent,
wondering if their child
is going to be all right.

Are they doing as they have been told?
Who are they hanging around with?
And should they really be seen
with those less than desirable people,
who everybody says
are sure to be trouble with a capital 'T'?
And you know all about that Holy Spirit bit,
the part that most people,
would rather leave in the margins
of their memories,
where it's convenient to forget
and only drag out the details
on special occasions,
like weddings, funerals
and getting Easter eggs.
Isn't this Holy Spirit thing
supposed to be just as important?
You know, it's the bit
that Jesus said would be with us
all the time,
even when we feel useless,
powerless and everything-less?
Lord,
help me to appreciate
all that you are,
everything that you can be
to me,
and every person
on this large lump of earth.
Amen.

Pete Townsend

God's love

1460 Dear God,
I know that you will always love me
and listen when I talk to you.
Help me always to show my love
through being a good listener.
Amen.

Heather Ellis

1461 Dear God,
Your love for us goes on forever and ever.
Help me to go on loving you, Lord.
Amen.

Heather Ellis

1462 Dear God,
you are never too busy
to show us your love.
Help me to show my love for you, Lord,
by finding time to pray each day.
Amen.

Heather Ellis

1463 Dear God,
I love you with all my heart,
soul and strength.
Amen.

Heather Ellis

1464 Dear God,
Thank you that love comes from you.
Keep on sending your love please.
Amen.

Heather Ellis

1465 I will share my love with others,
just as you shared your love with me.
Thank you God for giving us your love.
Thank you that you care.
Amen.

Heather Ellis

1466 When I go to sleep at night
I know you and your angels are near,
watching over me
and keeping me safe.
Thank you God for looking after me.
Amen.

Heather Ellis

1467 I am amazing!
Thank you God for making me special.
You know everything about me.
I am made with your love and care.
I am happy to be me!
Amen.

Anon

1468 We know you
love us to bits
and that you can
do everything.
Help us to
believe your
promise that we
shall live with you,
in joy, for ever.
Amen.

Denis O'Gorman

1469 Dear God,
thank you for your
love. Please help
us to know that
you are always
near to us.
Amen.

Denis O'Gorman

1470 Dear Lord,
you love us so
much and always
want to take care
of us. Thank you,
God.
Amen.

Denis O'Gorman

1471 Dear Lord,
you love us when
we are good and
even when we do
wrong. Thank you
for your love.
Amen.

Denis O'Gorman

1472 Dear Jesus,
it is difficult to understand
how much you love and care for us;
open our eyes,
give us your light
and help us to feel safe with you.
Amen.

Denis O'Gorman

1473 God, our heavenly Father,
you love us more
than we can ever understand.
Help us to share your love
with everybody we meet.
Amen.

Denis O'Gorman

1474 Lord God,
we like to give you little things
but most of all we know
you want our love.
Thank you for giving us your love.
Amen.

Denis O'Gorman

1475 Dear Father God,
we run to you
because you are full of love.
Everything we have
comes from you.
Thank you for the lovely things
you have made for us.
Amen.

Denis O'Gorman

1476 Father God,
we know you love us
and are always waiting
for us to come to you.
Take us in your arms
and hold us tight,
today, tomorrow and for ever.
Amen.

Denis O'Gorman

1477 God, you made us out of your love
and you want us to love you.
I give my love to you this day.
Help me to show your love to others
by the way I deal with each of them.
Amen.

David Adam

1478 God, you are always with me.
You keep me in your love
and you protect me from evil.
Help me to remember that you never leave me
and you are always happy to hear my prayers.
Amen.

David Adam

1479 Lord God,
you know I am often in the midst of troubles
and there are dangers all around.
Keep me in the protection of your love
and in the life which is eternal.
Amen.

David Adam

1480 God, you love me always.
Even when I have done things
that make you sad
you still love me and always love me.
Thank you, God.
Amen.

David Adam

1481 God, thank you for your love and protection.
Whatever happens in this world,
you still love me and care for me.
Help me to know your power
and to be aware of your presence.
Amen.

David Adam

1482 God, I know that you love me
and wait for me to turn to you.
You are always ready to hear me and help me.
Let me remember you
and your power every day.
Amen.

David Adam

1483 God, you are all-powerful
and a generous God,
always ready to help us
and give us of your goodness.
Thank you for my life and all I am able to do.
Amen.

David Adam

1484 Lord God, I am loved by you
and seek to love you.
You love all your creation –
help me to love it too.
Teach me to love others
as I know I am loved.
And thank you for all who love me.
Amen.

David Adam

1485 Lord God, you are wonderful,
greater than all treasures.
I am happy to know you love me
and are with me.
Help me to do what you would like me to do.
Amen.

David Adam

1486 Lord our God, you are the only God
and I love you with all my heart,
with all my mind and with all my strength
today and every day.
Amen.

David Adam

1487 God, you love me
and want me to spend time with you.
In the stillness you offer me your peace,
your power and your presence.
Help me to be still and quiet before you.
Amen.

David Adam

1488 God, I thank you for your love
and that you are always with me.
Jesus, help me to know you are always with me
and that I can talk to you about all I am doing.
I know you want to keep me safe
and in your peace.
Amen.

David Adam

1489 God, teach me to be still and quiet before you,
so that I may know your love for me
and give my love to you.
In the stillness help me to know
you are always with me
and that you care for every one of us.
Amen.

David Adam

1490 Thank you, God, for inviting me
to know you and love you.
I seek to enjoy your presence
and the wonderful world you have given us.
Amen.

David Adam

1491 God, you were there at the beginning
of the world
and the beginning of life.
Thank you that you are always with me.
You never leave me.
You are always ready to help me.
Amen.

David Adam

1492 Lord God, you care for me and love me.
You never leave me but are always there,
ready to help me and give me strength.
Help me to love you
and put my trust in you each day.
Amen.

David Adam

1493 Lord God,
I often do not know where I am going
or what will happen next,
but I know that you are always with me
and you love me.
Thank you, God.
Amen.

David Adam

1494 Lord Jesus, you are with me,
always with me.
Though you are hidden,
help me to know you are always there
and ready to be my friend.
Amen.

David Adam

1495 Christ before me.
Christ on my right.
Christ behind me.
Christ on my left.
Christ beneath me.
Christ above me.
Christ in my heart.
Christ in all who love me.

David Adam

1496 As the clouds hide the sun,
so you are hidden from me, O God.
Let me know that you are always there,
you are always with me.
You love me and never leave me.
Amen.

David Adam

1497 God, thank you that wherever I go
you are there.
You never leave me
and are always ready to help me and hear me.
Amen.

David Adam

1498 Good and glorious God,
you have made me out of your love
and for your love.
Touch my heart with the joy of your presence,
that I may give myself in love to you.
Amen.

David Adam

1499 Lord God, you are a generous and loving God,
giving us more than we deserve.
You are full of compassion,
slow to anger and of great kindness.
Help me to work for you
and to do your will out of love and joy.
Amen.

David Adam

1500 Father God, thank you for your love
and for the love in my home.
Help me to show your love and kindness
to others
and to remember you are with me every day.
Amen.

David Adam

1501 God, I rejoice in your love for me.
I seek to love you with my whole being:
with my heart, my mind,
my soul and my strength.
As you love me
help me to learn to love you better
and to love others.
Amen.

David Adam

1502 Lord God, you give me your love
and count me as one of your children.
Help me to give my love to you
and to reveal your love for others
through my actions and words.
Amen.

David Adam

1503 Lord God, you have created me out of love
and for your love.
You ask me to show your love to all,
as you love everyone.
Help me to learn to love those who are against me,
even when I cannot love their actions.
Amen.

David Adam

1504 Father God,
thank you for loving me.
I give you my love with all my heart.
Amen.

David Adam

1505 God, I know that you are always with me
and that you love me
because you have promised me –
and you always keep your promise.
Thank you.
Amen.

David Adam

1506 God, help me to know that you love everyone,
even me.
Because you love me always
let me learn to give my love to you each day.
Amen.

David Adam

1507 God our Father, thank you for your love.
Jesus loves me and I am happy.
I would like to give my love to you.
Amen.

David Adam

1508 God, I love you
for you have given me life
and many good things.
Help me to be kind
and willing to share with others.
Amen.

David Adam

1509 God, you are wonderful
and all things belong to you.
You give us all that we have
and you give us your love.
Thank you, God.
Amen.

David Adam

1510 God, you are always ready to listen to me.
I can come to you and say 'thank you'
and I can ask you to help me each day.
I am glad that I can speak to you.
Amen.

David Adam

1511 God, I am happy
because I know that you love me
and do not want me to be lost.
You want me to come
and give my love to you every day.
God, I love you.
Amen.

David Adam

1512 God, thank you for your love
and that you have given this world
for us to live in.
I thank you for my life and my home.
Thank you for all that you have done for me
and for Jesus our Lord.
Amen.

David Adam

1513 Thank you, God, for your love.
May I love you with all my heart,
with all my soul
and with all my mind.
Amen.

David Adam

1514 God loves you just
the way you are!

Susan Sayers

1515 Thank you, God, for loving us so much
that we never need feel unwanted
where you are concerned.
Thank you for showing us, through Jesus,
how important we are to you.

Michael Forster

1516 Lord,
life feels like a game of skittles –
you've guessed it! I'm not the ball.
Even when I try to keep my eyes open
to avoid taking a knock.
Bang! Out of nowhere the ball comes flying,
and I'm left staring at the sky.
Sometimes things seem to be going wrong all the time.
Is it really me or something I said?
I try so hard to do the right thing,
but I don't think that other people think the way I do.
Or do some people enjoy knocking me down?
It certainly seems that way.
You must know the feeling:
'can't do right for doing wrong'.
Sometimes I think that my face doesn't fit,
and it hurts like hell,
trying to squeeze into a mould
that's just not my shape.
Still, it's a good thing
that you don't turn your back
or pretend to be deaf
when my mouth opens and the verbal begins.
Lord, thank you
that no matter what,
you are for me,
and you want the best for me.
Thanks for being there, or rather, here.
Amen.
Pete Townsend

1517 Lord,
at times I would rather chew sand
than do what you want.
I'm not being a pain,
just trying to find my way about.
The trouble is,
although I'm not trying to be a pain,
I'm in pain
because I have a tendency to walk into things,
to trip over the obvious,
to attempt a backward somersault
with a bag over my head.
I think I'm learning
that your love for me
is so great
that following your ways
makes a lot of sense.
Amen.
Pete Townsend

1518 Lord,
although the desert sands may freeze,
and the oceans dry up,
your love remains.
Although the mountains may crumble,
and the sky turn black,
your love remains.
My Lord, you are King.
Even though I see death and destruction
and rivers of tears,
my Lord, you are King.
Even though I see hatred and violence
and broken hearts,
my Lord, you are King.
Let me remember you
when the clouds gather
and the rain falls.
Let me remember you
when the thunder sounds
and my feet tremble.
My Lord, you are King.
You keep me secure
in your warm embrace.
Your love is as high as the heavens
and as deep as the oceans.
My Lord, you are King.
Amen.

Pete Townsend

1519 Well, Lord, it's me again.
You know, the one who has a bag of chips on their shoulder.
I'm not depressed or anything,
I'm used to looking and feeling
like the contents of a dustbin.
It becomes a way of life,
looking at everything through grime-coloured eyes.
I know I should be thankful for what I am,
and what I've got, but I'm not.
Why does it seem as if I'm not quite,
somehow, well sort of, you know,
a full cream biscuit?
And, why does it seem like what I am
isn't anywhere near as interesting,
or amusing, or head-turning as anybody else?
Come to think of it,
I don't stand out in a crowd,
and I don't even stand out in a room on my own.

Continued overleaf

I feel as if people pay more attention to the wallpaper
than they do to me.
But then this morning, I read that you are the one
who put me together inside my mother's body . . .
the wonderful way you created me.
Everything you do is marvellous . . .
Whoopee!
Mega whoopee!
A full cream biscuit whoopee!
Hang on a moment while I climb out of the dustbin.
Hello, it's me again.
I'm alive and I thought I really ought to say thanks.
Thanks for taking an interest in me,
and loving me just the way I am.
Amen.

Pete Townsend

1520 Father, thank you for loving us so much that when we get it wrong you always let us start again, and try again.
Amen.

John Wright

1521 Lord God, it is so easy to pass on the good news of your love and to love each other.
Help us to do it more and more.
Amen.

John Wright

1522 Lord, I know you love me even when I ignore you.
Help me to love you back, and to love others,
in the way Jesus showed.
Amen.

John Wright

1523 God our Father, teach us that love is more important than things, that people matter more than possessions, and that you matter more than everything.
Amen.

John Wright

1524 Father God,
thank you for loving us
and making us special.
Amen.

Denis O'Gorman

1525 Father God,
you know us and you love us.
Please help us to be strong
and do what is right.
Amen.

Denis O'Gorman

1526 Father God,
all that we have,
we give to you,
but most of all
we give you our love.
Amen.

Denis O'Gorman

Thank you, God

1527 Thank you, God.
Even though I can't see you,
I know you are always near
and will never leave me.
Thank you, God, for watching over me.
Amen.

Heather Ellis

1528 Father God,
thank you that you never get tired
and that you and your angels
watch over me while I sleep.
I am glad you are looking after me.
Amen.

Heather Ellis

1529 Thank you God for making me.
Thank you for letting us know
that we are special.
Including me!
Amen.

Heather Ellis

1530 Thank you that we are all different.
Thank you that you know how we feel.
Thank you that you lived as a child and an adult.
Thank you that you know how we feel.
Amen.

Nick Harding

1531 Thank you, Lord,
that you can help us
as we believe in you.

Ashley Guest

1532 Dear Lord,
please help us to
be grateful for all
the gifts we have
and to remember
to say, 'Thank you'.
Amen.

Denis O'Gorman

1533 Dear Lord,
thank you for
giving us
everything we
need.
Amen.

Denis O'Gorman

1534 Dear Lord,
thank you for all
the good things
you give to us.
Help us to be
happy with what
we have.
Amen.

Denis O'Gorman

1535 Lord,
thank you for all the
good things you
give to us. Help us
to be generous and
understanding.
Amen.

Denis O'Gorman

1536 Lord,
we want so
many things,
especially when
we see others
with them.
Help us to say
'Thank you' for all
the good things
that you have
given to us.
Amen.

Denis O'Gorman

1537 Thank you, God,
for making each of us so special.
You know and love every one of us.
Help us to give our special love to you.
Amen.

David Adam

1538 God, thank you for loving me,
for giving me food to eat.
I know that you care for me
and for everything that you have made.
Amen.

David Adam

1539 Lord, thank you that you have called me
to be the salt of the earth.
Help me to work to improve my life
and the area in which I live.
May I show that it is a joy
to be alive and to know you.
Amen.

David Adam

1540 Thank you, loving God,
for this wonderful journey called life!
Thank you for always leading us
forward toward the new,
but thank you also for the good things from the past.

Michael Forster

1541 Thank you, God,
for your goodness and special love.
May your love never leave this school.
Amen.

Michael Forster

1542 Thank you, Jesus,
that I can come to you at any time.
You make me feel very welcome.
Amen.

Michael Forster

1543 We really want to thank you, God,
for being there for us.
Thank you for always wanting the best for us
and leading us toward new life.

Michael Forster

1544 Thank you, God,
for being the kind of God you are!
Thank you for loving, and loving and loving!
Thank you for showing your love in people
who love us for who we are,
not for what we can do!

Michael Forster

1545 Thank you, God!
Thank you so much for people
who haven't taken no for an answer
where other people's needs have been at stake!
Thank you for people who get things changed
(even if at times we get embarrassed by them!).

Michael Forster

1546 Thank you, Lord, for all that's not obvious!
Thank you for the things we only find
when we climb mountains, or dig deep,
or look or listen more carefully.
Thank you for a wonderful, multi-layered creation!

Michael Forster

1547 We want to say 'thank you', God,
for people who care;
people who find their own importance
in helping others.
Those people change the world for us all!
Thank you!

Michael Forster

1548 What a wonderful world!
There's so much we don't understand!
So much for us to ask and learn about!
Thank you, God, for the unanswered questions!

Michael Forster

1549 Just sometimes, God, we meet really special people:
people who seem to see the good in us
even when we're having a bad prayer day!
Thank you for them!

Michael Forster

1550 It's a tough call, you know, God,
being asked to love like that.
We can't do it, of course,
but perhaps we could get a little closer than we do!
You can do it, though, can't you!
You love like that all the time
– and often it hurts you.
Thank you, God, for all your love.

Michael Forster

1551 Thank you, God, for every kind person.
Thank you for people who've helped us
when we've been in any kind of trouble.
Thank you for the love you've put into the world.

Michael Forster

1552 Now we actually stop to think of it,
you really do give us an awful lot, don't you!
Thank you, God!

Michael Forster

1553 Thank you, God, for surprising us.
Thank you for old people with fresh, vibrant minds.
Thank you for children with so much to teach us.
Thank you for oddly dressed people
who are full of love.
Thank you for the unexpected!

Michael Forster

1554 Thank you, Lord of hope,
for the way you surprise us with joy,
and show us the extraordinary and the wonderful
in the ordinary things of life.

Susan Sayers

1555 God of faithfulness,
we thank you for the way
you always keep your promises
and never let us down.

Susan Sayers

1556 Thank you, Father,
for transforming our suffering and our mistakes
again and again and again.

Susan Sayers

1557 Lord Jesus,
thank you for setting us free.
Help us to let others be free as well.
Amen.

Susan Sayers

1558 Lord God, there are so many wonderful things
in your creation that we take for granted.
Open our eyes to see it all
as an expression of your love for us,
and help us to live thankfully.
Amen.

Susan Sayers

1559 Lord, we thank you
for the extraordinary generosity of your love,
which takes us by surprise and refreshes us,
and which always appears
where we least think to look for it.

Susan Sayers

1560 Lord, we thank you
that we can trust you completely
and you never let us down!

Susan Sayers

1561 Oh give thanks to the Lord,
for he is good,
for his steadfast love endures for ever.
Amen.

From Psalm 136

1562 Father, we thank you for the glimpses of glory
you give us in this life, for your friendship
and your promise to be with us always.

Susan Sayers

1563 Thank you, loving God,
for giving us space and support,
guidance and forgiveness,
challenge and reassurance.

Susan Sayers

1564 Good Shepherd of the sheep,
we give you thanks that in you
we are able to live through good and ill
with abundance of life.

Susan Sayers

1565 Dear Jesus, you are my shepherd
and I am one of your lambs.
Thank you for loving me
and looking after me.
Amen.

Susan Sayers

1566 Living God, we thank you
for showing us the Way,
in human terms that we find easier to understand.

Susan Sayers

1567 Father God,
thank you
that every hair on my head
is numbered,
every grain of sand
is counted,
every sparrow that falls
is remembered,
every person on this planet
is counted
as being loved by you.

Tony Bower

1568 Creator God,
thank you
that you
are bigger than me,
bigger than all I can see,
bigger than the universe,
bigger than the galaxies,
bigger and bigger
than anything
because you
created
EVERYTHING.

Tony Bower

1569 Lord,
we thank you
for LIFE,
it is a gift,
a precious, precious
gift,
and each new day
is like a present,
waiting to be unwrapped,
waiting to be opened.
Lord,
we thank you
for this priceless gift
and pray
that by the way
we make the most of it,
we will show you
just how grateful we are.

Tony Bower

1570 Dear Father God,
thank you
that you are Alpha,
the beginning,
and you are Omega,
the end,
you are like a circle,
we cannot see
where you begin
or where you end,
but we know
that you are there
and have been here
forever.

Tony Bower

1571 Father God,
thank you
that wherever we are
and whatever we've done,
you are there
and you care.
Thank you
that we can talk to you
in prayer.

Tony Bower

1572 Father God,
in all the good times
we praise you,
in all the hard times
we praise you,
in all our schooldays
we praise you,
in all our holidays
we praise you,
in all our lives
we praise you.

Tony Bower

1573 Creator God,
for our families
we thank you,
for our friends
we thank you,
for our school
we thank you,
for our world
we thank you.

Tony Bower

1574 Loving heavenly Father,
we thank you
for hope
when all seems hopeless,
we thank you
that you find us
when we feel lost,
we thank you
for love
when we feel lonely,
we thank you
for light
when we are in the dark,

Continued overleaf

we thank you
for peace
when we have troubled minds,
we thank you
for your gentleness
when we feel fragile,
we thank you
for your kindness and
goodness
when life is harsh and
horrible,
we thank you,
for being faithful
when we have been let down.
We thank you,
Father God,
we thank you
for being
you.

Tony Bower

1575 Father God,
thank you
that there is so much
to thank you for,
for your goodness,
your kindness,
your graciousness
to us,
for your love,
for your peace,
for your forgiveness,
that you've granted us,
for your Son,
for Jesus,
who died for us,
for your Spirit,
your desire
to help us
and live with us.
We thank you
and praise you
for who you are,
how great you are
and how great
is the love that you
have lavished on us,
that we can be called
children of God.

Tony Bower

1576 Loving heavenly Father,
thank you
for all the many, many, many things
that bring us
happiness and joy.
Our family
our friends
our pets,
playing sport
playing music
playing games,
singing
acting
reading
writing
sunsets
sunrises
snow
snowmen
Christmas
presents
birthdays
parties.
Father God,
the list could go on and on.
There are so many things that bring joy
and I want to thank you for the joy
that you give
by loving us every single day.
Tony Bower

1577 Dear Father God,
thank you
for kindness,
kind words
kind actions
kind thoughts
which help people
feel better,
that make the world
a better place.
Please help us
to be kind
in all that we say
and do
today.
Tony Bower

1578 Life-giving God,
thank you
for peace,
the peace and quiet of the countryside,
the peace that comes when all is still and calm
and thank you
for the peace that you promise
when things are far from well,
the promise to be with us
and help us.

Tony Bower

1579 Dear Lord,
thank you
that there are times to play,
times to eat
and times to work.
Sometimes I want to eat biscuits
before tea,
or play
before I've finished my work.
Please help me to wait
and be self-controlled.

Tony Bower

1580 Lord,
thank you
that you are good,
you are never bad,
never naughty,
never unkind,
but always, constantly,
consistently good.
All that you do is good.
All that you say is good.
Please help us
to be like you.

Tony Bower

1581 Thank you
for choosing to love us.
Please help us
to choose
to love
today.

Tony Bower

1582 There's so much
I want to share,
that I can't think
which words I want
to say first.
They are all jumbled up
in a heap that's labelled
'Things I want
to thank Jesus for'.
So, Jesus –
thank you
for it all.
Every single bit.

Susan Hardwick

1583 Thank you,
God,
for my special friends –
and for giving me life.

Susan Hardwick

1584 Dear God –
THANK YOU
THANK YOU
THANK YOU
thank you, thank you
for EVERYTHING.
I wish I deserved
everything you bless me with.
You really are
very, very
generous and kind,
'cos you pour
your blessings down, anyway,
whether I deserve them
or not.

Susan Hardwick

1585 For the world in which I live
thank you, God.
For all I am able to do
thank you, God.
For all who provide me with food
thank you, God.

Continued overleaf

For all who love me
thank you, God.
For your love and generosity
thank you, God.
Amen.

David Adam

1586 Thank you, God, thank you.
You have given us a wonderful world
and lots of beautiful creatures.
Thank you for our homes and families.
Thank you, God, thank you.
Amen.

David Adam

1587 For eyes to see,
thank you, God.
For colours and patterns,
thank you, God.
For the beautiful world and all its animals,
thank you, God.
For books to read and pretty pictures,
thank you, God.
For kind faces and good people,
thank you, God.
Amen.

David Adam

1588 Dear God,
help us to be thankful
for the things we have.
Amen.

Caroline Vallance.

1589 Dear God,
thank you that we can talk to you
about anything and everything.
Thank you that you listen to us
and answer our prayers.
Amen.

Caroline Vallance

1590 Dear God,
thank you for the great things you give us.
Help us to appreciate them
and not just want more and more.
Amen.

Caroline Vallance

1591 Thank you, God, for your love:
for not wanting to possess us,
but wanting us to be happy
and wanting us to be free.
Thank you for the wonderful life you have given us.

Michael Forster

1592 Thank, you, Lord God, for Solomon's wisdom.
He knew you were greater than we can ever imagine.
Thank you for being truly God –
so great we can never understand you.
But thank you, also, for showing yourself to us
in a way that really helps.
Thank you for Jesus.

Michael Forster

1593 Thank you, God,
for giving us more than just ourselves to think about!
Thank you for being all
that we will ever need to worship.
Thank you for filling your world
with wonderful reminders of your love.

Michael Forster

1594 Thank you, God,
for being a God of love.
Thank you for the rules you've given us
which help us to live well and be happier;
and thank you for loving us
even when we find it difficult to keep them.

Michael Forster

1595 Thank you, loving God,
for not being too predictable!
Thank you for doing unexpected things
and using the people we least expect, as well.

Michael Forster

1596 Thank you, amazing God,
for doing such wonderful things.
Thank you for caring about people,
and for sending Jesus
to show us just how much.

Michael Forster

1597 Thank you, God,
for making ordinary people special.
Or is it really that, as far as you're concerned,
nobody is ordinary?
Thank you, anyway,
for loving us so much!

Michael Forster

1598 Thank you, loving God,
for hopeful people
who are always patiently looking out
for what you are doing.
Thank you for all the signs of hope you give us.

Michael Forster

1599 Thank you, loving God,
for the sheer wonder of your love for us.
Thank you for your promise
that you will love us for ever,
even though we can never do enough
to deserve a love like yours!

Michael Forster

1600 Thank you, God, for loving everybody,
even those whom other people find difficult.
Thank you for loving Zacchaeus,
and thank you for loving us.

Michael Forster

1601 Thank you, Jesus, for being our King
of life and love.
Thank you for loving us so much
and for offering us your new life.

Michael Forster

1602 Thank you, Jesus, for walking with us
when the journey through life gets difficult.
Thank you for helping us to see
where the hope is.

Michael Forster

1603 What a wonderful thing life is!
Thank you, Jesus,
for coming to share our life
and for making it really worth living.

Michael Forster

1604 Thank you, Lord Jesus,
for calling us to be your friends
and to help spread the Good News.
Help us to live the kind of life
that makes other people want to know you as well.

Michael Forster

1605 Loving God, thank you for challenging us
and trying to show us your truth,
even when we don't find it easy.
Thank you for loving us so much
that you don't give up on us.

Michael Forster

1606 Lord,
sometimes trying to express my feelings
makes me feel
vulnerable,
hurt,
sensitive,
stupid,
useless.
But at other times I feel
glad,
happy,
gobsmacked,
astonished,
and, not very often,
totally speechless.
Thanks for being there.
Thanks for being you.
Thanks for standing by me
even when you have every right to walk away.
I may not always be honest with you,
and I definitely can't be honest with some people.
But you know that grin I have
hides a thousand hurts.
I like being real with you,
because you are real to me
even when I can't get a handle on you.
Thanks,
thanks for being who you are.
Thanks from me, to you.
Amen.

Pete Townsend

1607 Thank you, God, for the world you made for us . . .
Thank you, God, for everything.
Thank you, God, for the life in your world . . .
Thank you, God, for everything.
Thank you, God, for the life you have given all of us . . .
Thank you, God, for everything.
Thank you, God, for the food we enjoy . . .
Thank you, God, for everything.
Thank you, God, for all the things you give us . . .
Thank you, God, for everything.

Nick Harding

1608 Father God,
thank you for giving us so many good things.
Help us to grow in your love.
Amen.

Denis O'Gorman

1609 Father God,
we thank you for all the good things you give us.
Help us to love you more and more.
Amen.

Denis O'Gorman

First Communion

1610 Heavenly Father,
the bread is very small
and we only get a sip of wine,
but we know that your love is very big –
enfolding all the people in the world –
because you gave your Son
to die on a cross
as a sign of your everlasting love.
Amen.

1611 From this day on
may the truth of God's word
grow strong in your heart
and may the gentle love of Jesus
fill your life
now and always.
Amen.

Confirmation

1612 Almighty God,
as the faith of . . . . . . is confirmed we ask that he is upheld
and supported in his beliefs by all present today.
May this significant milestone in his faith journey
be a source of inspiration for him and a creative
opportunity for the church.
We pray that through your grace and his faith,
his life may be strengthened and your kingdom extended.
We ask this through Jesus Christ, our Lord.
Amen.

Rupert Bristow

1613 Almighty God,
we pray for those being confirmed today.
May your high expectations, Lord, be matched by their
faithfulness.
On this special occasion, when their baptism is
transformed into confirmation by your grace and their free will,
let this church rejoice and their school(s) applaud.
May the sacraments deepen their spiritual experience of
you and encourage them in the exploration of their faith.
In a moment's silence let us pray for the individual(s)
being confirmed . . . . . .
Let us pledge ourselves to doing all we can to support
them in their commitment.
We ask this through Jesus Christ, our Lord.
Amen.

Rupert Bristow

Praying

1614 I love to pray.
Today I felt like praying
for someone I know in my tent!
I am glad that I can pray anywhere.
Thank you God for prayer.
Amen.

Heather Ellis

1615 Dear God,
we know that
you are here and
that you listen to
our prayers. In
this moment of
quiet, we open
our hearts to ask

Continued overleaf

or tell you about
something
important to us.
Amen.

Denis O'Gorman

1616 God our Father,
listen to our
prayers today and
watch over us
with your love.
Amen.

Denis O'Gorman

1617 Father God,
you listen to every word we say
and even if sometimes you say 'No'
we know that this is always
for our good because you love us
and keep us from harm.
Amen.

Denis O'Gorman

1618 Dear God,
help us to understand
that you are our loving Father
and that we can talk to you
in any way.
Amen.

Denis O'Gorman

1619 I love to pray.
I prayed that you would keep me safe
today and you did!
Thank you God for prayer.
Thank you for keeping me safe.
I promise to pray every day.
Amen.

Heather Ellis

1620 Dear God, holy Spirit of love,
light up this darkened world
and come into my heart
as I pray to you today,
so that I may be filled
with your love and joy
for ever and ever.
Amen.

Denis O'Gorman

1621 Lord,
how on earth do I stop feeling
screwed up, washed up, tied up,
scrunched up, fed up, messed up,
and dried up,
without allowing all my bodily functions
to stop working?
Because, Lord, you've got to admit,
I do a really good imitation of a wreck,
without a rehearsal.
It's not that I go out of my way
to make a complete
donkey of myself,
it's just that some things
are natural!
When I'm threatened,
and mocked,
I must try to wise up, and remember
that some people
are a bit touchy at times
and that it's far better to talk to you
than listen to a load of monkeys talking bananas.
So, Lord,
I'm not saying that even sharing my thoughts with you
is going to guarantee that I won't put my foot
where it isn't wanted,
but at least I'm really glad to know
that you're always with me
and would prefer a quick yelp of help
to a long silence which ends in ouch!
Amen.

Pete Townsend

1622 Lord,
I can't always say exactly when I may need your help,
or precisely where I'll need it,
but I think I'll always know why
I need your help,
your love,
your understanding,
and the occasional bit of patience
for those times when nothing I say or do seems right.
Why I need you around is simply because,
no matter how hard I try not to
screw everything up with such finesse,
whatever I try to do
always ends up with my own,
totally unique,

Continued overleaf

absolutely unmistakable,
foot in mouth,
finger in the eye,
tread on foot trademark
that everyone knows
is my way of doing things,
that nobody else would have thought of
(or wouldn't even dream of doing if they had any sense).
What I'm saying, Lord,
is that even when I do my best,
it isn't always the best that everyone expects.
So, could we come to some sort of arrangement,
where you get involved in my everyday life,
every single day of my existence,
to make sure
that we all get used to having
a touch of the extraordinary
in our ordinary lives?
Amen.

Pete Townsend

1623 Lord,
getting confused
seems to be an occupational hazard
of living.
Everyone has an opinion
and everyone insists they're right!
Words seem to surround me
like a dust cloud on a hot day.
They blur my vision and dull my senses.
I'm not sure which way to turn.
Do this, do that,
don't do this, don't do that.
What am I supposed to do?
I need to be able
to pick out the truth
from a pile of garbage.
I need to see the truth
stand out like a neon light
on a dark night.
Help me, Lord,
to know you,
to see, hear and know the truth
in a land of confusion.
Amen.

Pete Townsend

1624 Lord, I hope you're there.
I'd feel really stupid if I was talking to myself!
It would be like being in a football ground
when the team was playing away.
Or at a cinema when the film had finished two hours ago.
It might be like singing a song which had no tune,
or trying to read a book in the dark.
All a bit pointless really!
So, God what is the point?
Why am I here?
Why do I feel so alone at times?
Why don't I hear you speak?
Why does everything feel such a mess?
Why?
I need to hear your voice.
I need to feel you near.
I need to know your love.
I need you.
But I don't know how any of that can happen.
I don't know what you want from me.
Still, here I am,
I'm listening – are you?
Amen.

Pete Townsend

1625 Lord,
at times –
well, if I'm honest, quite a lot of the time –
I feel as if my head
is in a blender.
My thoughts whizz around,
until everything
is in a complete mess.
It makes my stomach churn,
and my legs feel odd.
If I could close my eyes,
stick my fingers in my ears
and scream,
then I would, if it made
any difference
to the way I feel.
You may have noticed
that when I tried that last time
people gave me funny looks
and wondered
if I was quite right in the head.
I couldn't admit to them
that my head felt full of spaghetti

Continued overleaf

and if I had told them
it wouldn't have made any difference.
But telling you how I feel
seems to make all the difference.
Thank goodness for that.
Amen.

Pete Townsend

1626 Dear God,
help us to know you and to be ready to tell you everything that matters to us.
Each of us has something we really want to share with you,
and we are all going to keep very quiet now so we can think about it really hard.
Pause
Hear what we say, God,
help us with the answer and let us know that,
whatever happens, you are always our friend.
Amen.

John Wright

1627 When things are going really well
in the future I will remember
to thank you.
When I am tired or ill
in the future I will ask
you to help me.
When I feel sad and hurt
in the future I will ask
you to comfort me.
I will always remember
to thank you.
Amen.

Nick Harding

The Lord's Prayer

1628 Our Father in heaven,
hallowed be your name,
your kingdom come,
your will be done, on earth as in heaven.
Give us today our daily bread.
Forgive us our sins as we forgive those who sin against us.
Lead us not into temptation but deliver us from evil.
For the kingdom, the power, and the glory are yours,
now and for ever.
Amen.

1629 Our Father, who art in heaven,
hallowed be thy name;
thy kingdom come;
thy will be done;
on earth as it is in heaven.
Give us this day our daily bread.
And forgive us our trespasses, as we forgive those
who trespass against us.
And lead us not into temptation, but deliver us from evil.
For thine is the kingdom, the power and the glory,
for ever and ever.
Amen.

Our Father

1630 Father God,
thank you
that we can call you
Father
Our Father
Dad
Daddy
because that's who you are,
the Father of humankind,
the Maker of us all
and we thank you
that we can call
on you,
depend on you
anytime,
night
and day
as we pray
'Our Father'.
Tony Bower

Who is in heaven

1631 Dear Father,
thank you
for heaven,
a place that is perfect,
somewhere that is called
Paradise.
It's hard to imagine
a place that we haven't seen
not even in holiday brochures,
a place that we haven't been to
but we know
it is going to be beyond good
because
you are there.
Tony Bower

Hallowed be your name

1632

Heavenly Father,
your name is special,
holy,
separate,
different from any others;
because no one
in the whole of creation
is the creator
but you,
no one can compare
with you,
no one;
and no one can be called God
but you.
Please help us
to use your name
and to say your name
with respect
and remember who it is
we are speaking to.

Tony Bower

Your kingdom come

1633

Father God,
thank you
for your kingdom,
a kingdom
that has no geographical
boundaries,
a kingdom that starts
in our hearts:
the place
where your love and rule
start,
affecting the way we act,
the way we think,
and the ways in which we live.
In a world
where we see so many bad
things
going on
in earthly kingdoms
we do pray for,
and long for,
your peace,
your love
and your kingdom
to come.

Tony Bower

Your will be done on earth as it is in heaven
1634

Loving God,
thank you
that everything you do is good,
and all that you are is good,
every desire that you have is
good,
and your will for us is good.
Please help us,
to say 'yes'
to you
and to say 'yes'
to your will
in our lives,
that we will do the things
and act in the ways
that will please you
by doing all that is right
and all that is good
and pleasing in your sight.

Tony Bower

Give us this day our daily bread
1635

Father God,
thank you
for providing us
with all that we need
because you know
our needs
even before we ask.
Please help us
not to be full of greed
but to give to those
who are in need.

Tony Bower

Forgive us our trespasses as we forgive those who trespass against us
1636

Father God,
thank you
that you do forgive us
when we say sorry
to you.
You wipe out what we've
done wrong
like pressing delete
on a computer,
whatever we've done
vanishes from your screen
because you mean it
when you say
you will forgive us
when we confess to you.
Please help us
to be like you
and show grace
and forgiveness
to those
who are willing to say
'sorry'
to us.

Tony Bower

Lead us not into temptation but deliver us from evil
1637

Dear Lord,
you know all about us,
and the words that we say
and the things that we do.
You know
what tempts us
to be naughty.
Please help us
to be led by you
on the right path,
and not to go
in the wrong direction.
Please help us
pay attention
to you,
so that we will follow
where you lead us.

Thank you
that you can,
and you do,
protect us
from evil,
and lead us
in your ways
which are good.

Tony Bower

1638 Our Father in heaven,
your kingdom come,
your will be done
on earth as it is in heaven.
Your kingdom come . . .
because we are honest and do not cheat,
because we are fair and do not steal,
because we listen and do not laugh at others,
because we are friends and do not gossip,
because we love and do not hate,
because we share and do not grab.

Ray Simpson

1639 Our Father, in heaven,
forgive us for the
wrong things we
do, as we forgive
those who do
wrong to us.
Please help all of
us to learn to say
sorry and mean it.
Amen.

Denis O'Gorman

1640 Lord, sometimes we pray 'thy kingdom come, thy will be done, on earth as it is in heaven.'
Help us to make the choices that make the world, our earth, more the place you want it to be.
In Jesus' name, we ask.
Amen.

John Wright

Graces

1641 The grace of our Lord Jesus Christ,
and the love of God,
and the fellowship of the Holy Spirit,
be with us all evermore.
Amen.

1642 The grace of our Lord Jesus Christ,
and the love of God,
and the fellowship of the Holy Ghost,
be with us all evermore.
Amen.

1643 Almighty God,
we give thanks for this food: for those who grew it;
for those who brought it here; for those who prepared it;
for those who cooked it; and for those who serve it.
Now we ask for your blessing on those who eat it.
Amen.

Rupert Bristow

1644 Almighty God,
as we sit down to eat our lunch, let us remember all that has gone into the preparation of this meal.
Help us to be aware also, Lord, of those in the world who are short of food and water, for whom our meal would be a feast.
Amen.

Rupert Bristow

1645 Almighty God,
you provide for our every need.
Help us to appreciate what is now before us.
Bless this food to our use and strengthen us in your service.
Amen.

Rupert Bristow

1646 Heavenly Father,
we are looking forward to our meal.
Let us do justice to this food, remembering that we cannot take it for granted.
Thank you for the skills of all those involved in providing our lunch today.
Amen.

Rupert Bristow

1647

Heavenly Father,
this food you give to us.
Our praise we give to you.
Amen.

Rupert Bristow

Morning, noon and evening prayers

Morning

1648

Father God,
thank you
for this new day.
Please help us
to make the most of it
in work, rest and play.

Tony Bower

1649

Father God,
thank you
that whatever I'm feeling –
sad or bad,
good or glad,
lonely or mad –
you are always the same.
You are always loving,
always good,
always kind,
always fair,
always there.
Thank you
that you know all about me.
You know how I am feeling,
you know how I am doing
and you care for me,
this new day.

Tony Bower

1650

Creator God,
thank you
for the light of another new day.
Even if the sun doesn't shine
and the rain sets in,
we can still enjoy this freshly created day.
Thank you.

Tony Bower

1651 Dear God, light us up.
When I wake up,
may I feel the sun is shining on me
because you are smiling down on me.
Chase away bad, dark thoughts.
Make me smile.

Ray Simpson

Noon

1652 Stop!
It's the middle of the day.
I get too full of myself.
Please God,
calm me down.
Now stay still.

Ray Simpson

Evening

1653 Loving heavenly Father,
thank you
for the day that we've had,
whether some of it was good
or some of it was bad.
We thank you
for being there,
always there
even when we sleep,
even when we dream
you are wide awake.
Thank you that you will be
there to greet us
tomorrow.

Tony Bower

1654 Mr Sun, you settle down.
God made you, God made me.
Dear God,
help me to think before I speak
and settle down with you.

Ray Simpson

Arrow prayers

1655 God help me,
God lead me,
God show me.

Rupert Bristow

1656 Today's a big day for me.
Make it a big day for you too, Lord.

Rupert Bristow

1657 Let nothing be in moderation
when we worship you.

Rupert Bristow

1658 Even the ordinary is extraordinary.
So let me do the small things well.

Rupert Bristow

1659 Empower me to do your will.
Equip me to do it well.

Rupert Bristow

1660 Help me to get the balance right
between family, work and you, Lord.

Rupert Bristow

1661 I am yours, Lord.
Show me you are mine.

Rupert Bristow

1662 Be close, be near, take away my fear.

Rupert Bristow

1663 Give me the energy to prepare
and the preparedness to surprise.

Rupert Bristow

1664 O God, help me face my class.
Bring out the best in me and in my students.

Rupert Bristow

1665 Raise my sights to your horizons, Lord.

Rupert Bristow

1666 Jesus, be my teacher,
Jesus, be my friend.

Rupert Bristow

1667 Give me the power to be creative in these moments of peace.

Rupert Bristow

1668 Be with me as I am put to the test.
Help me to remember how your Son was tested for me.

Rupert Bristow

1669 Help me to be more patient with others and less impatient with myself.

Rupert Bristow

1670 Lord, help me and hold me;
love me and never leave me
Lord, help me to take responsibility when I need to
and to let go when you say so.

Rupert Bristow

1671 Bring me patience and peace when I really want to let fly.

Rupert Bristow

1672 It's awfully difficult just now, Lord.
Calm me with your presence, fill me with your wisdom.

Rupert Bristow

1673 Help me to hear in the noise and listen in the silence.

Rupert Bristow

1674 Help me today, Lord, to listen and to learn, and to do all you would want of me.

Rupert Bristow

1675 Grant me peace and integrity when the pressure is on and the going gets tough.

Rupert Bristow

1676 Give me the perseverance to see this task through to the end. Thank you, Lord.

Rupert Bristow

The Bible

1677 Dear God,
your Bible shows us how to live the right way.
Sometimes we don't follow your rules,
we're sorry.
Help us do what is right every day.
Amen.

Heather Ellis

1678 I want to learn about you, Jesus.
So where can I read about you?
Oh yes, I can find you in Matthew,
Mark, Luke and John, in my special Bible.
Amen.

Heather Ellis

1679 Lord,
thank you for the Bible
and the guidelines for living it contains.
Help us to live our lives well.

Ashley Guest

1680 Dear Lord,
thank you for the Bible
and all the wonderful things that it contains.
Help us to understand it as we read it.

Ashley Guest

1681 Jesus,
this Bible book
is brilliant!
There are so many stories.
So much adventure
and excitement.
Some stories
I don't really understand.
But others
make sense
and I learn something from them.
It's an amazing book, Jesus.
Help me read it
and understand it
more and more
each day.
Amen.

David Gatward

1682 Lord,
the stories of what you did are incredible.
Help us to find out more about you.

Ashley Guest

1683 Lord God, I want to know about you, and Jesus, and what I should do. Help me to read in your library, the Bible, to find the answers.
Amen.

John Wright

1684 Lord God, help us to tune in to you through the Bible,
to receive your message so we can know you, worship you and live the way you want us to.

John Wright

1685 We offer you our thanks and praise
for the scriptures that remind and inspire us,
and for your living Spirit which enables us.

Susan Sayers

1686 Thank you, Lord, for using Isaiah
to help us recognise Jesus
as your Son.
Thank you for making it possible
for us all to be free.
Amen.

Susan Sayers

Knowing God

1687 Father God,
I want to know you always.
I am going to hold on tight
because I never want to let you go.
Amen.

Heather Ellis

1688 Dear God,
never let me be
afraid to show
that I believe in
you.
Amen.

Denis O'Gorman

1689 Father God,
we know that you
love us dearly.
Help us to share your love
with everybody we meet today,
so that they may know
you love them too.
Amen.

Denis O'Gorman

1690 Lord, I don't understand philosophy,
I can't get my head around psychology,
and theology leaves me cold.
I'm not trying to make trouble,
or cause anyone a problem.
I just want to be honest,

well, as honest as I can be.
Don't get me wrong,
I'm not saying I know it all,
I'm glad I don't,
know it all, I mean.
I want my faith to be real,
not based on some second-hand account,
or a set of rules which make me choke.
If I'm going to believe in you,
properly, not some Sunday saint,
or weekday wonder,
but real, like a proper relationship
between two hearts,
then help me see the truth
of who you are,
and what you mean to me.
Amen.

Pete Townsend

1691 Lord,
you'll have to speak up,
I can't hear you very well.
The sound of my own voice
is almost deafening
with a dustbin
over my head.
It's not the best place to be,
underneath a container for rubbish.
But perhaps it's the best place
for the dustbin.
I wasn't pushed,
I didn't stumble or trip.
I'm sitting here
by choice
because it's how I feel
about myself.
Excuse me,
what was that you said?
You want to come and join me?
Surely you can find a better place to be.
Pardon?
You can't think of anywhere better
than here with me?
Hang on a minute, I'm coming out.
There's not enough room for two
and anyway, I feel much better now there's you and me.
Amen.

Pete Townsend

1692 Father God,
may we feel your power in our lives,
and show it to all around us.
Amen.

John Wright

1693 Lord, be my spade – there when I need help.
Be my wellingtons – there at special times.
Be my tea – an essential part of life each day.
Amen.

John Wright

1694 Father God,
we are your children and you love us.
Help us always to follow your teaching.
Amen.

Denis O'Gorman

Going to church

1695 Dear Jesus,
the Church is your world family. You have
given treasures to each member of this family.
And we don't know what they are.
Help us, in our church, to find different
treasures like
the Bible,
the Holy Spirit,
friends,
stillness,
communion,
beautiful art,
the saints,
the poor,
celebrations,
prayer
and . . .
(Add other things you think are treasures.)

Ray Simpson

1696 Lord,
I really can't get my head around
all this 'thee, thou and therefore' stuff.
It drives me round the bend and over the hill.
What does it all mean?
Is it some sort of code for the initiated?
A kind of secret language
that only those in the know understand?
Do we need a translator or interpreter
to explain what's going on
and what we need to do?
Should there be a sort of 'idiots' guide'
to help us say the 'right' things at the 'right' time? –
so that we don't stand up when we should be sitting down.
Perhaps you could suggest
that someone puts a few dictionaries
next to the hymn books,
although I really think
that we'd never sing a word or a note.
We'd be too busy looking in the dictionary
trying to find out
what we were singing about,
or what we were trying to say
if only we knew what we'd said!
I think we need
the Holy Spirit
to descend on a few of the congregation
and get them to speak
in a language
that we can all understand.
Until that time,
you'll have to guess what I mean
'cos the only word I've got sorted
comes at the end of a line. Amen.

Pete Townsend

1697 Lord,
this church thing,
is at best a bit odd,
and at worst,
the most boring time I've ever had to spend
(apart from sitting through a documentary on painting ceilings).
But the funny thing is, Lord,
that when you look around
at all these bodies
gathered in one place
to chat about you,
sing a bit,
and listen to the vicar
try and tell a joke
without giving away the punchline,
or forget he was telling a joke
in the first place.
Then,
when we're having a cup of tea,
and a biscuit if some little grubby fingers haven't nicked them all,
there seems to be an odd assortment of people
who, for one reason or another,
want to know more about you.
And, Lord,
I'm really glad
that you love
every size, shape, colour, texture and hue,
and you don't care one little bit
about status, prestige, earnings, cars,
gadgets or designer clothes,
because you care about the person,
the body inside
which is vulnerable, sensitive and needs
a lot of TLC.
So, thanks,
thanks that you love me, and him, and her
and every single fragile human being,
wherever and whatever.
Amen.

Pete Townsend

1698 Lord,
I'm really finding life
kind of frustrating.
So many things
demanding my attention,

wanting my time,
eating away at my sanity
until I can't remember
what it was I was supposed to be doing
in the first place.
Sometimes I walk into a room
and then spend the next ten minutes
wondering what I'm doing there!
I look around for a sign,
a clue to my action.
Why, when, how, what for?
And Lord,
if I'm honest
that's exactly how I feel
when I go to church.
It's not that I don't want to be there
but it would be nice
if I had a clue
as to what I was supposed to be doing there!
It's a good job that my faith
isn't in tradition, buildings or committees,
or even how many times
someone remembers my name,
but my faith is in the One
who gave his all for me.
Amen.

Pete Townsend

Miscellaneous

Firework night

1699 Loving God,
thank you
for fireworks,
for the ones that EXPLODE
with a loud BANG,
for fireworks
that fizzle and crackle,
for fireworks
that whizz,
for fireworks
that burst into beautiful
colours,
for fireworks
that spin in a cartwheel,
for fireworks
that make and create
the Niagara Falls,
for fireworks
of all colours, shapes and sizes
we thank you.

Tony Bower

1700 Father God,
thank you
for bonfire night,
for fire and smoke,
for toffee apples and hot dogs,
for sparklers and more
sparklers,
for fireworks and even more
fireworks,
we thank you for this
wonderful night
and pray that you would help
us to be safe tonight.

Tony Bower

1701 Wow, God, the colours are wonderful.
The fireworks are so good.
Wow, God, the rockets are so high
and the bangs are so loud.
Wow, God, the shapes are so amazing,
and the patterns so great.
Wow, God, the fireworks are wonderful.

Nick Harding

Birthdays

1702 I love birthdays!
Friends come round, we have fun
and there are presents to be opened.
Your love is the best gift of all.
Thank you God for birthdays.
Amen.

Heather Ellis

Parties

1703 Dear God,
thank you for parties and celebrations. Thank you for party food and drink. Please help all those who don't have enough to eat to get all that they need.
Amen.

Gill Thorniley

Holidays

1704 Dear God,
thank you for fun days and holidays,
for days when we can run and jump and sing.
Please help those who feel sad when others around are happy.
Amen.

Gill Thorniley

Remembrance day

1705 Our Father God,
thank you
for all of the soldiers
who fought for our freedom,
who stood up
for what is right.
Please help us
to stand up today,
be brave and strong
in always doing
the right thing.

Tony Bower

1706 Dear Father God,
thank you
for all the people
who were willing
and prepared
to sacrifice
and give their lives
so that we may live
freely
today.

Tony Bower

1707 We remember those who were willing to fight in wars
long ago,
and we offer our thanks.
We remember those who are fighting now,
and we ask for strength.
We remember those left behind, sad or worried,
and we ask for comfort.
We remember places in the world where there is still war,
and we pray for peace.

Nick Harding

Education Sunday

(Usually, but not exclusively, celebrated on the ninth Sunday before Easter)

1708 Almighty God,
as we celebrate all that education can offer us and all that we can bring to education, we give thanks for the role of the church in our schools and the contribution of schools to the life of our church.
Help those who teach and those who learn to build on these links.
Grant wisdom to governors of schools and to PCC members, to diocesan and council officers, and to national government in sustaining and developing the educational system in all its depth and breadth.
And in their growth of understanding and knowledge, may all pupils seek to love you, as you love them.
We ask this through Jesus Christ, our Lord.
Amen.

Rupert Bristow

1709 Almighty God,
on this special Sunday we pray for the schools and colleges we serve.
May those who study prosper and grow in their learning.
Enable those who teach, support, administer or govern to carry out their duties with commitment and energy, knowing they have the support of this congregation through our prayers and in our actions.
Show us, Lord, new ways of expressing and developing the church's partnership with our schools and colleges.
We ask this through Jesus Christ, our Lord.
Amen.

Rupert Bristow

Being poorly

1710 Dear God,
thank you for the times when we are healthy. Please help us when we are ill. Thank you for all those who look after us when we are ill: for family, doctors, nurses and all the others who care for us.
We pray now for all those we know who are ill, and pray that you will bless them.
Amen.

Gill Thorniley

Other

1711 You have shown me the path of life;
your presence will fill me with joy.

Susan Sayers

1712 O God, how we need you!
We thank you for supplying us
and coaxing us forward
with such tenderness and affection.

Susan Sayers

1713 Here I am, Lord – body, heart and soul.
Grant that, with your love,
I may be big enough to reach the world,
and small enough to be at one with you.

A prayer of Mother Teresa

1714 We praise and bless you, God of our making,
for the way you draw us deeper
into the meaning of life.

Susan Sayers

1715 For all you have in store for us, we thank you;
we look forward to walking into the future
of your promise, alive with your life.

Susan Sayers

1716 We are the Church
and you are our God.
You fill us with love every day.
We are the Church
and you are our God.
We're a body of people who pray.

Susan Sayers

1717 Lord, in all I do today,
remind me that there's just one way
to do things that I do best,
to put my mind and heart at rest.
And that's to put in your great hands,
my life, that you alone have planned.
Amen.

Anon

1718 Actually, God, we know we often complain a lot,
but really we're glad to be a bit crowded.
We like being close to people, and to animals,
and we want to thank you for all the beauty
you've put into your world – our 'ark'.

Michael Forster

1719 Some people live in really crowded places,
and there's not much fun in that.
Please, God, help the people in your world
to share the space you've given us
so that everyone can have enough.

Michael Forster

1720 Loving God,
we don't always listen to you very well.
We miss the chances you give us
to help others, or to make new friends,
or perhaps just to enjoy life more.
Please forgive us and teach us to listen
– to you and to each other!

Michael Forster

1721 Sometimes, God, we get things out of proportion.
The things you give us to use
start taking over our lives.
Please forgive us when we lose sight of you
and the kind of life you could give us.

Michael Forster

1722 Thank you, God, for life!
And thank you for all the things that make it really good,
whether they're hi-tech, low-tech
or just not tech at all!
Thank you for all the good things we enjoy!

Michael Forster

1723 Please, God,
bless all people who think too badly of themselves:
people who are afraid to do anything
because they're convinced they'll fail.
Please help them to know that they're loved,
and help us to show them that for you.

Michael Forster

1724 Let's pray for people with good intentions,
but no time to turn them into reality.
Please, God, bless busy people,

and help them find time for you
– and each other
– and themselves.

Michael Forster

1725 We want to say yes.
Honest, God, we do.
It's just that so many things get in the way
and we get sidetracked.
Can you help us to change, please?

Michael Forster

1726 Sometimes it just seems that there's no hope.
Thank you God, for being there,
and for the people – like these women –
who make you easier to see
by being there themselves.
Please encourage and strengthen them.

Michael Forster

1727 Please God, bless all people
who do little things for others.
Let them know they're appreciated.
Oh, and while you're at it,
can you inspire some other people
to do little things for them?

Michael Forster

1728 Lord, we welcome you into our homes,
our streets, and our communities;
where we are blind to your presence,
give us sight;
in the ordinary and the remarkable,
help us to recognise our true and living God.

Susan Sayers

1729 Lord, keep us safe
as we travel through life.
Help us to love what is good
and hate what is evil.
Amen.

Susan Sayers

1730 Jesus, we haven't seen you
but we know you love us.
We want to get to know you
and enjoy your company.
Amen.

Susan Sayers

1731 Loving Heavenly Father,
thank you
that giving a little
can make a lot of difference;
one kind word,
a small act of kindness
all act like a pebble
thrown into the sea,
as we watch
and we see
ripples
spreading out,
reaching out
to others,
in other parts
of the world,
where our help,
our small gift
can make a big, big
world of difference.

Tony Bower

1732 Lord,
thank you
for walks
that we can go on,
short walks,
long walks,
medium-sized walks,
walks to the shops,
walks to school,
walks in the country,
walks in town,
walks in winter,
walks in summer,
spring and autumn too,
walks up hills,
walks down dales,
walks along city streets,
walks by riverbanks,
walks on sandy beaches,
walks on rocky ledges,
we thank you
for the joy of walking.

Tony Bower

1733 I'm thirsty,
but not for Coca-Cola,
or lemonade,
or orange juice,
or Appletiser.
I'm thirsty,
but not for
blackcurrant,
Ribena,
grapefruit juice
or any other tantalising drink.
I'm thirsty for you God,
thirsty deep inside,
thirsty to know you God.
I want to drink in
all that is good,
all that is right,
all that is healthy
and I'm not talking about
something liquid
but a right way of living.

Tony Bower

1734 I'm often in a rush,
running so fast,
as if I'm going to run
right in to tomorrow.
I'm always busy doing things,
playing out,
playing in,
playing on
my computer.
I'm always up to something,
even when I shouldn't be.
I need to stop sometimes
and be still,
calm down,
sit down
and settle down.
Be still
not just in my body
but in my mind
and my heart
and know that no matter what
is going on
and no matter what
is happening
and I am doing

Continued overleaf

you are still God,
always have been,
always are
and always will be.

Tony Bower

1735 Father God,
thank you
that your word
is like a light
being switched on
on a dark, dark morning;
your word
helps us to see
what is right and
helps us to know
which way to go.
Your word
is like a lamp
leading us,
guiding us,
so that we can see
where we're going
and know that what we are
doing
is right.
Please help us
to keep looking
to your word
so that we will live our lives
in the light
of your ways.

Tony Bower

1736 Father God,
in this life
lots of things fail us,
our cars won't start,
the TV is on the blink,
there's gunge in the sink,
our friends fall out,
the rain keeps us inside,
we can't find that THING!
And people we love
get ill.
Sometimes life can be sad
and life can be hard,
but in all things

and at all times
your love never
ever
fails us;
you never break down,
you never go on the blink,
you never fall ill,
you never leave us,
you are always there
and you always,
always care
for us.

Tony Bower

1737 Loving heavenly Father,
before the world was made
you loved us.
Before we were born
you loved us.
When we do wrong things
you love us.
When Jesus died on the cross
he showed
you love us.

Tony Bower

1738 Creator God,
thank you
for food
and drink
and all the other things in life
that I think
are important:
like the clothes I wear,
the way I comb my hair,
the body
that you've given me,
and all the things
I can do and play
every single day.
Please help me
not to worry
about all of these
important things
but to know
that the thing
I really must do
is to trust in you.

Tony Bower

1739 Jesus,
I know
that I can't do everything
on my own.
Sometimes
I need the help
of other people.
Sometimes
it's school work
and other times
it's more difficult,
like standing up to someone.
Help me, Jesus,
to accept people's help
and at the same time
to help others
who may need
my help.
Amen.
David Gatward

1740 Jesus,
sometimes
there are things that I have to do
where I need people to help me,
or I need to help other people.
We have to work together.
It can be difficult,
because you have to think
of these other people.
You need to be patient,
and listen to them.
You have to be helpful
and willing to learn.
But it is so great
when you work as a team
and get it right!
I like that, Jesus.
Amen.
David Gatward

1741 Jesus,
how can I show people
your love?
You see,
I know you love me
and that you love everyone,
but I want to help
and show people
how much you really love them!
I can do things
like help people,
and be friends with them.
I can be happy,
and hug them!
Is that good enough?
Will that help?
I'll start right away!
Amen.

David Gatward

1742 Jesus,
I'm really tired.
I can hardly keep my eyes open.
All I want to do
is sleep,
and sleep,
and sleep.
I've had a great day
and done so much.
Thinking about it,
I can't help but smile
and laugh
and yawn
all at the same time!
I know, Jesus,
that sometimes
I don't do much with my days.
But today,
I really feel
like I lived every hour.
It's been great
and I'm exhausted.
Watch over me, Jesus.
Amen.

David Gatward

1743 You
always know
what is best
for each person
and creature
you have made.
So,
I pray that
the right things
will happen
for all your
creation.

Susan Hardwick

1744 God –
you have made me
strong and brave,
and with
a mighty roar.
Help me
to use these,
and all my gifts,
in the service
of others.
May I always give
all glory to you.
Then others will want
to praise your name
and to serve you, too.

Susan Hardwick

1745 Dear Jesus –
the bright sun
has disappeared.
I'm feeling sad.
Please will you
roll away the clouds.
Make the sun
shine again.
Whenever I feel
like this,
please help me
to remember,
all the good things
I have
and that I do,
and all the beautiful
people in my life.

Susan Hardwick

1746 God –
I wish –
I wish –
I wish for so
many things,
that I don't know
what to
ask for first.
I suspect
I'll just have to
wrap them all
into a bundle
and give them
to you.
Then,
you can choose
which ones
are right
and best
for me.
Thanks for being
so wise
and understanding
of all my needs.

Susan Hardwick

1747 Jesus –
we made
a thank you list.
Now,
we've made a
wish list.
It's full of things
we want you
to help us
be and do.
So – here it is.
Help us always
to be kind
and not selfish.
Help us always
to think of others
and not just
ourselves.
Help us always
to be thankful
for all the
good things
in our lives.

Continued overleaf

Help us always
to be loving
and caring.
Help us always
to grow
every single day
more
and more
like
YOU.

Susan Hardwick

1748 Thank you
for a lovely birthday,
for all the fun
and presents,
for another
year of life.
I want to enjoy
every age of
growing up.

George and Angie Allen

1749 You surround me
with your love.
When I was small
I felt your loving
arms around me.
I did not need to
fear with you close
beside me.

George and Angie Allen

1750 Wherever I go
and whatever I do,
you will
never
leave me.

George and Angie Allen

1751 I am ill in bed.
I know I will
get better.
Please make it soon.
Thank you
for the people
looking after me.

George and Angie Allen

1752 I love having a pet.
Thank you
for another life
and the gift
of looking after them.
They are so beautiful
to look at
and hold.

George and Angie Allen

1753 I am so sad that
my pet has died.
Thank you
for their life
and all the joy
and happiness
they gave.

George and Angie Allen

1754 I am not afraid
when I am
away from
home and
family.

George and Angie Allen

1755 God our Father,
we ask you to hear our prayers.
Bless us with your love and compassion.
Send your Holy Spirit
to set our hearts alight
with the flames of faith and love.

Katie Thompson

1756 Glory to you, O God,
for you provide my daily needs.
You have made me for yourself
and I hunger for your love
until I come to your presence.
In you alone am I truly refreshed
and restored to the fullness of life.
Glory to you, O God.
Amen.

David Adam

1757 Dear God,
please help us today
to have the courage
to tell the truth
and not to lie,
whatever we are faced with.
Amen.

Caroline Vallance

1758 Dear God,
help us not to moan about things being unfair.
Help us to make a difference when we can.
Amen.

Caroline Vallance

1759 Dear God,
help us to be self-controlled today
in all that we say and do.
Amen.

Caroline Vallance

1760 Dear God,
thank you that you understand
what it is like to be tempted.
Please help us to be strong enough to say no
when we are faced with temptation.
Amen.

Caroline Vallance

1761 Dear God,
help us to be the sort of people
who are prepared to be changed on the inside,
where it really matters.
Amen.

Caroline Vallance

1762 Thank you, God, for loving all that you have made,
and never wasting anything.
Thank you for your promise of a new start
whenever things go wrong.
Thank you for rainbows, and all they mean.

Michael Forster

1763 Thank you, loving God,
for making life unpredictable!
Thank you for making faith such an adventure,
when we never know
where you're going to lead us next.
Give us grace to make the journey,
to live by faith in you
and care for one another along the way.

Michael Forster

1764 Sometimes it's hard to be faithful.
Sometimes other things seem more exciting.
Sometimes being your friend means making choices
that we don't want to make.
Forgive us when we try to take short cuts
and help us to trust you and stay with you.

Michael Forster

1765 Loving God, bless all the people
who struggle with difficult decisions,
who can't be sure that what they're doing is right
until after they've done it.
Help them to have faith in you,
and to do what they honestly believe is right.

Michael Forster

1766 Dear God,
if you came to church,
I would feel happy.
I might
clap
or laugh
or cry
or dance
or paint
or sing
or show you my toys
or just sit quietly.
Help us make church like that –
ready for you to turn up any time.

Ray Simpson

1767 Dear God,
teach us . . .
to dance like clouds that play,
to laugh like sun that glistens,
to flow like streams that sing,
to fly like birds that chirp,
to dream like rainbows that gleam,
to have fun with you.

Ray Simpson

1768 Glory to God, the angels sing,
and I join in.

Susan Sayers

1769 Put your hand in God's hand
and he will guide your steps.

Susan Sayers

1770 A promise is for keeping.
Only make one if you
mean to keep it.

Susan Sayers

1771 We cannot understand
the whole picture yet.
One day we will
understand it better.

Susan Sayers

1772 Sometimes God
transforms a situation
by transforming
our perceptions of it.

Susan Sayers

1773 Help us to accept the things
we cannot change,
the courage to change
the things we can
and the wisdom to know
the difference.

Anon

1774 When we can
no longer walk,
God carries us.
When we get ourselves lost
the Good Shepherd is out
searching for us
and hears our bleating.

And when he finds us
he lifts us on his shoulders
and brings us safely home.

Susan Sayers

1775 Sometimes we have no energy
or health to pray,
but that is when we are upheld
by the love
and prayers of others.

Susan Sayers

1776 If everything feels tightly
knotted and tangled,
stop tugging at it
and allow God
to work on it.

Susan Sayers

1777 It is only in the dark
that we can see the starlit sky.

Susan Sayers

1778 Let God's peace melt all your
fears away.
Let his courage strengthen you.
Let his love surround you.

Susan Sayers

1779 May God touch your pain
with healing,
and restore you to wholeness
of body, mind and spirit.

Susan Sayers

1780 God bless you
and fill you with hope,
wash your wounds
and bind them up,
so that
you may
know the
fullness
of healing –
physical,
emotional
and
spiritual.

Susan Sayers

1781 It's very hard, Lord, to get this right,
and most of the time we don't.
Please forgive us when we throw away good ideas
just because they're 'old',
and equally when we hang on so tightly to the past
that we miss out on the future you have for us.

Michael Forster

1782 Loving God, please bless all those
whose memories are important to them.
Especially very old people,
who are so rich in experience.
As you lead us on the journey of life,
towards your wonderful future,
help us to treasure the past as well.

Michael Forster

1783 Loving God, we pray for people
who take themselves too seriously.
Help them to lighten up.
And when they've done that,
help us to follow their example!

Michael Forster

1784 Thank you, God, for open-minded people,
who don't write us off when things go wrong for us.
Thank you for people who are always willing
to give other people a chance.

Michael Forster

1785 Sometimes, we only live for today
and don't hear your warnings.
Then we get ourselves into trouble
by making wrong decisions.
Please help us to be more open,
and to hear your voice
even through unexpected people.

Michael Forster

1786 Thank you, God, for loving us
even though we're not perfect.
Thank you for seeing the good
as well as the bad in us.
Thank you for new beginnings.

Michael Forster

1787 We're sorry that sometimes we get frightened
and react against new ideas
without giving them a chance.
Help us to be open to you
when you speak through people we find difficult.

Michael Forster

1788 We're sorry, loving God,
for not always appreciating the life you give us.
Please help us to make the most of every day
by helping make life better
for all your people.

Michael Forster

1789 Loving God,
some people seem to have to wait a long time
before they experience real life.
Please help them to know your love,
and to trust in you for the future.

Michael Forster

1790 Dear Lord,
please guide us
and keep us safe
from all harm.
Amen.

Denis O'Gorman

1791 Where there is hate, let me bring love.
Where there are quarrels, let me bring peace.
Where there is darkness, let me bring light,
Where there is sadness let me bring joy.

Thought to be a prayer said by St Francis of Assisi

1792 Make our hearts good, Lord,
because we know
the way we are on the inside
affects the way we act on the outside.

Ashley Guest

1793 Thank you, Lord,
that you made me unique.
Help me to appreciate that and to be
careful to watch the words that I speak to others.

Ashley Guest

1794 Dear Lord,
bring your peace to our hearts,
our minds and our lives
where we need it today.

Ashley Guest

1795 Let us look at the candles we have lit
remembering those we have thought
about today.
May these candles represent our love and care.
'The light shines on in the dark and the
darkness has never overcome it' *(John 1:5)*.
Amen.

Jill Fuller

1796 Lord, thank you for 'OUCH'!
Without it I wouldn't know what to say.
Like the 'ouch' when I stub my toe,
or the 'ouch' when I try to move a solid object with my head!
Especially the 'ouch'
when someone stabs my ego
with a well-aimed word.
I think 'ouch' is such a useful word.
It has the ring of pain
where other words have no echo.
I understand 'ouch' when it registers in my brain,
like it affects the parts
that other words can't reach.
I can feel the 'ouch'
even though I'm not hungry,
as I watch the skeletal forms
crying in their stillness on the TV screen.
I can feel the 'ouch'
even though I'm not grieving,
as I read about the fingers of death
pointing at the innocent.
I can feel the 'ouch'
even though I'm not in the line of fire,
as I listen to the powerless voices
of refugees walking to misery
I don't always understand,
I can't say I know why.
But you've been there before me,
you know the misery.
You gave us the choice to anaesthetise pain,
to ignore the hurting and point the finger of blame.

Without the 'ouch'
I might not recognise pain,
and then it would be too late
when pain recognises me.
Amen.

Pete Townsend

1797 Father,
I'm sorry if I seem to have a bag over my head at times!
It's not that I don't notice things,
I just don't always see them!
You know how it is;
so much to do and so little time to do it.
Or maybe I don't have a lot of time
for those things which seem hard.
I don't use excuses;
I really do like to watch an obscure documentary on TV!
You can always learn something,
and it's better than seeing what you don't want to see.
If I look too hard,
I might see something which needs to be done,
like talking to someone I don't really know.
It's nice, me and you,
two's company and three's a crowd.
But I seem to remember
that Jesus liked talking to crowds!
Amen.

Pete Townsend

1798 Dear Lord, do you know the latest?
I heard it from a reliable source,
I got it from a friend who lives next door to someone,
whose second cousin saw a friend in the supermarket.
I'm not one to gossip, I speak as I find!
I don't cause trouble, I just say what's on my mind.
You know what they say, 'a trouble shared is a trouble halved'!
I'm doing a favour,
just spreading the load.
It's no skin off my nose,
I'm happy to help.
So, if you feel a bit busy and need someone to tell,
don't hesitate to call me, I'm always in.
I mean, how can I feel sorry for someone,
if I don't know what's what?
I don't want the gory detail,
just the juicy bits will do!
Now, what was I going to tell you?

Continued overleaf

I bet you know already.
Still, good news will keep,
until the next time I hear a scandal
which needs a little 'help'!
Amen.

Pete Townsend

1799 Lord,
why is this relationship thingy
so tough?
Come on, why couldn't you have sorted this out
before you allowed two people
to become mutually exclusive?
If you're honest,
and isn't that something you're quite big on?
you have to admit
that we're an odd species.
I don't agree that women come from one planet
and men from another.
I think they are from different universes.
Did you have a bit of a giggle
when you took a rib from Adam
and made him a companion?
I think you may have conned him
by saying that it would only cost a rib,
'cos you forgot to say
it would cost him an arm and a leg later
just to keep her happy!
Hey, I'm only joking,
it works both ways.
She likes to be flattered
and given gifts
while he's trying to find the courage
to whisper, lovingly in her ear,
he's supposed to be going down the pub with his mates.
Being honest
is too tough at times.
To admit that you might,
just a fraction, a teeny-weeny bit,
be out of order,
and saying it out loud,
feels like you've just confessed
to being a serial bone-cruncher
(she's a vegetarian you know).

I know, I'm avoiding the issue,
just like I do
when me and my significant other
have a blazing row
about why it's OK
for me to be wrong, and not admit it,
when she is forced to plead guilty
when she hasn't a clue
what I'm on about.
Saying sorry
through gritted teeth
not only sounds strange
but doesn't do your teeth any good either.
I need, no, I think we both need
to ask for your help
whenever we're finding the going tough,
which is pretty much
most of the time.
But all I can ask
is that you'll be with us,
love us, and hug us,
when the last thing we feel like doing
is hugging each other.
Amen.

Pete Townsend

1800 Here I am, Lord.
Help me to live your way
and help me to work with others
so that we can be part of your team.

Susan Sayers

Intercessions

Authority

1801 God of power,
we pray for those who are in authority
and in positions of influence and responsibility;
may they be earthed in humility,
courageous in integrity,
and mindful of the need to serve.

Susan Sayers

1802 We pray that all who have authority and power
in our nation and our world
may use it for good,
upholding and instigating what is right and fair,
and listening to the needs of those they represent.
May we recognise our responsibility
to support and stand up for God's values.

Susan Sayers

1803 We bring those whose authority and decisions
affect the lives of many people
and the health of the planet.
We pray for sensitivity and honesty,
and the strength to retain integrity
even in positions of power.

Susan Sayers

1804 Lord God, we pray for the world we inhabit;
for those who lead, and take important decisions,
and for those who follow or are coerced,
or who have no voice.
We pray for mercy and justice,
compassion and integrity.
We pray for protection against evil
and strengthening of goodness.

Susan Sayers

1805 Lord of life,
we pray that in all meetings and conferences
where important decisions are taken,
hearts may be turned to honour what is just and true,
compassionate and constructive.
We pray that in all areas
where there is corruption, deceit or distrust,
consciences may be sensitised afresh
to know what is right
and strive towards it.

Susan Sayers

1806 Dear God,
we pray for the leaders in the world, who have to make hard decisions.
Please help them to make good choices.
Amen.

Gill Thorniley

1807 Almighty God, give us such love for the world
that we may pray with longing and desire,
'Your kingdom come.'
Give our leaders the grace to see
their work as service and their role as stewards;
and sharpen both the recognition of needs
and the commitment to just provision.

Susan Sayers

1808 May the leaders of this nation
and of all the nations
be drawn increasingly to understand
God's ways of justice and righteousness,
and be filled with the longing
to do what is right and honest and good.

Susan Sayers

World

1809 Lord God, the world lurches from crisis to crisis,
and there is much misleading and misdirecting;
help us recover the natural sense
of what is right and just, honest and good,
so that our hearts are inclined
to hear the voice of your leading and respond to it.

Susan Sayers

1810 We pray that our world may be lit
by this light in the darkness
to bring freedom and hope
wherever there is oppression,
recognition and respect where there is none,
and in all conflicts
positive ways forward.

Susan Sayers

1811 Holy God, give all the nations
and peoples of our world
such respect and love for creation
that we learn to take proper responsibility
for the resources we share
and the universe we inhabit.
Give us courage to make good decisions
even if they involve us in conflict or discomfort.

Susan Sayers

1812 Lord, we want to pray
about all the unresolved conflicts in our world.
We ask you to give us your desire for peace,
your spirit of discernment,
your understanding of unspoken needs,
and your capacity for forgiveness.

Susan Sayers

1813 Father, from the conflicting needs
and agendas of the world
we cry for mercy,
for a deeper understanding of one another
and a greater desire for co-operation and peace.
We pray for sensitivity in handling
delicate negotiations
and the wisdom which respects and listens.

Susan Sayers

1814 Holy God, breathe your life into the universe;
breathe responsible caring, honesty and compassion,
breathe right values and good stewardship,
peace and reconciliation, vision and hope.

Susan Sayers

1815 We bring to you, Lord,
our nation, our world, our universe;
all the areas that are fastened shut to hold you out;
all the bewildered confusion
about who we are and why we are here;
all the doubts and insecurity,
and all the searching for inner peace.

Susan Sayers

1816 Walk with us, Lord, down the streets
of our cities, towns and villages,
drive with us down the motorways
and fly with us down the air corridors.
Meet all those who are curious, searching,
or moving in the wrong direction.
Let your presence be sought
and recognised in all the world.

Susan Sayers

1817 Good Shepherd of the sheep,
we pray for the world we inhabit –
the world we have inherited
and will pass on to successive generations.
Teach us to look after it carefully and wisely,
to share its gifts more fairly,
and work together to ease its sufferings.
Turn the hearts of those who are excited by evil things
and encourage the timid to speak out
for what is wholesome and good.

Susan Sayers

1818 Living God, our planet,
with its frenzied life on its fragile skin,
is unnervingly small and vulnerable to evil.
Sharpen our consciences to sense your direction
and protect us from all that draws us away from you.
Guide our leaders in the way of truth
and realign us all to the values
which are built on you.

Susan Sayers

1819 God of glory,
may the whole world come to know you
and give you honour and praise.
Encourage us all to stand up to the devil,
when he prowls,
firm in our faith,
and strengthened with your power.
May your kingdom come and your will be done.

Susan Sayers

1820 For all the peoples of the earth
to know you and honour your name.
For the healing of the nations
and a new thirst for righteousness and purity
at every level and in every aspect of society.
For a dissatisfaction with the pursuit of pleasure
and all that distracts us from our true calling.

Susan Sayers

1821 For the grace and power to live out our faith
in the real and challenging world,
among those we meet and eat with,
whose lives we share,
without compromising that calling
to be the body of Christ,
living God's integrity and purity,
forgiveness and love.

Susan Sayers

1822 We bring before you, O God,
the particular problems of our age and our culture;
renew in us a commitment
to community and mutual trust,
give a sense of value to all
who despise others and themselves;
protect the vulnerable and sensitise the hearts
of all who have become anaesthetised
by images of violence.

Susan Sayers

1823 We pray, Lord, for peace in our world and our lives;
that our faith in your gift of peace
will allow us to bring pardon where there is injury
and forgiveness where there is hatred.

Katie Thompson

1824 Let the world in which we live be transformed by love;
may peace overcome war,
friendship replace loneliness
and selfishness turn to generosity.

Katie Thompson

1825 Lord, we pray that, as caretakers of creation,
we will look for and see your love
reflected in the world around us,
and take responsibility for protecting and cherishing
all living creatures.

Katie Thompson

1826 Lord God,
help us to recognise you
in the world around us,
and, by our living love,
to show how much we care for you.

Katie Thompson

1827 Father, we pray that we will satisfy our neighbour's
hunger for love by giving them a smile,
sharing a glass of water,
or simply making time to talk and listen.

Katie Thompson

1828 Let us pray for people who thirst for peace and
reconciliation;
may we commit ourselves
to work for international justice and peace
by defending human rights throughout the world.

Katie Thompson

1829 Let us pray for nations and people
who hunger for justice, equality and an end to poverty;
may we as Christians
recognise the dignity and rights of our neighbours
and do everything we can to satisfy and meet their needs.

Katie Thompson

1830 God our Father,
may we find the treasure of your loving kingdom
in the people and world around us.

Katie Thompson

1831 Blessed are those who hunger for what is just and fair;
may political leaders, citizens of rich countries
and Christians everywhere
ensure that we share the goods and resources of the world fairly,
for the happiness of all.

Katie Thompson

1832 Blessed are the poor and homeless;
may they open our eyes, which are so often blinded
by selfishness and greed,
to see their needs and allow us to experience
the happiness which giving with love can bring.

Katie Thompson

1833 Lord, we pray for the homeless, the hungry and the unemployed;
with our loving help and encouragement
may they find happiness in their troubled and difficult lives.

Katie Thompson

1834 Lord, we pray for an end to injustice, violence
and fear in our world;
may governments and leaders work tirelessly
for peace and equality
so that all people can enjoy the happiness they deserve.

Katie Thompson

1835 We pray for peacemakers in our world;
may we support their brave efforts
to heal injustice and reconcile differences and bitterness
in countries and communities divided by fear and hatred.

Katie Thompson

1836 Heavenly Father,
may we be filled with the joy of your love,
and gladly go out to share it with the whole world.

Katie Thompson

1837 Lord, we pray for the world you have made;
may we care for and protect the gifts of creation
which bring us so much joy and pleasure.

Katie Thompson

1838 Loving Father,
fill our lives with joy
and help us to share all that you give us,
so that we can make this world
a happier place for everyone to live.

Katie Thompson

1839 For all peoples and nations of the world;
may the light of Christ shining in our lives
help us to change the darkness of hunger, poverty and
injustice into the joy of sharing, caring and equality
for everyone.

Katie Thompson

1840 For the poor and the hungry;
that we who have plenty may always be ready
to help our brothers and sisters who have little.

Katie Thompson

1841 For understanding, forgiveness and peace in our world;
that leaders and nations will work together
to build one kingdom of love.

Katie Thompson

1842 Father, we pray for people whose lives are shattered
by war or violence;
may your kingdom come
through the efforts of all who work
to bring peace to troubled lives and nations.

Katie Thompson

1843 Father, we pray for the homeless and the unemployed;
may your kingdom come
through our love for one another,
as we help anyone who is in trouble or afraid.

Katie Thompson

1844 For all who work to build God's kingdom on earth;
may the Holy Spirit guide and inspire them
to live by Christ's commandments
to love God and one another.

Katie Thompson

1845 For nations and communities divided by conflict and fear;
may the Holy Spirit guide and strengthen them
to love their enemies,
to do good to those who hate them,
and to forgive rather than condemn.

Katie Thompson

1846 We pray for understanding and acceptance in our world;
that as Christians we will find a way
to your generosity of heart,
by welcoming and supporting
those who have wandered far from your path.

Katie Thompson

1847 We pray for those who strive for material wealth
above everything else;
that as Christians we will find a way
to show them by our daily lives
that it is more important to have treasure in heaven
than here on earth.

Katie Thompson

1848 We pray for people who suffer hardship or persecution
because of their faith;
that as Christians we will find a way
to uphold the rights of every person
to have the freedom to worship without fear.

Katie Thompson

1849 Lord, we pray for those who suffer injustice,
exploitation and discrimination;
by our Christian love for you and for our neighbour
may we take effective action against evil
and defend everyone's right to life.

Katie Thompson

1850 Lord, we pray for nations and families
devastated by conflict and hatred;
by our Christian love for you and for our neighbour
may our care and loving support for them
turn sadness to joy, hatred to forgiveness,
and bring the gift of your peace to their lives.

Katie Thompson

1851 Lord God,
we cannot love you unless we love one another.
Help us to become people of forgiveness and compassion
who recognise your face in the people we see around us.

Katie Thompson

1852 We pray for the homeless and refugees
who have lost everything they own;
may we never turn away from our neighbour in need,
but respond with loving generosity and welcoming
kindness.

Katie Thompson

1853 We pray for those who are poor;
may our love enrich the lives of our neighbours,
and may our support for aid agencies
help to improve the quality of their care.

Katie Thompson

1854 May all the families on earth
be blessed with mutual love
and caring consideration one of another;
may arguments and misunderstandings
be properly resolved,
and difficult relationships refreshed and healed.

Susan Sayers

1855 Thank you, Father, for the order and variety,
simplicity and complexity of this universe.
Thank you for all that humankind is able to do;
may all these gifts be used wisely and well,
for the good of all, including those as yet unborn.

Susan Sayers

Sick and suffering

1856 God of wholeness,
we remember those who are aching today
in body, mind or spirit;
knowing that nothing is unredeemable,
we ask that you will bring good
even out of these barren places.

Susan Sayers

1857 Lord God, there are some who are going through
very distressing, painful and worrying times.
We stand alongside them now,
and ask for them your comfort, reassurance,
healing and peace of mind.

Susan Sayers

1858 We pray that all those whose lives
are fettered by the past,
by rejection, guilt, pain or anxiety,
may be set free and encouraged to live to the full.

Susan Sayers

1859 Holy God, we bring to you those we know
who are suffering with prolonged illness,
debilitating pain, and emotional distress.
Lay your hands on them to bring relief and healing,
courage to live through this dark time,
and the inner strength which only you can give.

Susan Sayers

1860 We pray for all who are oppressed,
downtrodden or despised;
we pray for those who will not eat today
and all who live in the degrading circumstances
of poverty and powerlessness;
we pray for a heart to put injustices right
and strive for a fair sharing of resources.

Susan Sayers

1861 Wherever there is illness, unhappiness,
injustice or fear;
wherever people feel frustrated,
imprisoned or trapped;
give us a greater sense of loving community,
a heart to put right whatever we can,
and the willingness to stand
alongside one another in our sorrows.

Susan Sayers

1862 Lord, we pray for peace of mind and spirit
in all those who are distressed or enveloped in pain.
May they know the reality of your inner healing,
and may even the worst situations
become places of growth and new life.

Susan Sayers

1863 Lord, in the shock of sudden illness and pain,
and in the wearing endurance of long-term weakness,
give your peace and tranquillity,
your healing and hope.

Susan Sayers

1864 We pray for all who are too exhausted
or overwhelmed by circumstances and pressures
to be able to pray;
surround all those who are troubled
and heavily laden
with the revitalising assurance of your presence,
your understanding and your love.

Susan Sayers

1865 The world's misery and pain
and desperate need of healing
are clear to see and affect us all.
We pray now for this damaged world
with all its weakness, longings and failings,
with all its potential and hope.

Susan Sayers

1866 We pray for all who suffer through others' sin;
all victims of abuse or oppression or apathy;
all whose adult lives are distorted and misshapen
by early damaging experiences
which need your healing.

Susan Sayers

1867 We bring all for whom illness or injury
has caused disruption, uncertainty
and the prospect of long-term change;
all who find their lives are spinning
out of their control;
give them working knowledge
of your total loving and unchanging presence,
so that in all the changes and troubles of life
they may be assured of your everlasting protection.

Susan Sayers

1868 We stand alongside all those who are suffering,
whether in body, mind or spirit,
and long for your healing and comfort,
your strength for perseverance
and your patience in the dark times;
we long for your living Spirit
to envelop and sustain them.

Susan Sayers

1869 Holy God, breathe your life into those who suffer;
breathe comfort and wholeness,
forgiveness and new confidence,
breathe peace of mind
and the knowledge of your love.
Susan Sayers

1870 If the terrible suffering of extreme poverty,
injustice and oppression
is to be addressed realistically,
then take away our greed and complacency
and our assumptions
about appropriate living standards,
and teach us sacrificial self-giving
of time, energy and resources.
Susan Sayers

1871 Lord God, we pray for those who cannot think,
for the pain or anguish which engulfs them;
for all whose lives are troubled and insecure;
for those who have little energy left to rejoice.
Bring healing,
and the resources to cope with suffering,
and give us the grace
to carry one another's burdens in love.
Susan Sayers

1872 We bring to you, Lord,
those whom life has damaged,
and all who find it difficult to trust in you;
we bring you those who need refreshment and hope,
comfort, healing and inner serenity.
Susan Sayers

1873 Walk with us, Lord,
through the times of suffering and pain,
alerting us to one another's needs
and providing for us in whatever ways
are best for us.
Help us to trust you through the dark times;
breathe new life and hope
into those who are close to despair.
Susan Sayers

1874 Good Shepherd of the sheep,
we pray for the weak and vulnerable,
for those who must live
depending on others for every need,
and for those who are bullied, or constantly despised.
We pray for a greater reverence, one for another,
for a greater willingness
to uphold and encourage one another;
we pray for healing and wholeness.
Susan Sayers

1875 Living God, you can use
and transform all our experiences.
We lay before you now
those who are travelling through a time
of pain or anguish, tragedy or conflict
which is hard to bear.
We stand alongside them in their suffering,
and offer it to your transforming, healing love.
Susan Sayers

1876 Lord of life,
we pray for all who feel out of their depth,
all who are drowning in their pain,
sorrow or guilt.
Set them free, O God, and save them,
support them to a place of safety
and fix their feet on the solid rock of your love.
Susan Sayers

1877 We pray for those who are full of tears,
and cannot imagine being happy again;
we pray for the hardened and callous,
whose inner hurts have never yet been healed.
We pray for wholeness and comfort and new life.
Susan Sayers

1878 God of glory,
may our homes, schools, shops, offices and factories
become places where your glory
is seen and experienced
in the ordinary things, the everyday routines,
the pots and pans of life.
Fill us to overflowing with ongoing thankfulness
both in the sunlight and in the storm.
Susan Sayers

1879 God of glory,
with your special affection
for the discarded and marginalised,
the weak and the vulnerable,
we pray for all those who find life
an exhausting struggle
or who long for some respite from pain or depression.
Support them in their troubles,
bring healing and reassurance,
and touch them with the gentleness of your peace.

Susan Sayers

1880 For those whose lives feel empty or cheated,
or filled with pain, or worry or guilt.
For all whose hopes and dreams are in tatters;
all who are in any way imprisoned.

Susan Sayers

1881 We pray, Lord, for people who are filled with doubt
and uncertainty;
that the faithful witness of Mary and Joseph her husband
will help them to walk from the darkness of doubt
into the light of certainty.

Katie Thompson

1882 We pray, Lord, for those who need to be forgiven
or show forgiveness;
that our faith in your desire and power
to forgive our sins and make us forgiving people
will change our hearts and lives for ever.

Katie Thompson

1883 Let the lives of the poor and those in need
be transformed by love;
may each of us do whatever we can
to relieve their suffering and hardship,
and may we never take for granted
what we are fortunate to have.

Katie Thompson

1884 Let suffering and pain be transformed by love;
may your healing love bring comfort and strength
in times of loneliness and despair.

Katie Thompson

1885 Let us pray for people who are imprisoned
by loneliness and fear;
may our friendship and love free them
to take their rightful place in your kingdom.

Katie Thompson

1886 Let us pray for the sick and all who suffer;
may our visits and prayers comfort them,
and our loving care fill them with joy and hope.

Katie Thompson

1887 Blessed are those who suffer
and are imprisoned for sharing the Good News;
may their faithful witness
fill them with happiness and consolation,
knowing that the kingdom of heaven belongs to them.

Katie Thompson

1888 We pray for those who are filled with doubt and uncertainty;
may they find faith in Jesus the risen Lord,
and be filled with the gift of his peace.

Katie Thompson

1889 Lord, we pray for people who cure the sick and care for them;
may their skill and love bring comfort and happiness
to those who suffer.

Katie Thompson

1890 Lord, we pray for people who are alone and filled with despair;
may our friendship and love fill their lives
with joy and fresh hope.

Katie Thompson

1891 For people who live in the darkness of hatred and fear;
may the light of Christ shining out from us
warm cold hearts and help others to see a new way
forward through forgiveness and friendship.

Katie Thompson

1892 For people who are sad or lonely;
that, like Jesus, we may always be ready to reach out to others
with a hand of friendship and a welcoming smile.

Katie Thompson

1893 Father, we pray for the sick and all who suffer;
may your kingdom come
through the love and compassion
of all who visit and care for them.

Katie Thompson

1894 Lord, we pray for those who are sick
and all who suffer in mind or body;
by our Christian love for you and for our neighbour
may we discover the face of Christ your Son
in those who are bruised by pain and suffering.

Katie Thompson

1895 Dear Lord,
help us to remember,
both prayerfully and practically,
those in the world who are
struggling to survive through famine,
disaster or war.
Amen.

Ashley Guest

1896 Thank you, Father, for all those who care for the sick,
the unstable, the ungrateful and the difficult.
We pray for all who are on the receiving end
of hate, deceit, suspicion or abuse,
and for those who cause others pain
and distress of any kind.
We pray for your healing and transforming.

Susan Sayers

1897 May those for whom the days and nights
creep past in pain or sorrow
be given comfort and hope;
may the frightened find reassurance
and the anxious find peace of mind.

Susan Sayers

1898 Healing God, lay your hands on those who suffer,
so that they may know the support of your presence
and find wholeness and peace in your love.
We pray especially for those who are locked
into the conviction
that they are beyond your forgiveness.
May they quickly discover
the freedom of your acceptance.

Susan Sayers

Faithful departed

1899 God of life,
we pray for those whose earthly lives have ended;
we remember those who have died
violently and tragically, suddenly and unprepared.
We give you thanks for lives well lived
and for happy memories.
May they rest in the eternal peace of heaven.

Susan Sayers

1900 Lord God, even as we pray now,
there are those journeying through death.
We pray for them, for all who have recently died,
and for all those left without their loved ones,
grieving, or numbed with shock.

Susan Sayers

1901 We pray for those who have died,
and those who miss them
and are finding it very hard to cope with their loss.
We pray for all those who have no one to help them
through that last journey.

Susan Sayers

1902 Holy God, we pray for those
making the journey through death,
and for those who have died to this earthly life.
Thank you for all they have given us.
Comfort those who miss them,
and through your mercy receive us all, in our time,
to live in the peace and joy of your eternity.

Susan Sayers

1903 We pray for those whose life expectancy is short,
for the babies and children who have died
while we have been praying;
for all who have come to the end of their earthly life
and made that last journey through death;
thank you for your welcoming mercy
and the promise of eternal life.

Susan Sayers

1904 Wherever earthly lives have come to an end,
and people are grieving the loss of their loved ones,
fill these places with the eternal peace
of your presence
and prepare us all through our lives on this earth
for everlasting life with you in heaven.

Susan Sayers

1905 Lord, we pray for those approaching death
with fear, resentment and anger,
and for all who counsel the dying and the bereaved.
We pray that those who have died will know
the joy of everlasting life with you.

Susan Sayers

1906 Lord, through the journey of death
and in the grieving of those who mourn,
gather us up into the everlasting arms of love
and comfort us,
and bring us to life in all its fullness.

Susan Sayers

1907 We pray that those who have gone through death
may know the brightness of everlasting life
in your company;
may we, with them, come to experience
the glory and joy of heaven.

Susan Sayers

1908 We remember those who,
freed from the ageing and pain of their bodies,
can live now with you
in the peace and joy of heaven.

Susan Sayers

1909 We commend to your love and mercy
all those who have made the journey
through death,
especially any who have died unprepared,
or violent deaths.
We thank you for your understanding
and compassion
and pray that they may know the forgiveness,
peace and joy of heaven.

Susan Sayers

1910 We pray for those who have come
to the end of earthly life;
have mercy on them.
May they, placing their faith in the God of life,
share in the light and joy of heaven for ever.

Susan Sayers

1911 Thank you, loving God,
for your promise to be with us always,
and not just until we die.
We remember with affection
those of our parents who loved us into existence
and now live in eternity.
Gather up into your loving arms
those who have recently died
and comfort all whose memories
make them aware of loss today.

Susan Sayers

1912 Holy God, breathe your life into the dead and dying;
breathe courage for the journey
and the realisation that you can be trusted.
Breathe life that lasts for ever.

Susan Sayers

1913 Father, through the life-giving death of Jesus,
may the dying turn to you
and know your merciful love;
may the grieving be comforted,
and may we all one day share
with those who have died
the eternal joy of your heaven.

Susan Sayers

1914 As we celebrate the new life of Resurrection,
let us pray to the one true God,
who brings us all to life.
Lord God, we pray that the Church
may proclaim with joy your message of hope
for the world;
may our lives, as well as our worship,
testify to the truth of the Resurrection;
broaden our vision of what is possible
through new life in you.

Susan Sayers

1915 Lord God, we thank you for lives well lived,
and commend to your keeping those who have died.
Through the Resurrection hope,
may they know the joy of heaven.

Susan Sayers

1916 We bring to you, Lord,
those who approach death with great fear
and those who die unprepared to meet you.
Have mercy on us all,
forgive us all that is past
and gather us into your everlasting kingdom
of peace and joy.

Susan Sayers

1917 Walk with us, Lord, through the valley of death;
may our love and prayers support those
who walk that journey today.
Draw close to them and welcome them
into the joy of heaven.

Susan Sayers

1918 Living God, we remember those who have died
and pray for them now.
Lead them out of their pain
into the light of eternity,
and keep us all in the Way that leads us
to share that everlasting life with you.

Susan Sayers

1919 Lord of life,
we pray for those who have died
and now see you as you really are.
We ask for mercy and forgiveness,
and commend them to your keeping for ever.

Susan Sayers

1920 We commend to your eternal love
those we remember who have died,
and we pray too for those
who miss their physical presence.

Susan Sayers

1921 God of glory,
teach us to understand death
in the context of your eternity,
so that our fears are calmed as we approach it.
Welcome with merciful love
those who have recently died
and shelter their loved ones, too,
in the shadow of your wings.

Susan Sayers

1922 For those who walk the dark journey of death
and all who have come through it
into your presence;
for mourners distressed by regrets
or angry with God at their loss.

Susan Sayers

1923 We pray, Lord, for those who have died
and departed from this world;
that their faith in Christ your Son,
who is the Resurrection and the Life,
will lead them to everlasting life in your kingdom.

Katie Thompson

1924 Lord, we pray for those who have died in your peace
that they will enjoy the happiness of eternal life
in your heavenly kingdom.

Katie Thompson

1925 We pray for our loved ones who have died;
that they will be filled with the joy of the Resurrection
as they share your eternal glory.

Katie Thompson

1926 Lord, we pray for all who rest in peace with you;
may they be filled with unimaginable joy
as they live for ever with you in your heavenly kingdom.

Katie Thompson

1927 For those who have died and those who miss them;
may the light of Christ and the promise of eternal life
turn the darkness of sadness
into the joy of hope and peace.

Katie Thompson

1928 For those who have died and are at peace with you;
that, welcomed into your heavenly kingdom of love,
they will enjoy eternal life and glory there.

Katie Thompson

1929 We pray for all who have died;
we give thanks that in life they have followed the way
which has led them to the peace and glory
of eternal life with you.

Katie Thompson

1930 Blessed are those who are saddened
by the loss of someone they love;
may their hope in the Resurrection
and the promise of eternal life
bring them comfort, and turn their sadness to joy.

Katie Thompson

1931 Dear God,
we remember those who are dying and those who have lost loved ones. Please bless them and help them in their time of need.
Please help all those who are accused and punished unjustly.
Amen.

Gill Thorniley

Church

1932 Lord God, make yourself known
to the people who come into our churches,
or who pass by and sometimes wonder,
but have not yet come in;
make us better bearers of your life
to those who need you
but have never met you.

Susan Sayers

1933 We pray that the light of God
will shine in all the dark corners of the Church,
and set us free from prejudice,
small-mindedness and hypocrisy;
that as members of the Body of Christ
we can move freely through the power of God
wherever we are called to go,
available and active in God's service.

Susan Sayers

1934 Holy God, we bring before you all that we are,
with as much honesty and openness as we can.
We know your Church is weakened
by disunity, misplaced priorities,
complacency and fear.
We pray for a new awakening of our calling
to be the people of God;
give us a fresh understanding of your will
and empower us with nothing short of your life
lived out in us.

Susan Sayers

1935 Wherever the Church is asked
to give leadership on sensitive issues;
whenever the current world
expectations of behaviour
need to be challenged in the light of God's love,
give us the wisdom and guidance we need.

Susan Sayers

1936 Lord, we want to pray for stronger faith
and the courage to live up to our calling;
for the grace to act always
with the generosity of spirit you show to us,
until the whole Church models the wisdom
which the world counts as foolishness.

Susan Sayers

1937 Lord, in all the daily concerns of parish life,
and in the great issues facing the whole Church,
may we never lose sight of your priorities
but see everything through the eyes of compassion,
with honesty and integrity.

Susan Sayers

1938 Lord, we pray that as Christians
we may listen more attentively
and with greater urgency than ever before
to the words of Jesus;
give us more awareness of your presence with us,
both in our worship and in our daily ministry,
giving us the courage to live out your truth with joy.

Susan Sayers

1939 Father, wherever the Church is dry and parched
may the water of your Spirit well up
to refresh and renew,
to bring life and strong new growth.
Lord, make us more aware of our thirst for you,
so that we come to you ready and eager
to receive your living water.

Susan Sayers

1940 Holy God, breathe your life into the Church;
breathe holiness and deepening faith,
breathe energy, inspired teaching and fervent praise;
unblock the channels and make us more receptive
to your gentleness and your power.

Susan Sayers

1941 Lord of life,
we pray that the Church
may be alive with your risen life,
refreshed and revived by the breath of your Spirit,
purified and refined like gold and silver,
so that we truly offer the possibility
of saving love to the searching world.

Susan Sayers

1942 God of glory,
may your light shine in our church community
as you work among us
and bless us with your presence;
we offer you the gifts you have given us
and our various ministries;
we offer you ourselves,
in the area you have placed us.

Susan Sayers

1943 We bring before you, O God,
the needs of the Church,
in its weakness and its potential;
revive and refresh us, teach and direct us,
inspire all who preach, teach
and gossip the Good News,
and uphold all who suffer for their faith in any way.

Susan Sayers

1944 Lord, we pray that ordained and lay people
who live and teach the Christian faith
may touch the hearts of others
and help them to understand your Word
and to nurture their gift of faith.

Katie Thompson

1945 Let the Church and her people be transformed by love;
may we shine in the darkness of our world
and brighten the lives of others,
filling them with joy and hope.

Katie Thompson

1946 Lord, we pray that Christians everywhere
will live the forgiving love of your Son Jesus
who welcomed sinners, befriended the tax collectors,
and cast stones at no one.

Katie Thompson

1947 Lord, we pray that our family the Church
will share the love of your Son Jesus
by helping those who have lost their way
to rediscover your endless love.

Katie Thompson

1948 Father, we pray that as Christians
we will serve you and one another
by becoming instruments of love in your hands,
by feeding the hungry, clothing the naked
and befriending the homeless and unwanted.

Katie Thompson

1949 Father, we pray that we will be encouraged and inspired
by the lives of the Saints
and all who dedicate their lives to sharing
and living your gospel of love.

Katie Thompson

1950 Lord, we pray for Christians throughout the world;
as faithful followers of Christ your Son
may we find true happiness through serving you
and our brothers and sisters.

Katie Thompson

1951 Jesus told us to come to him like little children
with all our worries and troubles.
Let us pray now for our own needs
and the needs of our world:
we pray for the Church and all its people;
may we share the gospel of peace by our living example
of acceptance, understanding and forgiveness.

Katie Thompson

1952 With simple trust and humble hope
we come before God our loving Father
with all our needs:
we pray for the leaders of the Church,
our government and the nations of the world;
that their wisdom and understanding
will fill people with hope for a better future
in a fairer world.

Katie Thompson

1953 For the Church and her leaders;
may the light of Christ guide and direct them
to lead us to our loving Saviour,
just as the light from a star
directed the wise men on their journey.

Katie Thompson

1954 Lord, we pray for our family your Church;
may we continue to grow in faith and love
as, filled with your Holy Spirit, we take our rightful place
in the one loving Body of Christ.

Katie Thompson

1955 For the Church and all your people;
that having heard and understood
the Good News that Jesus came to share,
each of us in our own way
will share that message of hope and love
with the rest of the world.

Katie Thompson

1956 Lord, we pray for the Church throughout the world;
by our Christian love for you and for our neighbour
may we lay the foundations for your kingdom
in our daily lives.

Katie Thompson

1957 Loving Father, whenever we start to get offended
by your generosity or open-mindedness,
give us the grace to repent and join your rejoicing.
Guard the Church against self-righteousness
and all rules and limits which you would not own,
but keep always before us the rule of love.

Susan Sayers

1958 Merciful God, break all habits
of destructive behaviour
in our homes and families, our friendships
and in all the homes of this parish.
Develop our ability to celebrate what is good
and face what is not with honesty.

Susan Sayers

1959 Lord God, give us understanding
to keep your law of love
so that we walk in the path of your commandments,
for that is what we really want to do.
Help us to encourage one another in living your way
and protect one another from falling.

Susan Sayers

1960 Unchanging God, change us from the heart
until the whole Church awakens to your love
that reaches out, nurtures and celebrates,
neither holding back from what is difficult,
nor rushing where angels fear to tread.
We pray for sensitivity and courage.

Susan Sayers

School

1961 Walk with us, Lord, in our life journeys,
guiding, teaching and correcting us,
as we learn the lessons of loving
in our homes, our schools and our communities.
Susan Sayers

1962 Good Shepherd of the sheep,
we pray for our school,
our fellow pupils, friends and neighbours,
and the members of our families.
We ask not for popularity at all costs,
but the grace to do your will
and be your witnesses
to what it means to live lovingly,
both when this is easy and also when it hurts.
Susan Sayers

1963 Lord of life,
we pray for the streets
and schools we represent.
May they be places where the truth of your being
is proclaimed daily by the way we live
and handle the everyday situations,
through your leading.
May our words and actions
speak of your faithful love,
your graciousness and your purity.
Susan Sayers

1964 Holy God, we pray for a greater awareness
of your presence in our homes and places of work,
in our cars and in public transport,
in the shops, schools and hospitals,
and wherever people meet together.
Teach us how to live lovingly,
with honesty and compassion;
teach us how to live thankfully,
and work on our habit of grumbling.
Susan Sayers

Ascension Day

1965 God of love, as we celebrate this festival
of Jesus' entry into heaven as Saviour and Lord,
we pray for unity in the Church
and reconciliation and renewed vision.

Susan Sayers

1966 As we recall the shout of praise in heaven
as the Lamb of God appears,
we pray for all who are hailed as heroes
and given great honour on earth;
for all who worship anyone or anything
other than the true God.

Susan Sayers

Other

1967 We pray that there may be a revival of longing
for your kingdom to come,
and a renewed commitment to working for it;
for a desire to live out our faith and worship
in our daily lives this week.

Susan Sayers

1968 Father, wherever our attention
has wandered from your calling,
wherever we have fallen short of your will for us,
and failed to keep the spirit of your law of love,
forgive us and transform us,
so that we walk again
the path that leads to life.

Susan Sayers

1969 Lord, in the local issues of this community,
and in the difficulties and dilemmas
on the world stage,
may we look for the face of Christ
and fix our attention on his underlying values
of love, justice and mercy.

Susan Sayers

1970 We pray for those who do not know you
or dismiss you as irrelevant to their lives;
we pray for those who influence
and encourage others
in what is evil, destructive or depraved,
and ask for your protection
of all who are vulnerable and in danger.

Susan Sayers

1971 We bring all those who find it so hard to believe,
so hard to trust in a faithful loving God;
we bring those who teach the faith;
all who preach and chat the Good News.
Give the right words
for each situation and each person,
and enable the seed to take root and grow.

Susan Sayers

1972 Holy God, breathe your life
into our homes and places of work;
breathe increased patience and understanding,
and the courage to live the Christian life
when to do so brings ridicule or demands sacrifice.

Susan Sayers

1973 If our workplaces and neighbourhoods and homes
are to display and respond to your values,
then make us more fervent in prayer,
more courageous in self-discipline
and, above all, more loving in outreach.

Susan Sayers

1974 Living God, may the Way which Jesus shows us
be the Way we live out our daily lives
around the table, in the daylight and the dark,
in the misunderstandings, the tensions and the rush,
in the eye contact, the conversations and the growing.

Susan Sayers

1975 Lord of life,
your love for us is so great
and our love for you so small.
Thank you for accepting what we are able to offer;
and ignite us to a blaze of love.

Susan Sayers

1976 Heavenly Father,
faith helps us to pray,
and prayer helps us to believe.
Enliven our faith,
and warm our hearts with the love
which leads to eternal life with you.

Katie Thompson

1977 Father, we pray that you will give us the strength and courage
to allow ourselves to go wherever you send us,
and to do whatever you ask.

Katie Thompson

1978 Father, we pray that our eyes will open to see Christ your Son in the faces of our neighbours,
and that our hearts will open
to respond lovingly to their needs.

Katie Thompson

1979 Lord God,
you sent your beloved Son
to be our Servant King,
and to teach us your loving ways.
Fill us with the Holy Spirit
and help us to serve you and one another
according to your commandments of love.

Katie Thompson

1980 Blessed are those who work to bring peace to our world;
may they bring love where there is hatred,
forgiveness where there is anger,
and lasting happiness where there is sadness and despair.

Katie Thompson

1981 Almighty God,
through Jesus your Son
you shared the secret of lasting happiness with us,
and showed us how to find and keep it.
By our words and actions in life,
may we enjoy eternal happiness in heaven.

Katie Thompson

1982 Loving Father,
listen to our prayers
and answer them as you know best.
May the joy of Christ's resurrection
and your unending love
shine out from us as happiness
and touch the lives of others.

Katie Thompson

1983 God our Father,
you sent your beloved Son Jesus,
who is the Prince of Peace,
to transform our world with his love.
May our living love touch the lives of others
and bring them the gift of your peace.

Katie Thompson

1984 We pray for those who have wandered away from you
and from the love of families and friends,
that a change of heart will lead them to search
for those they have lost,
and rediscover the joy of love and reconciliation.

Katie Thompson

1985 We pray for all Christian people;
that your peace and joy will grow in our hearts and lives
as we serve you and one another.

Katie Thompson

1986 Loving Father,
help us to always walk as children of the light,
shining out in the darkness,
and touching the lives of many
with the warmth of your love.

Katie Thompson

1987 Almighty God,
may we live in Christ's love
by serving you and one another,
and never take the love we share for granted.

Katie Thompson

1988 Lord,
fill us with your love,
so that your kingdom
will grow in us and through us.

Katie Thompson

1989 Father,
make us grow in love for you and one another,
and give us the courage to do your will,
so that your kingdom may come.

Katie Thompson

1990 For people who are searching for your kingdom of love;
that they will accept the invitation you give to everyone,
and have the courage
to follow the path which leads them there.

Katie Thompson

1991 For people who have wandered away from you;
that, trusting in your gentle forgiveness and tender love,
they will choose to change their hearts and lives,
and take their rightful place in your kingdom.

Katie Thompson

1992 Heavenly Father,
hear the prayers of your children,
and help us to follow you faithfully.
When we struggle,
help us always to choose your loving way,
so that we may belong to your kingdom.

Katie Thompson

1993 For those who have lost their faith and their way in life;
may the Holy Spirit search for them
and lovingly guide them back to the path
which leads to eternal life.

Katie Thompson

1994 For wisdom and understanding of God's way;
may the Holy Spirit guide us
and help us to accept that God's way
is often not the human way,
and that we must trust in his goodness.

Katie Thompson

1995 Heavenly Father,
as we follow the way of Christ,
keep us faithful to you
and forever close to your love and friendship.

Katie Thompson

1996 Loving Father,
as we make our way through life,
let us help one another to follow the path
which leads to your heavenly kingdom.

Katie Thompson

1997 Jesus taught us to ask God for all our needs,
and, confident in his love, we gather together
to pray for all our brothers and sisters:
we pray for countries facing famine, flood, drought,
and any kind of disaster;
may we never pass by and ignore
the troubles of our neighbour,
but do everything we can to provide for all their needs.

Katie Thompson

1998 Thank you, Father, for disturbing our complacency
and challenging us to move forward with you,
assured of your company and your love.

Susan Sayers

1999 Thank you, Father, for what we have been forgiven
and for the opportunities we have each day
to learn the joy of forgiving others.
Smash through our self-righteousness
and keep us learning in humility at your feet.

Susan Sayers

2000 Thank you, Father, for the love
which forgives again and again,
and is prepared to trust us
with the care of your people
even after we have let you down many times.
Teach us to minister to one another's needs
with compassion, sensitivity and discipline,
so that all are affirmed and encouraged.

Susan Sayers